Civilizations die from suicide, not by murder.

Arnold Toynbee, (1889 - 1975)
English historian & historical philosopher

Benjamin Franklin, upon being asked what kind of government the Continental Congress decided upon, replied:

"A republic, if you can keep it."

There is a tide in the affairs of men

Which, taken at the flood,
leads on to fortune;
Omitted, all the voyage of their life
Is bound in shallows and in miseries.
On such a full sea are we now afloat,
And we must take the current
when it serves,
Or lose our ventures.

Shakespeare's *Julius Caesar*

IF YOU CAN KEEP IT
The Arrogance And Cost
Of Convenient Assumptions

By

N. C. Munson

Allen-Ayers Books – Ponce Inlet, Florida

ISBN-13: 978-1496013026
ISBN-10: 1496013026
Library of Congress Control Number 2008900204
Published by Allen-Ayers Books, February, 2008
Ponce Inlet, Florida, United States of America

ALSO FROM N. C. MUNSON:

NOVELS (as Noel Carroll)

Circle of Distrust
Accidental Encounter
Delayed Awakening
Never By Blood
Broken Odyssey
Starve The Devil
The Exclusion Zone
A Long Reach Back
Light Years of Fear
Carroll's Shorts

SHORT STORIES

Slipping Away
The Galapagos Incident
Silent Obsession
Recycled
The Collection
Butterflies
Stairway Through Agony
Beyond Sapiens
End of The Beginning
By Invitation Only

HUMOR-SATIRE (as John Barr)

Hey, God; Got A Minute?
Soul Food

Contents

FORWARD - EMPIRES COME AND GO--9

CHAPTER 1 – FOUNDATION--12
STATUS OF THE AMERICAN EXPERIMENT=--14

CHAPTER 2 - THE CASE AGAINST US --22

CHAPTER 3-1 - RELIGION AND POLITICS--26
STRONGLY BELIEVING-29

CHAPTER 3-2 - PROGRAMMED INTOLERANCE--31

CHAPTER 3-3 - RELIGION AND MEDICINE-39
CONDOMS TO AFRICA--39
FAMILY PLANNING--42
ABORTION AND ALTERNATIVES--43
STEM CELL RESEARCH--46
ECONOMICS-51

CHAPTER 3-4 - RELIGION AND SCIENCE--55
IMAX, GALILEO AND TERRI SCHIAVO--55
EVOLUTION--57

CHAPTER 3-5 - RELIGION & POLITICS UMMARY--61

CHAPTER 4-1 - NARROWING ENERGY SOURCES--67
THE INEVITABILITY OF SACRIFICE--76
THE TERRORIST FACTOR--78
NARROWING ENERGY SOURCES – SUMMARY--80

CHAPTER 4-2 - GLOBAL WARMING --82
SUMMARY--92
POOR SENSE OF ECONOMICS--98

UNFAVORABLE BALANCE OF PAYMENTS--99

CHAPTER 5-2 - POOR SELF DISCIPLINE--104
    EDUCATION--105
    OUR CURRENT SCORE--111

CHAPTER 5-3 - DISTORTED PRIORITIES--114
    CRIME AND PUNISHMENT--114
    CONFLICTS--116
    AFFIRMATIVE ACTION--119
    WELFARE--121
    AUTHOR'S BIAS--125
    JUSTICE--128

CHAPTER 6 - BROKEN BORDERS--130
    ALICE IN WONDERLAND LOGIC--135
    THE EFFECT ON OUR COUNTRY--136

CHAPTER 7 - LITIGIOUS SOCIETY--143
    ADDICTED TO LAWSUITS--143
    TWO SIDES--146
    LAWSUIT ABUSE IN AMERICA--147
    CLASS ACTION SUITS--151
    MEDICAL MALPRACTICE SUITS--152
    PROPOSED SOLUTIONS TO LAWSUIT ABUSE--154
    SUMMARY--157

CHAPTER 8 - SELECTION OF POLITICAL LEADERS-159
    INFLUENCE PEDDLING--163
    PORK SPENDING AND SUBSIDIES--168
    CORRUPTION AND DECEPTION--172
    SOCIAL SECURITY--177
    SELECTION OF LEADERS--180
    MISPLACED LOYALTY--186
    SUMMARY --188

CHAPTER 9-1 – IRAQ--194

INTELLIGENCE--197
ENTRY INTO IRAQ--209
LEGALITIES--216
RETREAT INTO CHAOS--218
EFFECT ON THE MIDDLE EAST--222
EFFECT ON THE UNITED STATES--223
SUMMARY--226
ADDITIONAL THOUGHTS--239

CHAPTER 9-2 - FANATICAL ISLAM--242
BACKGROUND--242
CONFLICT--244
CLASH OF OPPOSITES--251
THE GROWING DANGER--253
CIVILITY VS. CIVILIZATION--260

IRAN AND NUCLEAR WEAPONS--265
A DANGEROUS DIVERSION--267
SUMMARY- THE SLEEPING GIANT-270

CHAPTER 10 – CONCLUSION--276
STATUS OF THE AMERICAN EXPERIMENT--277
RELIGION ENCROACHING ON GOVERNMENT--279
ENERGY CRISIS--281
ECONOMICS, EDUCATION & SOCIAL CONSCIOUSNESS-283
BROKEN BORDERS --288
A LITIGIOUS SOCIETY--290
SELECTION OF POLITICAL LEADERS--292
IRAQ--294
FANATICAL ISLAM--298
CLOSING THOUGHTS-- 299

This book is dedicated to our grandsons who someday will awaken to the fact that we, a generation or two ahead of them, gathered the world unto ourselves in such a way as to not only deprive them of what we so insisted our fathers bequeath to us, but left them holding the bill.

FORWARD-
EMPIRES COME AND GO

I write this book because I fear the loss of a good thing: our country. I see disease, deadly if not treated, metastasizing into our vital organs. I see this and wonder how many others see as well, and whether those others are aware of what that disease can do if we continue to avert our eyes and minds to its presence. I wonder also whether anyone is aware that we do not have all that much time left to decide.

A while back, under the pseudonym John Barr, I wrote a satiric piece entitled *Hey, God; Got A Minute?*[1] It was a conversation between a simple man and an understanding deity, its theme being to, through humor, provoke the reader into thoughtful examination of his most treasured beliefs and to examine, with as little bias as his emotions would permit, those of these beliefs he seldom challenged. For example, we are quick to proclaim a "miracle" when a baby survives an airplane crash that saw the horrible deaths of hundreds of people—If the one is a

---

[1] Satirical novel, ISBN 0-9658702-2-7, *"Good questions to ask the next time the Big Guy calls you in for a chat."*

"miracle," then what label do we place on the hundreds who died?

Reality is that our world is made up of billions of individuals with billions of interpretations of thousands of contrasting opinions, all of these individuals praising themselves for the richness of their reasoning and the paucity of everyone else's. Awareness of this should instill in each of us a sense of tolerance, understanding and, most of all, humility in what we so fervently profess to others.

No two persons ever read the same book."
Edmund Wilson, critic (1895-1972)

But this is <u>not</u> a book about religion. It is about our country. It is about the "monsters" facing us all and how much of this is of our own making. The mention of religion is to reflect upon the similarity between religion and political ideology, each placing belief above fact, each rarely able to challenge deep-seated opinion, each loath to consider with any degree of sincerity, ideas that conflict with its own.

Neither is this book about one political group or another. No one party has a corner on either ideas or mistakes. Being a Democrat, Republican, liberal or conservative matters less than whether one understands and respects history, in this case the ebb and flow of empires, their birth in passion, their ultimate death through apathy and complacency

. To the extent we educate ourselves to such history, we might yet avert what is otherwise inevitable and enjoy a while longer the blessings of liberty and prosperity that our founding fathers fought so hard to obtain for themselves and their posterity. What we Americans do now will be read by future historians with an eye toward understanding why the great experiment that was the United States of America succeeded or failed.

> ***"No nation in history has survived the ravages of time."***
> Colorado Governor Richard D. Lamm

The first chapter of this book will deal with the subject of religious incursion into politics, and will thus appear to be picking on the religious right. The chapter following that will address the energy crisis, which points fingers at both left and right. Subsequent chapters will touch on educational standards and personal responsibility and will appear in this to "attack" the left. Such will be the trend throughout; i.e. the intention is not to take sides but to point out the harm we citizens, left or right, inflict upon our mutually-owned country.

Reality in both religion and politics is that each too often accepts without thinking the full litany of teachings put forth by those they allow to speak for them (preachers and political leaders). Too often one believes because one is told to believe, told that to accept membership in this or that faith (or political party) requires complete devotion to all the rules and concepts specified within that group's "holy" book. The "novitiate" is required to support and even argue these beliefs.

Such "conviction" is less than commendable. True conviction is not about *deciding* to believe; it is about evaluating each situation then coming to a considered conclusion, even if that conclusion is not what one would prefer it to be. Belief is not synonymous with truth. Belief can lead us in unproductive directions bringing harm to others or to ourselves, either through commission or omission.

CHAPTER 1
FOUNDATION

"To doubt everything or to believe everything are two equally convenient solutions; both dispense with the necessity of reflection."
Poincare

The message in the above is that we aid our understanding when we reflect upon every piece of information that penetrates our senses, recognizing as we do so that no one alive or dead has ever had a lock on the truth. Where one says black, another says white or gray, each influenced in his choice by environment and personal bias. As said by Saint Thomas Aquinas, "The light of religion makes us see what we believe." This works equally well if we substitute "politics" for "religion." The undisciplined political mind too easily sees what it wishes were true. Two news commentators, one left-wing and one right-wing, will watch the same event yet "see" different "truths" in what lies before them. Particularly if they form their opinion without "the necessity of reflection."

"One who professes to know truth has an obligation to fully and fairly consider opposing opinion. If he fails to do so, if he fails to challenge himself

with all the doubts and counter-
arguments that man can devise, then
the beliefs he holds are less than
commendable. They are little more
than recordings in a stagnant mind, to
be replayed upon Pavlov's call."
John Barr[2]

We diminish ourselves when we believe or doubt everything in our party's "book of acceptable beliefs." One should not have to first search through a party line (or church doctrine) before making up one's mind. More commendable is to examine each item on its own merit (perhaps in the privacy of one's home where no one can witness this "heresy"), using reason rather than bias and offering criticism or praise as each appears to deserve it, then making a selection without regard to whether this conforms to party litany. A conservative, for example, might find logic in legalizing drugs ("take the profit out of crime"), while abhorring the thought of abortion. A liberal might rebel against welfare while supporting civil rights.

The point is that it is less than intellectually honest to force-feed an opinion, popular or unpopular, into one's catalog of beliefs. When we assume an end point, what we <u>want</u> to believe, then structure our arguments to support that end point, we fool no one, not even ourselves. This is one of the pillars of "denial."

"Good ideas should take precedence over rigid adherence to any particular political ideology."
Mayor Michael R. Bloomberg, New York City

---

[2] Ibid, page 35.

Right or left, ideology today too often *dispenses with the necessity of reflection*, even when there is strong indication that alternatives exist that will produce more desirable results. It is like wearing blinkers while claiming to see the world. Horses are calmed by such programmed ignorance, but should we follow the teachings of a horse, console ourselves as the animal does through ignorance? Our country is soon to be passed on to our children then a short time later to our grandchildren, and the care we are taking of it today will not escape their notice. Our conscience should be clear in what we bequeath to them. We should feel comfortable in the knowledge that we reasoned well and did not force upon them the burden of our prejudices, that we placed a greater emphasis on pursuing truth than perpetuating belief and that we acted, not with passion, but with reason.

"It is denial to a pathetic degree when one fights so hard to protect a single thought to the exclusion of painful challenges to that thought."
Howard Gardner, *Frames Of Mind*

STATUS OF THE AMERICAN EXPERIMENT

There is little evidence at the moment that we are able to reason without rancor or bias, that we can suspend valued beliefs even when, as in Iraq, we face a situation that can do serious and probably long-term damage to our country. There is also little evidence that we look beyond the near term, or that our concern for the future of our children and grandchildren rises above platitudes and slogans. This does not reflect upon the love we feel for them; rather it testifies to how seriously we consider the necessity to pass on to them what our parents passed on to us.

In 1787, Alexander Tyler, a history professor at the University of Edinburgh, spoke of the fall of the Athenian Republic 2,000 years ago,

> *"A democracy cannot exist as a permanent form of government. It can only exist until the voters discover that they can vote themselves largesse from the public treasury. From that moment on, the majority always votes for the candidates promising the most benefits from the public treasury with the result that a democracy always collapses over loose fiscal policy, always followed by a dictatorship. The average age of the world's greatest civilizations has been 200 years.*

> *"Great nations rise and fall. The people go from bondage to spiritual truth, from spiritual truth to great courage, from courage to liberty, from liberty to abundance, from abundance to selfishness, from selfishness to complacency, from complacency to apathy, from apathy to dependence, from dependence back again to bondage."*

We invite the truth of the above in our apathy and complacency, in becoming too set in our ways, too comfortable in the wisdom of our thoughts and too reluctant to bridge interference with those thoughts. We are too quickly persuaded by light and transient arguments that say it is reasonable to turn off concern and turn on a sit-com. If an opinion is demanded of us—selection of a candidate or referendum on a local, state or national matter-we seize on preconceived notions rather than reasoned examination of the issue. The latter is simply too demanding.

Step by tiny step, we are losing the America of our forefathers. And we have only ourselves to blame. We cannot point to Republicans, we cannot point to Democrats, we cannot even point to politicians per se. We cannot blame the courts for being too lax (or too harsh). We cannot blame the oil companies for their vigorous pursuit of profits or resistance to energy alternatives. There is only one entity deserving of blame, and it lies closer to home. Consider the following (first appeared in the Daytona Beach News Journal).[3]

> *1 - FEDERAL BUDGETS are rocketing out of sight, with ramifications to our economy that are absolutely frightening, for us as well as for our posterity. How is our government able to pursue policies that openly ignore this? Is it possible that the "informed" electorate, from whom our government receives all power, has its eye on the wrong ball? The phrase "weakening of the dollar" may sound esoteric and command little of our thinking, but if this weakening happens too quickly, as now appears likely, it will bring disruptions in jobs and prices throughout America. Many of the items we enjoy today come from abroad, and a weaker dollar will drive*

---

[3] Noel Carroll, Opinion Editorial, Daytona Beach News Journal, March 17, 2005.

up not only the price of imports, but the price of American-made competitive products as well.

The problem is that we are asking foreign countries to buy more and more dollars to support our debt. Or restated, we are asking them to pick up the bill for the spending excesses of Americans. Is it so surprising that they are, at long last, beginning to say no?

HOW IMPORTANT IS THIS TO THE ELECTORATE? In the last election the weakening of the U.S. dollar ranked well below the issue of same-sex marriage.

2 - INTEREST RATES are poised to rise significantly, not only to combat inflation as the Fed is determined to do, but because of increased competition for dollars between business and a government that needs more and more to cover its rapidly-increasing debt. Very few of us escape the results of this increase. Prices rise, as does unemployment. Jobs, those needed now and those needed as our children mature, are not created due to the high cost of investment dollars.

HOW IMPORTANT IS THIS TO THE ELECTORATE? In the last election, keeping "under God" in the Pledge of Allegiance was deemed more important.

3 - We have a rapidly growing FUEL CRISIS in this country, and in ignoring it we feed the very people who publicly vow to destroy us. Yet we, the electorate, dare any politician to get in the way of enjoying our gas-guzzling SUVs or suggest higher gas taxes to encourage conservation. Clever politicians, wishing to remain in office, and correctly measuring the mood of the people, smile obsequiously at our excesses rather than employ the "bully pulpit" to gather us together in a nation-saving cause.

HOW IMPORTANT IS THIS TO THE ELECTORATE? In elections since the crisis began in 1973, flag burning was more of an issue.

An increasingly favorite tactic among politicians is to seize upon issues that require little thought but generate great emotions. The above suggests the electorate accepts the lighter and more transient issues as reason enough for making a voting decision. Such issues are easier to understand; they are promoted by important faces, those of movie stars and rock singers. And who can vote down a person who so strongly defends mother, apple pie and baseball?

There is a serious stew of problems brewing in our country, and the electorate appears either not to notice, or, if a tug of recognition has begun to leak through, not to consider it their problem. They say, "That's what we hire politicians to do! If they don't perform, we'll throw the bums out and get someone new, someone young and exciting, someone who will tell us what we want to hear and trouble our collective conscience no more!"

Aware, as a growing number of people are, that there is a crisis that could threaten everything we have managed to secure for ourselves in the two-plus centuries of U.S. history, how do we respond when it next comes time to choose our leaders. Shall it be more of the same; shall we muddle along with our heads stuck in the sand like ostriches, ignorant of the dangers flying at our exposed bodies? Will we nod in meek acquiescence to a clever campaign manager who once again promotes the petty (but emotional) over the critical?

Yet it is both unfair and dishonest to blame the politicians. Politicians are prostitutes, they give their "customers" what they want. Were we "customers" to revise our preference, the prostitutes would assume a new position. We have the choice, we vote them in, we decide what is important, even if it is not. Therefore the fault for the mess we are in "lies not in the stars, but in ourselves."

Increasingly, we minister this nation like a bad marriage, one in which the parties consider themselves tied for life and no longer obligated to court one another. Such a marriage has a better-than-even chance of failing, whether it is between a man and a woman or between citizens and a country.

There was a restaurant near the waterfront in Philadelphia's historic area, a famous restaurant called Bookbinders. It had been there since American civil war days. An attraction for most of those years, it seemed by this author (who lived nearby) to be taking its customers for granted. True, it was a landmark, an attraction for tourists all over the world, but it arrogantly assumed it would always be so, that its reputation would carry it regardless of what care its owners gave to the business. The owners were cautioned by well-meaning locals in the 1990s that their service was slipping, that they were developing a reputation of not listening to customer complaints and suggestions, that they took too little care in the preparation and presentation of their food. But their reaction was always a knowing smile and little else. "We are Bookbinders!"

Even before closing their doors in 2001, they had begun to hemorrhage badly.[4]

To the extent we recognize no obligation to 'court' one another, to become involved in maintaining this marriage of individuals we call a nation, we might, like Bookbinders, ultimately find the blessings of what was once ours to enjoy fade to a distant memory. As husband and wife should wake up each morning reminded of the care needed to maintain their ever-shifting relationship, so should we as a people daily consider ways of maintaining the unique nature of American democracy. Not as it is today, and perhaps

---

[4] Three years and 21 million dollars later, Bookbinders reopened as a modern new restaurant. It is yet to be seen whether they will recover fully.

not as it has ever been in its past, but along the lines of what was intended when this magnificent invention eked out of the minds of our colonial forefathers.

That is not to say <u>revisiting</u> the ideas of our forefathers is not a good thing. Ideas fit the times, and the times change. We should never use as an excuse for action (or inaction) that our forefathers did not intend this or that, or that they would not approve. Whatever government we wish to construct for ourselves should not be restricted to what our forefathers elected for themselves. We should praise the wisdom they exhibited at a time when so much less was known than is known today, but we need not surrender to them the right to extend their choices beyond their life span. That was their time on earth; this is ours.

<u>Legitimate</u> change is not what we need to guard against. Legitimate change saw the exit of slavery and the recognition of equality between the sexes. Legitimate change put a limit on the power of individuals and institutions, giving birth to the middle class whose spending power continues to drive our economy today (more on this later). What we do need to guard against (beyond apathy and complacency), is change based on ideology, change attempting to import credibility by cloaking itself in patriotic words and religious doctrine, and exuding such cleverness in how they do this that we gravitate toward acceptance of what is often not in our best interests.

Our founding fathers deliberately made change difficult, demanding of us that we think hard about each revision and that we place compromise above decree. They did not think it wise for a majority to "rule" a minority, and indeed, since the early days of our country's birth this has been a moral imperative. The filibuster, the insistence that it takes more than a simple majority to end a debate—often frustrating to both parties—, permits a say to the minority that would otherwise devolve to smoldering resentment (or worse). And, since majority and minority are ever changing, it could also morph into a "get even" philosophy when the inevitable happens and a reversal of roles occurs.

Yet even while wrapping themselves in the banner of patriotism and invoking our founding fathers as gods to be honored and followed, the collection of power for themselves is vigorously pursued by both far right and far left. The result is a steady erosion of our founders' collective wisdom. Those practicing the extreme behavior they condemn in their opponents, never seem to notice how closely they resemble those opponents. And the people fail to notice that 'their' government is less theirs to command.

It is difficult to convince left and right ideologues that they are blinded by their own delusions, that their ideology is too much in the forefront of their argument, that it is poorly reasoned and overly consuming. Like many of history's destructive fanatics, they see only an opportunity to establish once and for all the 'inescapable truth' that they see so clearly.

CHAPTER 2
THE CASE AGAINST US

We regard ourselves as world leaders, envied by every nation on the globe and blessed by God above any of these nations. We do not regard as relevant the poor attention we give to helping the deity keep it this way. We also do not regard as relevant what history has taught us, specifically that empires come and go, and that an examination of the latter often reveals an *arrogance of convenient assumption*. "We Romans (or British, or Ottomans, or Egyptians) have 'arrived;' we are blessed, we are permanent, invincible and invulnerable to decay; everyone envies us and always will. We can relax and let the gods take it from here."

As the Roman Empire aged, there was more and more dodging of responsibility, including evading of the military draft that the Romans then had in place. There was no recognized need for sacrifice; they were at the apex of civilization; they had "arrived," (and so on). Like us, the Romans assumed too much.

The chapters to follow will deal with some of the monsters gaining strength in our country. What I hope they do **not** do is provide enlightenment to students of the next century on what brought about the fall of the American dream. Of late the monsters appear to be growing, feeding upon our way of life even as we raise our eyes in alarm and wave angry fingers at those responsible—the other guys.

It is left to the reader to decide which 'monster' takes priority over which, this being one of the things we citizens seem unable to agree upon. Those who find, for example, the religious incursion into politics not only acceptable but desirable will relegate this item to the bottom of the pile (or out of the "pile" entirely). I place it at the top because it shows not only a lack of understanding of what led our nation to greatness but, unchecked, has the potential of punishing us in many unpleasant ways. The last chapter, which addresses Islamic extremists, might be consider by many readers to be the most important of the "monsters" eating away at our country. I agree enough to place it where it will linger in the mind of any reader brave enough to wade that far into the book.

1 – **Incursion of religion into politics**. There are some who confuse politics with religion, forcing upon others ideas that are heavily influenced by their personal religious beliefs. Never is it presented that way. Rather it is presented as what to the perpetrator seems obvious: "What we believe is good; what you believe is less so, even as we respect your right to continue your flawed thinking."

We deny contraceptives to those most in need of them, civil rights to sexual behavior that displeases us, hope for the seriously ill (stem cells). We even deny evidence of humanity's ancient past (evolution). We deny all this not because there is solid logic in our reasoning, but because it conflicts with what we were taught to believe. Encouraged by the strength of our feelings to think we cannot be wrong, we insist that others come to grips with our way of thinking, even as such thinking is offensive to those others and has little to do with governing. We fail to see the close correlation between "strong religious beliefs" and fanaticism, smiling with approval at the former even as we frown at what we never seem to see in ourselves—the latter.

2 – **Narrowing energy sources and global warming.** The price of oil goes up and we panic into slowing down our purchase of gas-guzzling SUV's and take vacations closer to home. We quickly surrender whatever good this persuaded in us once oil prices retreat, as if now at a level less severe than yesterday, we are no longer threatened. We hide our heads in the sand and pray for more sources of oil, even when knowledgeable others show convincing evidence that our planet is being damaged from emissions the burning of this oil releases.

3 – **Education and Loss of the Middle Class.** We have become a weak and ineffective parent, excusing poor behavior in the name of progressive thinking. We blame others for our transgressions, stating that we were unduly influenced in childhood and thus should not be held accountable regardless of what we do. The one who "influenced" our bad behavior, of course, is also not responsible since his bad behavior was caused by yet another.

We fear accusations of racism or worse, and allow this to influence our social decisions. For reasons of convenience, we permit the "dumbing down" of America, in so doing damn an entire culture to second-rate status.

We throw prodigious sums of devotion and money at movie stars and athletes and almost nothing at those who find new cures for diseases or in other heroic ways provide a true benefit to society.

4 – **Broken borders**. With an eye toward votes and less toward the damage we encourage, illegal aliens are allowed to penetrate our borders by the millions. When the numbers swell to proportions that stir passions even in the meek, we wipe the slate clean by granting these law breakers legal status of some kind, showing no recognition of the incentive this gives others to seek for themselves the same success their brothers and sisters achieved by illegal behavior.

5 – **Our Litigious Society.** With arguments far reaching and weak at best, we permit outrages to our society (and to our economic well being) in the name of "defending the little guy." We permit lawsuits for every imaginable reason, both just and ludicrous, and fail to recognize the threat this poses to our way of life. We also fail to see the flaws so obvious in the arguments of those whose interests lie in continuing the practice.

6 – **Selection of political leaders.** We choose or reject leaders for the wrong reasons. We place "family values" above competence, preferring a good family man who leads our country into harm's way to a person of questionable values who has the knowledge and skills to guide us through difficult times. We place loyalty above conscience, even when such loyalty more serves one's leader than one's country.

7 – **Islam and Iraq.** Our country faces perhaps the greatest danger in its history from a rapidly-

expanding army of religious fanatics. Yet there is a great reluctance to face the problem, and even more reluctance to take action (including sacrifice) that might yet save us. We prefer to seize on arguments that tell us it isn't so, and we ignore the bias (or incompetence) of those offering the argument. The tale of Iraq demonstrates rather well our national confusion.

Each of these points will be taken up in a separate chapter, after which we will discuss what it all means and what, if anything, we can do about it, whether there is still hope of staving off a premature ending to the American experiment.

CHAPTER 3-1
RELIGION AND POLITICS

Our country began as a difficult birth, and few in the world, friend or foe, believed it would last. That it managed to do so until now is remarkable. It also bears examination. If we had to chose one area that most accounts for this success, we might chose the importance we placed on equality (however flawed *that* was to start regarding women and slaves). Disgusted with the systems of kings and aristocracy in the Old Country, we loudly proclaimed the value of opportunity combined with ambition. Any one of us could strive to be better or even best, regardless of humble beginnings and/or ill-regarded ancestors. "Only in America" was our slogan. Only here could a pauper truly become a prince, not by marrying well, but through hard work and application of whatever genius that person managed to acquire. We rejected the past, including many of the beliefs embodying that past. We would do it our way, a way we believed would make us a healthier nation with happier citizens, smarter and better off.

By all accounts, the result has been impressive. From nothing we have become the envy of the world. Not necessarily liked, for it is human nature to resent the successful, but at least respected. There were, to be sure, pockets of American behavior that we would like to bury in the past, but for most of our existence we were viewed as an admirable people.

As mentioned earlier, however, states, like marriages, can fail. Or at least become less than they once were. In the case of the American 'marriage,' the blemishes of late are ominous indeed. Our country is changing. For some this is not a problem, since "change" can be healthy and productive, as in sacrificing a current gain for a greater one in the future (e.g. going back to school). But some of the changes we are experiencing are *not* healthy and productive. They tamper recklessly with what got us to this point, what helped make this nation what it is, belief in the value of ambition, of individuals striving to make a better life for themselves. And, relevant to the discussion that follows, belief in the right of the individual to think and feel as he or she wishes without undue influence from the government. We are today tampering with this latter point in a dangerous way.

When we permit one religious group, even a majority group, to push their "certainty" over someone else's "certainty," we create the potential for serious (and entirely unnecessary) discord. This is happening today with the minority being asked to mimic more of the majority's <u>spiritual</u> thinking, both in speech and actions, and it matters little whether the minority resents this or whether it adds anything to the American dream. It is simply something the majority wishes, and being in the majority they see no need to be overly generous to those who fail to see things as clearly as they.

Only resentment can come from constructing policy whose purpose is to wave the flag of one's ideology in another's face, and resentment of this kind will not help us survive as a nation. It will fan flames that history has demonstrated time and time again are not easily doused. As admitted above, change can be a good thing, but this attempt to dilute the founding fathers' regard for the concept of maintaining a separation between religion and government is short sighted indeed. It is an unnecessary step in a counter-productive direction.

One of the wisest things our founding fathers ever did was to recognize the destructive power in religion, specifically the ready willingness of some to do harm to others (from subtle to mortal) who do not share their spiritual opinion. Our founding fathers, painfully aware of the extent of religious diversity in the world (and in their own colonies), with one religion so often at odds with its neighbor and equally as often showing such hatred and violence that the only predictable outcome was misery for all, wisely elected to declare a separation between that which we can handle and that which we clearly cannot (as history to that point had proven). In a stroke, they removed the impediment for banding together, none of us any longer having to resent his neighbor for being forced to take note of a religious opinion not his own. The result was a nation that could safely navigate the perils of governing without the impossibility of satisfying the widely diverse spiritual wants of its constituency. Restated, we were able to advance our country and the democratic concept without the constant drain of internal turmoil.

This is one of the legacies left to us by our founders, but it is ours only as long as we are wise enough to understand it, understand that the role of a government such as ours should be to protect our earthly rights, not our heavenly fates. Of late we are backsliding, and should this continue, we will be the epitome of the historical adage that "Those who fail to understand history are doomed to repeat it."

To the extent we forget the past (and indeed, the present, since much of the fighting around the world reflects one religion battling another), we sow the seeds of our own destruction. Countries come and go, and to keep ours going, we have to seek the same penchant for wisdom as those who brought it into being. If we do not, then we have only ourselves to blame if, step by tiny step, it begins to crumble. Religion exerting too much influence over governmental affairs is a 'monster' capable of strangling our society." With the emotion it engenders, there is the potential of creating chaos out of calm, hatred out of affection, misery out of pleasure. <u>Never in history has disregard for this truth profited a nation or its people.</u>

STRONGLY BELIEVING

It is argued by those pushing a religious agenda in government that they wish only to do good, that their agenda stems from the heart and represents strongly-held beliefs—on the surface, difficult to argue against. 'Strongly believing,' however, is highly personal and not a testimony to anything other than a suspicion of intractability. Osama bin Laden 'strongly believes,' but that should not impress a civilized world. The simple fact is that if one religion seeks to gain dominance over all others, it will encounter "strongly believing" people in opposition. All that will be accomplished will be a stirring of dangerous fires, with the oppressed daily inventing ways to take vengeance on the oppressor.

It is a sad commentary on us as human beings that we blot out awareness of this, that we cannot so much as entertain the thought that our neighbor might have a greater hold on truth than we. We live in fear that the sacred beliefs taught to us since childhood might be diminished should they suffer even a slight glare of examination, and we become positively deadly when others go so far as to suggest we are <u>totally</u> in error. As we do battle with a contrary opinion (with words or worse), we delude ourselves into thinking we are defending our god, doing his good work. We ignore the likelihood that our adversary believes he is doing the same. Closer to the truth is that such deadly intolerance of another's belief is evidence of insecurity in one's own.

In truth, the strength of one's beliefs has little to do with truth. If a majority, even a strong majority, proclaims a truth, does that make it so? And if they (in this case our government) vigorously pursue what they feel is a mandate to promote that 'truth,' is this commendable? Is Islamic Jihad commendable because so many people in the Middle East strongly believe in the inherent truth of it? Were the government witch-burners in Salem, who undoubtedly acted on strong convictions, right in what they did? Or the Christians officials of the Inquisition who had faith that they were exercising moral conscience when they burned alive those in opposition to their teachings?

"The role of the church is to bring about openness of mind and will to the demands of the common good, <u>not impose on those who do not share the faith</u> ways of thinking and modes of conduct proper to faith."
Pope Benedict XVI, Pope's Encyclical, February 3, 2006

It must be remembered that these government, et al groups and their followers did not consider themselves evil; quite the contrary. It is we who, filled with the wisdom of hindsight and reinforced by new "truths," now proclaim them to be so—even as we excuse similar behavior in ourselves.

What difference can we say truly exists between such groups of the past and those who would push a religious agenda today? Where is the dramatic new evidence that suggests their 'strong convictions' are any different (or potentially less destructive) than the 'strong convictions' of those whose behavior so appalls us at present? Or the 'strong convictions' of Protestants and Catholics in Northern Island, or of Jews and Muslims, or Hindu's and Buddhists, or whoever or whatever else is out there ready and willing to insist with sometimes deadly force that their way of looking at 'truth' is the only way that counts?

The spiritual beliefs of our government are less important than an understanding that their constituents are indisposed to the imposition of opinion where it touches the realm of their own spiritual beliefs. To the extent we ignore this simple truth, we are condemned to renewed and unending conflict in a country that had at its start a golden opportunity to avoid this with honor.

CHAPTER 3-2
PROGRAMMED INTOLERANCE

Right or wrong, born of good intentions or not, a strong hint of intolerance has seeped into our government in the last few years. Religion has become confused with patriotism, facts with faith, science with conviction. What had been a difficult progression toward a higher level of society freed from the capricious opinions of its leaders is regressing to embrace its ugly past.

"God save us from leaders who think He is guiding their hand."
John Barr

It has been argued that, while some 'strongly-believing' Christians are trying to move America toward a theocracy, they are in the minority. Yes, they are in the minority, but like so many clever minorities in history's past, they are capable of such deception that the weak among us are apt to follow[5]. An argument such as "They are trying to drive God from our classrooms" is accepted as valid rather than recognized as an attempt to replace substance with emotion. The irony is that such people sow the seeds of their own destruction as well as ours; i.e. they are not likely to appreciate what comes of this as governments and the spirituality of the people who run them change.

There is evidence that various levels of government all over the country are being "salted" with people more disposed to religious ideology than competence in the job. To the extent this is true, it leads us back to the destructive resentment our forefathers sought to avoid.

> *"Christians must begin to infiltrate the existing institutional order."*
> Gary North of the Christian Reconstructionist movement, 1981
> (Theocratic wing of the Christian right)

When, based on religious beliefs, we require the teaching of abstinence over condoms and other more effective means of family planning, we are taking a step toward a theocracy. When, based on religious beliefs, we attempt to imbue science classes with religious indoctrination, we are taking a step toward a theocracy. When, based on religious beliefs, we

---

[5] A classic example is the National Socialists Party in Germany in the 1930s.

approve or disapprove medicines or approve or disapprove research into promising relief for mankind's physical ills, we are taking a step toward a theocracy. Expressing indignation at the above (all of which are discussed further on) does not convince. Each is a step toward a theocracy, and to claim otherwise is, if not disingenuous, somewhere between convenient thinking and denial.

Also convenient thinking is the notion that our founding fathers were devoted Christians and that this means we are "required" to be as well (or that we must simmer in silence while those in possession of the "real truth" publically shout out their devotions). Neither part of this is correct. Consider these quotes from a few of our "founding fathers:"

George Washington rarely spoke about his religion, but his Freemasonry experience points to a belief in deism[6]. He became a Freemason in 1752 and remained one until he died.

James Madison (called the father of the Constitution) wrote in his Memorial and Remonstrance against Religious Assessments:

> *"During almost fifteen centuries has the legal establishment of Christianity been on trial. What have been its fruits? More or less in all places, pride and indolence in the Clergy, ignorance and servility in the laity; in both, superstition, bigotry and persecution."*
> *"What influence, in fact, have ecclesiastical establishments had on*

---

[6] Deism is a religious philosophy and movement that derives the existence and nature of God from reason and personal experience—Wikipedia.

society? In some instances they have been seen to erect a spiritual tyranny on the ruins of the civil authority; on many instances they have been seen upholding the thrones of political tyranny; <u>in no instance have they been the guardians of the liberties of the people</u>. Rulers who wish to subvert the public liberty may have found an established clergy convenient auxiliaries. <u>A just government, instituted to secure and perpetuate it, needs them not.</u>"

<u>"The purpose of separation of church and state is to keep forever from these shores the ceaseless strife that has soaked the soil of Europe in blood for centuries."</u>

"Religious bondage shackles and debilitates the mind and unfits it for every noble enterprise."

<u>Thomas Jefferson</u> denounced in many of his letters the superstitions of Christianity. He never admitted to any religion but his own.

"I have recently been examining all the known superstitions of the world, and do not find in our particular superstition one redeeming feature. They are all alike founded on fables and mythology."

"We discover in the gospels a groundwork of vulgar ignorance, of things impossible, of superstition, fanaticism and fabrication ."

<u>"Christianity neither is, nor ever was, a part of the Common Law.</u> The common law existed while the Anglo-Saxons were yet Pagans, at a time

when they had never yet heard the name of Christ pronounced, or knew that such a character had ever existed."

"I contemplate with sovereign reverence that act of the whole American people which declared that their legislature should 'make no law respecting an establishment of religion, or prohibiting the free exercise thereof,' thus building a wall of separation between church and State."

John Adams was a very religious man but was still appreciative of the fragility of the country he helped to create.

"As I understand the Christian religion, it was, and is, a revelation. But how has it happened that millions of fables, tales, legends, have been blended with both Jewish and Christian revelation that have made them the most bloody religion that has ever existed?"

"This would be the best of all possible worlds, if there were no religion in it!"

(It was during Adam's administration that the Senate ratified the Treaty of Tripoli (1797). Faced with Barbary pirates we could not control (Muslims), our government included the promise that, ***"The government of the United States is not in any sense founded on the Christian religion."*** The treaty was read aloud to the Senate, and each Senator received a printed copy.)

Benjamin Franklin, a rascal at times, had his own way of looking at the world.

"The way to see by faith is to shut the eye of reason."

"<u>In the affairs of the world</u>, men are saved, not by faith, but by the lack of it."

"Some books against Deism fell into my hands. . . It happened that they wrought an effect on me quite contrary to what was intended by them; for the arguments of the Deists, which were quoted to be refuted, appeared to me much stronger than the refutations; <u>in short, I soon became a thorough Deist."</u>

"I wish it (Christianity) were more productive of good works ... I mean real good works ... not holy-day keeping, sermon-hearing ... or making long prayers, filled with flatteries and compliments despised by wise men, and much less capable of pleasing the Deity."

""As to Jesus of Nazareth, my Opinion of whom you particularly desire, I think the System of Morals and his Religion...has received various corrupting Changes, and <u>I have, with most of the present dissenters in England, some doubts as to his Divinity</u>; tho' it is a question I do not dogmatize upon, having never studied it, and think it needless to busy myself with it now, when I expect soon an opportunity of knowing the Truth with less trouble." (He died a month later.)

Thus the convenient, self-serving assumption that truth is on the part of those who would nudge us ever closer to a theocracy is far from "truth" at all. Our founding fathers showed more wisdom than we are disposed of at the moment, as we are proceeding full speed ahead in a direction sure to harm us all.

The behavior of such people suggests they do not want any *less* of a theocracy than that which satisfies their 'strongly-held' beliefs. It is "give in and we will no longer have an argument." In pushing for this they have a tendency to interpret criticism of their actions as an attack upon their faith rather than upon the offensive behavior emanating from that faith. Most of us do not care what beliefs others hold as long as they do not attempt to make them ours. Many of our founding fathers might have been Christians, but that does not make us a Christian nation any more than the fact of their also being white makes us a white nation. It is not enough to say "we are the majority; we have the numbers on our side." Numbers do not import truth. If they did, the world would be flat and the sun would revolve around the Earth.

However one wishes to play with words, the founding fathers were intent on separating church affairs from State affairs. Thomas Jefferson, in addition to what is quoted above, inveighed against "*every form of tyranny over the mind of man*," his intent being to argue against what many of our colonial ancestors suffered in the "old country," the requirement that they think as their ruler thought in matters of religion. Invading our political realm with a religious agenda does exactly that. In a successful people's government, all beliefs have to be considered and properly addressed, not just those that support a leader's conscience.

"I increasingly witnessed a government that was more and more using theology and ideology to drive its policies and its people-stem cells, abortion, Plan B, the war and many more."
Dr. Richard H. Carmona, former G.W. Bush administration
Surgeon General

We are being led toward becoming a lesser people, as exemplified by the influence of ideology over medicine (more on this later). An FDA scientist resigned in protest when social conservatives interceded in the evaluation of the so-called "morning after" pill,[7] this while moderates of the same party remained silent. The narrow religious beliefs of our government are becoming the deciding factor in what medical benefits the people are permitted to enjoy.

Why do we permit such incursions into this basic freedom, which surely we do, either through commission or omission—those in sympathy with the views of government look the other way when a minority objects? And why after all the historical evidence available to us, do we not see the danger inherent in religion gaining too strong a hold over our lives? Catholics and Protestants in Northern Ireland; Muslims and Jews in the Middle East; Muslims and Hindus in India. From the past, the Inquisition; the bloody flip-flops between Catholicism and Protestantism in Elizabeth I's time; the War of the Roses and so many other wars fought in the name of protecting or promoting this or that faith. What is there in any of this that suggests we are better off by promoting one belief above another?

Or permitting those who persist in doing so to lead us?

Regardless of how strongly one feels one's beliefs, it makes no sense to tamper with what has worked so well to this point. The god that most Americans believe in can handle himself. He does not

---

[7] Susan F. Wood, assistant FDA commissioner for women's health and director of the Office of Women's Health; resigned August 31, 2005.

need self-appointed guardians purporting to speak in his name, defending him as if without their help he might not survive.

CHAPTER 3-3
RELIGION AND MEDICINE

There are large and well respected religions in this world, and the concept of faith per se is comforting to countless numbers of people. What is being written here is in no way an attempt to disturb that. Rather it is hoped that we Americans can retain the plusses of our spiritual beliefs without suffering the oftentimes crippling negatives. But unless we are willing to modify our opinion to reflect new input from an ever-changing and ever-developing world, we have no moral right to accost others and think in doing so that we are guiding them toward a greater truth. The "greater truth" in this instance, is that we lack sufficient conviction to permit a challenge to invade our sphere of protected opinion.

CONDOMS TO AFRICA

When a Catholic became president of the United States in 1960,[8] the fear was that he would tend to decide matters, not on what best served the American people, but on what best served the Catholic church. Much to the relief of Americans of all faiths, this did not occur. At the beginning of the twenty-first century, however, attitudes began to change. A new president made it clear from the start that his spiritual beliefs

---

[8] John F. Kennedy

would strongly influence his governmental decisions. This has manifested itself into pronouncements that may or may not have profited our spiritual well being, but have certainly made the world less well off in a secular sense.

A good example of this is our government's policy on condoms for Africans suffering from AIDS. The Bush administration <u>will</u> provide condoms to Africa and others, but there are strings attached. To be eligible for such aid, the receiving country must emphasize abstinence over condoms and condemn prostitution. Further, no family planning group may speak about abortions, legal or illegal. Brazil declined these conditions because it "stigmatized prostitutes" whose cooperation, Brazilian health workers claimed, was essential to their anti-Aids strategy. Cambodia is also not interested as they have become one of the world's few success stories in the struggle against AIDS, and have achieved that success partly by vigorously promoting the use of condoms.

Examining the results thus far, it is clear that we are doing little to combat AIDS in Africa; i.e. our current policy is <u>not</u> working. But then we operate with ideological blinkers on when we expect it would. Demanding that people who have almost nothing to call their own refrain from the one thing they do have that is free—sexual pleasures—is naïve at best. Worse, it suggests the partaking of sex is but an intellectual decision, which people of all walks of life can simply march away from. Even a brief examination of life around us (including the lives of politicians) proves otherwise.

History and human nature show sexual desire to be more than a flip-of-the-coin choice, and as we naively pretend otherwise, human beings are being infected with a killer disease from which they will likely not survive. We see this yet we wallow in moral confusion as the problem exacerbates. Tenaciously holding on to an abstinence program is hiding our heads in the sand and thinking all the bad of the world will go away. If the situation does not respond to such policy,[9] what moral high ground can we claim by continuing to pursue it?

In attacking the problem of AIDS in Africa, <u>we address, not the medical needs of these people, but the spiritual beliefs of the United States government</u>. Millions of Africans already infected with AIDS are destined to soon die, but equally as shocking, many more millions will become ill through sexual contact with the already-infected.

That people of good conscience find legitimate controversy in this cannot be denied, but it makes little sense to permit one unprovable point of view to rule over another, particularly when that point of view results in such deplorable waste of human lives. And particularly when that point of view is a religious one put forward by a leader who was elected to represent us in secular, not religious, matters.

> *"To impose a dogma-driven policy that is fundamentally flawed is doing damage to Africa."*
> Stephen Lewis, UN special envoy for HIV/Aids in Africa

It is not disputed that refusing condoms to organizations that offer counsel on reproductive health options is helping to spread HIV contamination. It is also not disputed that this contributes to a rise in unwanted pregnancies and abortions (or to more children being brought into families who already find it difficult to feed the children they have). It is a twisted

---

[9] The number of people contracting AIDS about equals the amount dying from the disease - UNAIDS/WHO AIDS Epidemic Update: December 2006.

sense of morals that would advocate this as a greater good. Our leaders err badly when they place conformity to their private brand of morality as a litmus test to qualifying for U.S. medical aid.

FAMILY PLANNING

President George W. Bush appointed as the head of Family Planning, a doctor who is vehemently opposed to family planning and who regards the distribution of contraceptives as: "demeaning to women, degrading of human sexuality and adverse to human health and happiness[10]." His group has made the medically-inaccurate claim that having an abortion greatly increases a woman's risk of breast cancer. This is clearly a person ill-suited to his job. It is also a sacrifice of science to ideology.

At the same time Bush permits funding to religious groups that oppose condom use. As reported by the Center for Health and Gender Equity:

> *"Religious fundamentalists, some financially supported by the US government and the office of the first lady, have become prominent in attacking condoms and those who distribute them."*

Recently the Supreme Court, flush with new conservative appointees, has found a certain type of abortion (partial birth) so offensive that they permit the baring of its use even if the life of the mother is at stake. It is now the law of the land that the threat to a

---

[10] *A Woman's Concern,* a Christian pregnancy-counseling organization.

woman's life will not necessarily have a bearing on the treatment selected by her physician.

ABORTION AND ALTERNATIVES

It is reasonable to say without fear of contradiction, that abortion is not an admirable choice when it comes to family planning—emotions engendered by the subject has a destabilizing influence upon our country. But not being admirable, it behooves us to find <u>realistic</u> means of avoiding it.

We are faced with inexorable truths: that young people <u>do</u> find ways to get together, that they <u>do</u> succumb to emotions (sexual desire), and that they <u>do</u> become pregnant when they do not want to. It does us no credit to deny all this, which we do when we preach abstinence alone. More commendable would be to focus on the bottom line, that as with AIDS in Africa and a poor choice to head family-planning, the policies of the Bush administration are making matters worse, not better. Recognizing, as certainly we should, the human misery we thus encourage, the reasonable in us should react, not with more of the same, but with policies that actually work. There is an inherent contradiction in claiming it is moral to ignore human misery in the name of morality.

The federal government spends $176 million a year on abstinence-only education,[11] and millions more are spent every year in state and local matching grants. The goal is to discourage intimacy outside marriage, but the program provides no instruction for safer sex in the "unlikely" event sex occurs. Indeed, it restricts "unfettered information." The program continues on even though a comprehensive study of abstinence

---

[11] Fiscal Year 2007

education found no sign that it delayed a teenager's sexual debut (authorized by Congress in 1997, the study followed 2000 children from elementary or middle school into high school[12]).

We cannot legislate against pregnancy. Pregnancy happened in the past and it will continue to happen as long as mankind is influenced by sexual desire. We show ourselves to be between immature and irresponsible when we abandon the reality of this in favor of wishful thinking. When young people are flush with emotions and opportunity, it is not logical to expect them to choose the sharing of a soda rather than their bodies.

Evidence shows that condoms do more to bring down abortion rates than pious moralizing, yet our government is dead set against advising the young of its properties, believing this encourages them to promiscuous behavior. We so fear one evil that we flee to a greater one. If abortion is to be avoided (and there appears to be little opposition to this), then we must educate the coming generation to alternatives. Teaching abstinence alone may accommodate a religious opinion, but it does not get the job done. Consider these comments by former U.S. Senator John Danforth:

> *"The Bush administration and Congress have turned over issues bearing on women's reproductive rights to far-right religious groups opposed not just to abortion, but to expanded stem-cell research, effective*

---

[12] A Mathematica Policy Research 9-year study showed no difference in the age of first intercourse between the study group and their peers.

birth control and AIDS prevention programs. The Food and Drug Administration continues to dawdle over approving over-the-counter access to emergency contraception for fear of inflaming members of the religious right who deem any interference with the implantation of a fertilized egg to be an abortion. This foot-dragging may be good politics from one narrow view, but it harms women and drives up the nation's abortion rate."

Universally despised or not, there are many sides to the issue of abortion-as-a-last-resort, and all arguments deserve to be considered. Special consideration should be given to the person most directly involved, the one who, for one reason or another, does not want to deliver another child into this world. That person should not be made to suffer and perhaps die because of the beliefs of others, beliefs that, by her actions, she obviously does not share.

Consideration should also be given to the fact that suffering and death are a fact of life when desperate women attempt to exorcise themselves of unwanted pregnancies. And the fact that this suffering and death is heavily skewed toward those too poor to acquire for themselves a safe procedure. If we blindly prohibit abortions without providing an alternative to avoiding pregnancy, we will encourage a back alley market in abortions—there is no shortage of evidence pointing to the validity of this. The law will <u>not</u> change sexual desire, accidental pregnancy and the use of abortion to resolve unwanted pregnancy, and shielding our eyes from this painful truth does us no honor.

It is important that this issue be openly discussed, that ideology does not block consideration of relevant data. We do not want to wake up one day and realize we have chosen emotion over intellect. Each egg in a female's body might be capable of producing life, but it would be monumentally absurd to suppose in this that God intends to see each and every one of these eggs through to a safe birth.

STEM CELL RESEARCH

The Bush Administration's attitude regarding stem cell research has resulted in less scientific effort being directed toward this promising area. The lesson here is that government backing, critical to much of this research, will come at a price: conformity to the moral dictates of the Bush Administration and its supporters among the religious right. There is a great debate in this country over the issue of stem cell research, and as with the issues addressed earlier, the focal point is one group's spiritual beliefs being imposed upon the rest of us.

> *"Stem cells have the remarkable potential to develop into many different cell types in the body. Serving as a sort of repair system for the body, they can theoretically divide without limit to replenish other cells as long as the person or animal is still alive .... Diseases that might be treated by transplanting cells generated from human embryonic stem cells include Parkinson's disease, diabetes, traumatic spinal cord injury, Purkinje cell degeneration, Duchenne's*

muscular dystrophy, heart disease, and vision and hearing loss. "[13]

The above is not disputed by either the political right or the political left, but there is great disagreement over the type of stem cells that might best serve this important medical purpose. Scientists are in general agreement that embryonic stem cells hold greater potential than adult stem cells, but those in opposition to the concept contend otherwise. Motivated by religion rather than science, they are pushing the less promising adult stem cells. That or the few lines of embryonic stem cells permitted under the President's guidelines, many of which lines are deteriorating or are contaminated or lack the diversity needed to conduct a wide range of studies.

Therapeutic cloning of stem cells is also prohibited if a researcher expects financial backing from the government, and as with restricting research to adult stem cells, this could have a serious impact on the research being conducted. We currently have no way of identifying which embryos carry the right gene for the disease being studied, which means the discovery process would suffer greatly were scientists not permitted to create stem cells that have the same DNA as a patient with a particular disease. The Bush administration not only refuses federal funds for such studies, but would like to ban the practice entirely. If this happens, a promising line of medical research will have to be abandoned.

"You can't do research with your feet bound and one hand tied behind your back."
Jerome Groopman, Harvard Medical School.

---

[13] National Institutes of Health

In fairness to all sides, there is a genuine ethics question here, and it is one that tugs at us all. Experimenting with embryos is, at least in some form, experimenting with human life. Some dismiss such life as far less than what we regard as human, while others feel it stacks right up there with the kind of experiments Nazi doctors performed on concentration camp inmates.

Louis Guenin,[14] in his *Ethics of Human Embryonic Stem Cell Research*, presents in encapsulated form the dilemma we currently face:

> *"Moral Treatment of Embryos In the case of embryonic stem cell research, the end that scientists hope to achieve is the relief of human suffering. That this is a humanitarian and worthy end is not in dispute. The controversy is about the means, namely, the consumption of donated embryos. More particularly, embryonic stem cell research and therapy would use donated embryos that, by virtue of donor instructions, will never enter a uterus. Is it permissible to use those means to that end? Ancient religious texts provide little guidance. The ancients did not understand embryology, did not imagine that scientists might create and nurture what we now understand as embryos*

---

[14] Louis M. Guenin is Lecturer on Ethics in Science, Department of Microbiology and Molecular Genetics, Harvard Medical School.

in the laboratory. Nor can we get an
answer from laboratory experiments.
There is no test for whether an embryo
is a person. Instead we are left to our
own devices, to our own moral
reasoning.

Dr. Courtney Campbell, of Oregon State University, in a report commissioned by President Clinton's National Bioethics Advisory Commission, suggests there is little inter-religion (or even <u>intra</u>-religion) consensus. With **Christians** there are, even within denominations, differing opinions on when life begins. **Christians** also disagree on whether or not it is wrong to experiment with embryos that will never enter a womb (discarded for one reason or another). **Jews** do not consider an embryo to have human status, and permit almost any action for the purpose of saving human life. **Muslims** are divided on when the soul begins. **Jews** and **Muslims** are both favorably disposed to cloning if for therapeutic reasons, but would draw the line on cloning for the purpose of organ harvesting. **Buddhists** believe a fetus becomes human soon after fertilization, but restricts the prohibition against the harming of life to <u>sentient</u> beings. (The other half of that is that it must be seen to <u>benefit</u> sentient life to be acceptable.) **Hindus** are uncertain and calling for time to think, but there is a general feeling that such cloning is permissible if the aim is to alleviate infertility or save lives.

It has been argued that, since President Bush permits embryonic stem cell research in some form that he <u>is</u> providing government funding where none existed before. But is this a valid argument? If a government declares clapping one's hands legal but adds that it must be done using only one hand, is this not a de-facto ban on clapping hands? Substantial discouragement can be as effective as official prohibition. A research facility <u>will</u> lose federal funds as a result of conducting "unapproved" research, and it takes a courageous (or wealthy) facility to carry on without such funds. There are reputable and talented scientists out there negatively influenced by this de-facto ban, some of whom have left the country for more enlightened pastures (see ECONOMICS below).

"The only explanation for legislators comparing cells in a Petri dish to babies in the womb is the extension of religious doctrine into statutory law.
John C. Danforth, former U.S. senator and an ordained Episcopal priest

Opponents of stem cell research have also argued that it raises false hopes in the afflicted. But how high would those hopes be if we did not conduct the research? What sense does it make to retreat from the study of diabetes just to spare the feelings of those currently ravaged by it?

Reason is being trumped by ideology, and it is hurting our country. We are tying the hands of those whose findings have the potential to produce real gains for humanity. There are excess frozen embryos from fertility clinics that could assist in the understanding of human disease and the reduction of human misery, yet they are destroyed in the name of preserving the sanctity of human life. Americans are being condemned to suffer because our leaders cannot separate politics from religion.

We cannot regain the time we lost, but we can resolve to require of future leaders that they show a willingness to represent us all, that they not be so governed by their spiritual beliefs that they neglect their secular responsibilities. Religious beliefs can vary to the point of absurdity.[15] Best for the leader of a free nation such as ours that he not let his spiritual beliefs become law imposed upon disbelieving others—which this reluctance to conduct stem cell research brings about.

ECONOMICS

One wonders what will yet be denied our world through human minds bent by intractable ideology. In Singapore, chewing gum is evil, but cloning embryos for stem cell research is not. In America, it is the opposite. Both are demonstrations of human reasoning, but viewed together they have a hint of comedy about them. A chewing gum advocate could come to this country to escape the imposition of unreasoned opinion upon his "vice." And (as is happening) our scientists can abandon the United States for Singapore's more reasoned approach to stem cell research. Both problems solved. But while the chewing gum immigrant might provide benefit to our country, the vanishing scientists will do quite the opposite. With them will go all the fruits of their inventions.

Beyond the obvious medical benefits of stem cell research, there are economic consequences for our country. The outcome of this research could bring about the next technological boom, rivaling Microsoft and other giants of Silicon Valley in growth and

---

[15] When Ben Franklin went to England to represent the colonies, he was surprised to find people singing on the Sabbath, something that was not permitted in many parts of his own country. Yet nothing bad was happening to these people. Ben said of it, "I am beginning to suspect that the deity is not nearly as angry at the offense of breaking the Sabbath as your average New England magistrate."

economic impact. Could, but will not. Instead, a smaller and less capable country is beating us to the punch. While we wallow in uncertainty and self-righteousness, South Korea is grabbing this huge market potential for itself.

It is painful to consider how many times in history progress has been delayed because the human psyche is so fearful of change. And so certain that the forces of nature and of nature's god will strike them ill should they so much as consider it. A solid example is the history of smallpox vaccination (1700s). The scientist who discovered the vaccine[16] was condemned by clerics as immoral and blasphemous. The concept of vaccination was said to usurp God's power to decide the beginning and end of life. Vaccination was said to be a tool of the devil. How many people died of smallpox as a direct result of such narrow thinking? How many will either die or live less promising lives because such minds still influence matters today?

Upon vetoing a congressional bill permitting a more liberal approach to stem cell research, President Bush stated with no indication that he saw the hypocrisy in it, "It goes against MY beliefs." If we are holding back for fear that we will let loose the Mengele in ourselves, then safeguards are sensible, fair and wise. But when something so potentially beneficial to mankind is defeated because of one man's opinion then we are being wounded by our own leaders. Millions of Americans suffering for want of an answer, and our response is religious ideology that shows embarrassing similarity to that argued by ideologues in the Middle East.

There is promise, but it has yet to run the gauntlet of religious fanaticism. University of Pittsburgh researchers have discovered that epithelial cells taken

---

[16] *Edward Jenner (1749-1823)*

from amniotic fluid could be a substitute for embryonic stem cells. They caution, however, that these cells do not live as long as embryonic cells and thus depend on a steady supply of discarded placentas. They warn also that there is a question of rejection, that over time the amniotic cells could develop the antigens that can trigger rejection, and that this could limit its ability to treat certain diseases.

Additional promise may be found in recent discoveries that mice and man are cousins 75 million years removed. They share genes to a remarkable degree (only about 300 of the mouse's 30,000 genes have no obvious counterpart in the human genome). This makes a mouse an excellent stand-in for human testing (assuming, of course, that the testing is performed by a scientist who believes in evolution).

"There's not going to be one shoe that fits all. We're going to have to see which ones are most useful for which clinical conditions."
Robert Lanza, scientific director at Advanced Cell Technology, Worcester, Mass.

When faced with a difficult choice, our president chose the American ayatollahs over the scientists, thus safeguarding his political position at the expense of real gains for humanity (and economic gains for our country). The heralded "compromise" (the small line of cells permitted for research) puts in mind a compromise on evolution vs. creationism. Or a compromise between a surgeon and a preacher over how to go about a heart transplant. It is doubted that this "compromise" will coax anything other than ridicule out of readers of history a hundred years from now. We will likely look as foolish to our children's children as the state of Tennessee and William Jennings Bryan do to us now.

John C. Danforth, In the Name of Politics, March, 2005

"It is not evident to many of us that cells in a Petri dish are equivalent to identifiable people suffering from terrible diseases. I am and have always been pro-life. But the only explanation for legislators comparing cells in a Petri dish to babies in the womb is the extension of religious doctrine into statutory law.

"... While religions are free to advocate for their own sectarian causes, the work of government and those who engage in it is to hold together as one people a very diverse country. At its best, religion can be a uniting influence, but in practice, nothing is more divisive. <u>For politicians to advance the cause of one religious group is often to oppose the cause of another</u>.

"Take stem cell research. Criminalizing the work of scientists doing such research would give strong support to one religious doctrine, and it would punish people who believe it is their religious duty to use science to heal the sick. ... We Republicans have allowed this shared agenda to become secondary to the agenda of Christian conservatives. As a senator, I worried every day about the size of the federal deficit. I did not spend a single minute worrying about the effect of gays on the institution of marriage. Today it seems to be the other way around.

"We think that efforts to haul references of God into the public square, into schools and courthouses, are far more apt to divide Americans than to advance faith. ... In the decade since I left the Senate, American politics has been characterized by two phenomena: the increased activism of the Christian right, especially in the Republican Party, and the collapse of bipartisan collegiality. I do not think it is a stretch to suggest a relationship between the two. <u>To assert that I am on God's side and you are not, that I know God's will and you do not, and that I will use the power of government to advance my understanding of God's kingdom is certain to produce hostility.</u>"

CHAPTER 3-4
RELIGION AND SCIENCE

IMAX, GALILEO AND TERRI SCHIAVO

Like the Taliban of yesterday's Afghanistan and the Mullahs of today's Iran, those in power claim the moral high ground to be theirs through "certainty of truth" and "strength of conviction." They protest that what they propose is best for the people, even if those people do not know this, do not agree with it and do not wish to be burdened by someone else's narrow interpretation of how they should conduct their lives.

It was widely reported in April of 2005 that a number of science museums felt the need to cancel the **IMAX** documentary, "Volcanoes of the Deep Sea," which suggested life might have originated at undersea vents. It was feared that this would "raise the hackles" of religious zealots who viewed it as contrary to their interpretation of the Bible. Beyond the religious aspect here, consider how quickly our nation would lose its potential if young people were not exposed to broad sources of knowledge.

"No leading world power in modern memory has become a captive of the sort of biblical inerrancy that dismisses modern knowledge and science."
Kevin Phillips How the GOP Became God's Own Party

This has happened often in history, yet those whose "hackles are raised" appear to be unknowing of the fact that they are so often proven wrong in calling for the suppression of new ideas. Witness, for example, the experience of **Galileo** almost four hundred years ago, when the cardinals of the Holy Office concluded that his contention that the Earth revolves around the sun was "foolish and absurd" as well as going against Holy Scriptures. As an alternative to being burned at the stake, Galileo was forced into house arrest for the remainder of his life.

"The number of people that can reason well is much smaller than those that can reason badly. ... But reasoning is like racing, where a single galloping Barbary steed easily outruns a hundred wagon-pulling horses."
Galilei Galileo (1564-1642)

There is an example closer to home, the unfortunate case of a brain-damaged woman on life support, **Terri Schiavo** of Florida. Loudly presenting their opinion, spokespersons outside the Schiavo hospice openly criticized Florida Governor Jeb Bush for not taking advantage of the power passed on to him by people like themselves, the right wing of the Republican party. They promised serious political repercussions if he did not act, <u>by any means necessary</u>, to prevent the pulling of the plug on Schiavo's life-support system. It appeared to matter little that such blatant exercise of power would be in serious contradiction to the law, and that it would be an act of anarchy in which the state police and/or the National Guard would have to choose between breaking the law or participating in a mutiny.

EVOLUTION

"As scientists compare human genes with those of other mammals, tiny worms, even bacteria, the similarities are absolutely compelling. If Darwin had tried to imagine a way to prove his theory, he could not have come up with something better, except maybe a time machine."
Francis S. Collins, Director of the National Human Genome Research Institute, NIH

Science and the technological advances that so often flow from it are critically important to the success of this country of ours, especially as we gravitate toward a global economy. To the extent we permit a disruption of the flow of ideas, in effect substituting ideology for science, we detract from this potential. We lose jobs, industries that might have been (e.g. stem cell technologies), tax revenues to insure our defense and the well being of our people. And we torment a large segment of our society that does not agree with such ideology and that cannot understand why it is so necessary that our supposedly-secular government encourage it.

Intelligent Design (I.D.) is a term used by conservative religious groups in their battle against the theory of evolution. Intelligent Design contends that

much of life is too complex to have happened by
chance, that the only valid answer to how we got here
is that there must have been an intelligent designer.
The issue this causes us to face, which is more
prominent now than it has been since the Scopes
"Monkey Trial" of 1925, is whether American children
should be taught I.D. in science class as an alternative
to evolution. Or at least on an equal plane with
evolution.

*"It takes scientific discipline to protect ourselves from
our own credulity, but we've also found ingenious
ways to fool ourselves and others."*
Daniel C. Dennett, author of *Darwin's Dangerous Idea*.

In general, educators are adamant in their
disagreement, arguing that religion is about
indoctrination and education is about exploration. They
do not feel I.D. belongs in a science classroom. They
go further to caution conservative parents that they
might not want their children exposed to all the
arguments <u>against</u> I.D. which would surely happen if
the class were to be truly educational and not just
doctrinal. Further, they argue that children are always
free to attend a school that supports what they prefer to
believe, but if they want an education, they must
expect their views to be challenged.

*"Global warming and tobacco's link to cancer are
junk science, but creationism should be taught in
schools?"*
(Author unknown)

A discussion of Intelligent Design in a formal
classroom might be welcome if one could trust that the
person doing the teaching would present it as theory

only, theory that has considerable basis in faith but little basis in fact. Under the climate in which I.D. is currently being promoted, however, there is little hope that this would happen. Or that such a presentation would be free of government ideological influence, either local or federal.

If evolution is what science (and considerable evidence) is proving it to be, the concern of I.D. advocates is valid—their beliefs will be tested. As with the tormentors of Galileo, who held to the belief that the Earth was the center of the universe, they will be forced by the continuing flow of new knowledge to change at least some of their opinion. Indeed, refusing to do so would pose an arrogant suggestion that God must conduct his affairs according to their expectations, that the evidence he has displayed to reasonable men and women for common inspection should be ignored. If the world really is as the evidence suggests, and if there really is a god, then logic suggests this is the way he "designed" it. It might well be that he is unimpressed with those who deny his works.

"If English was good enough for Jesus Christ, it's good enough for us."
Texas governor, Miriam "Ma" Ferguson (1925),
Barring the teaching of foreign languages.

Faith should not devalue reason. We have long known that all living organisms are related to one another genetically. We have DNA proof that monkey and man shared a common ancestor, and that 65 million years ago, the time when the dinosaurs disappeared, this ancestor looked somewhat like a shrew. Man and mouse each descended from a small mammal that split into two species toward the end of the dinosaur era, and notwithstanding all those years of separate evolution, only one percent of the mouse's genes have no obvious counterpart in the human genome. Rocks, bones and fossils tell very powerful tales that cannot be denied out of hand by anyone truly searching for an answer.

It is not valid to say that since evolution does not yet have all the answers, that this in some way vindicates I.D. Ignorance never suggests anything other than that we are, for the moment, ignorant. And protesting that, because another does have the answer, your answer must be correct, is illogical. ("You do not know, therefore I do.") Not having an answer is not a competing hypothesis.

"To teach intelligent design as science is to encourage the supercilious caricature of America as a nation in the thrall of a religious authority."
Charles Krauthammer, Pulitzer Prize winning columnist (and noted conservative),

Were our government not imposing their beliefs upon unwilling recipients (President Bush has stated that I.D. should be taught along with evolution), the discussion of I.D. vs. evolution would invoke the same ridicule as it did in Scope's time. But because of this influence, it is not a laughing matter. If left unchallenged, our children will be taught what has been called by many learned individuals, "junk science." Intelligent Design is not a valid hypothesis because there is no observable or experimental evidence to support it.

"The fact that a scientific theory cannot yet render an explanation on every point should not be used as a pretext to thrust an untestable alternative hypothesis grounded in religion into the science classroom or to misrepresent well-established scientific propositions."

John E. Jones III, U.S. District Judge,(Republican, appointed by Bush), Kitzmiller, et al v. Dover Area School District, et al.

Reason dictates that students should be told that, as evidenced by the fact that new discoveries are made every day, there is still much to be learned. This should not, however, be translated into proof of I.D. With I.D. a student might hear a lecture on the gaps in evolution theory but he should not then hear a conclusion not defended by fact and not warranted by what he just heard (as in "They do not know, therefore we do"). Seizing on a gap in knowledge, or even an anthropological fraud or two in a long line of powerful and highly credible discoveries, extends too far into the realm of the indefensible. This is using weak argument stretched to the limits and wherever possible taken out of context to support a desired result. Such tactics might someday impact badly upon the advocate's children and grandchildren as they seek to overcome their educational deficiencies.

"A faith that requires you to close your mind in order to believe is not much of a faith at all."
(Rev. Patricia Templeton, St. Dunstan's Episcopal Church)

Science sees confusion and attempts to provide explanation, wherever that explanation might lead. It begins with a hypothesis and a willingness to abandon this hypothesis in the face of contrasting information. I.D. starts with a desired conclusion that is not to be altered, even in the light of new information. It accepts only those arguments that appear to support this conclusion, and provides ever more artful justification of their claims.

"There [is] a growing need to demonstrate that the loud, shrill voices of fundamentalists claiming that Christians had to choose between modern science and religion were presenting a false dichotomy. …. The theory of evolution is a foundational scientific truth. To reject it is to deliberately embrace scientific ignorance and transmit such ignorance to our children. …. We believe that among God's good gifts are human minds capable of critical thought and that the failure to fully employ this gift is a rejection of the will of our Creator."

(Letter signed by more than 10,000 ministers, February, 2006)

True science will state that anything not supported by a substantial body of evidence cannot rise above the level of theory. When there are hypotheses covering gaps in evolution, they are stated as such, and additional information on the subject is treated with respect rather than fear. Science daily adds to our knowledge of what took place in Earth's past, and each new discovery cuts further into whatever gap previously existed. I.D. is not a pursuit of knowledge, and thus should not be presented to vulnerable young minds as science. Any community worried about the ability of its students to compete in a global economy would be wise to keep supernatural explanations out of its science classes

"Intelligent design can lead only to unintelligent students."

(Author unknown)

The fact is that evolution occurs, and on a daily basis (every year we must come up with a new flu vaccine to deal with a mutated flu bug). There is so much evidence available that we and all the billions of other past and present species on this planet have evolved and are <u>still</u> evolving, that one argues against it at considerable peril to one's reputation. Dinosaur, et al bones have been recovered from all over the world, most of them extracted with an eye toward preserving the story they tell. The earth around, over and under them is painstakingly dated, not to prove pre-construed opinion, but to learn and understand. Further examination reveals the nature of the creature, when it lived, what likely preceded it or came after, even in some cases what it ate. Others consider these data, confer with fellow seekers of truth then offer conclusions. When there is opposition to a conclusion, "truth" must be postponed until additional data surface.

We have found (and are still finding) abundant evidence of "transitional forms," one species on its way to being another. And we have discovered through DNA testing that we are direct descendents of a humanoid creature from Africa who looked substantially like us and lived some 200 thousand years ago. Beyond that, we find more and more bones each year that shed additional light on man's long transition from what he once was to what he is today. Recently scientists extracted a protein from the thigh bone of a tyrannosaurus rex some 68 million years old. From it they were able to determine the protein's sequence of amino acids and, through this, establish a closer match to the dinosaurs and modern day birds. The fact that proteins last so long means further discoveries could lead to further matches connecting the world of the dinosaurs to that of humans; i.e. we might someday be able to construct a true "family tree" that shows with a greater degree of reliability who exactly are our ancestors.

We err when we reject such evidence of our past. And we err even more if we think we have arrived at some end point in either evolution or religion, that it all ends in what we see and believe today.

CHAPTER 3-5
RELIGION AND POLITICS SUMMARY

"The result of this open espousal of one religious view is a censorious climate in which a growing number of pharmacists feel free to claim moral grounds for refusing to dispense emergency contraception and even birth control pills prescribed by a doctor. Public schools shy away from teaching about evolution, and science museums reject scientifically sound documentaries that may offend Christian fundamentalists. Public television stations were afraid to run a children's program in which a cartoon bunny met a lesbian couple."

John C. Danforth, former U.S. senator and an ordained Episcopal priest

In ignorance, denial or deliberate negation of the wisdom put forth by our founding fathers, an American political party, having reached power in such numbers that enabled them to claim the presidency and both houses of Congress, took it upon themselves to impose on people of all faiths their slant on religion. This has infiltrated many corners of our lives, none of them in a beneficial way:

> *1-Government agencies have been "salted" with people who demonstrate more of a propensity for religion than competence. These people are pushing a religious agenda and a narrow brand of Christianity as a national faith.*

> *2-Government heads have turned from reality regarding population planning and the prevention of sexually-transmitted disease.*

3-Officials rally against abortion yet they have established no realistic alternatives to unwanted pregnancies (which, in turn, assures a high abortion rate).

4-Stem-cell research has been slowed to the point where, not only will cures for stubborn diseases be longer in coming, but our country will suffer economically as more enlightened nations pick up the slack.

5-Our leaders attack whatever opinion conflicts with their religious views, as with the dispensing of birth-control products, and IMAX documentaries, and scientifically-sound Public Broadcasting presentations to our young.

6-Government encourages the debasing of science regarding our ancient past, pushing Bible-based intelligent design over evolution.

An individual's spiritual beliefs are his to enjoy, but when we permit such beliefs to infect public policy, we slow the advance of human knowledge and contribute to America's decline. We are poisoning the political atmosphere in the name of morality and closing our eyes to what this is sure to engender: resentment by those of our countrymen not in agreement with our government's religious views.

Religion is a subject that provokes great emotion. Throughout recorded history mankind has tortured, maimed and killed in support of spiritual beliefs, and few (if any) religions can claim to have escaped this. On the surface such behavior is illogical—how does silencing one's opponent add truth to one's point of view? It is as if we are so fearful of being wrong in what we believe that reminders of this must be met with anger, hate and violence. Restated, irrational behavior is our defense against doubt.

Logical or not, such behavior was both predictable and obvious to our founding fathers, who sought a way to tame the worst of it. We, however, even as we praise them for their thinking, feel comfortable in deviating from that thinking, taking no notice as we do so that we open the Pandora's box of resentment they fought so hard to contain.

There needs to be a better understanding of the harm we do when we brush aside the feelings of those who do not share the views of the majority. Tax dollars come from all Americans (Jews, Muslims, Buddhists, Hindus, and so on), and it is unlikely that any of these groups will see reason in another group's spiritual views being given preference over theirs. Or having those views thrust upon their children while they are engaged in a genuine pursuit of knowledge.

It might be easier to understand this point if we imagine how each of us would feel if Muslims grew in such numbers that they could exercise their "democratic right" to publicly promote Muhammad over Jesus (or whoever). Would we all shrug and say, "majority rules?" Would we be willing to recite "under Allah" in the Pledge of Allegiance? Would we be mollified by the argument that we do not have to participate, that we have the right to remain silent while the rest of the class bows toward Mecca or otherwise expresses their devotion to the "approved" religion? In the spirit of cooperation, would we accept the admonition that women should cover their faces and hereafter regard themselves as inferior to men? (Likely the latter provokes a smile of ambition among some men, even as they strive to keep this hidden from their wives.) Or would we finally begin to see the danger inherent in religion gaining too strong a hold over our lives?

The unfortunate way of this world is that one religion will always try to thrust its beliefs upon the vulnerable young as "irrefutable" fact that they doubt at the risk of their immortal soul. But it should not be a democratically-elected government that does this. The more we tamper with this simple truth, the more we begin to resemble citizens of a theocracy, such as Afghanistan under the Taliban or Iran under the Mullahs. Since our government represents every one of us, and since "every one of us" will never see eye to eye on the subject of religion, logic suggests religion should not be part of what we hope will be a democracy that will last.

"The whole problem with the world is that fools and fanatics are always so certain of themselves, but wiser people so full of doubts."
Bertrand Russell, English Logician and Philosopher, (1872-1970)

This new America we create in innocence, ignorance and sometimes arrogance is in reality a speedy trip to the past, to the time of the haves and have-nots, to larger and larger pockets of ignorance and to the desperate actions that so often stem from this ignorance. And to what has been throughout all of mankind's recorded history, highly destructive and totally senseless battles for supremacy, one religion vs. another.

CHAPTER 4-1
NARROWING ENERGY SOURCES

It should surprise no American that the cogs of economic machinery of this, the most powerful country on Earth, are heavily dependent upon cheap and readily-available energy. Restated, as energy supplies slow or rapidly escalate in price, the economy of the United States and the "good life" its citizens have long enjoyed can quickly change for the worse. Our economy is like a human brain, critically important yet exceptionally vulnerable to neglect. If we invite a stroke by failing to watch our cholesterol, or if we refuse a helmet during risky play, we could quickly fall into a life that compares poorly to the one we had.

The chief source of our energy today is oil, and our daily lives are built around it. Beyond gasoline and diesel for running our vehicles and heating our homes, oil is critical to many of the products that feed our economy: plastics, medicines, food items, petrochemicals. When the price of crude oil rises, all aspects of our society are affected. We spend more for driving, for flying, for clothing, for goods made out of petrochemicals, and for delivery of food and other products to our stores. And having to devote more of our discretionary income just to get to and from our jobs, we have less to spend for goods and services, which means the producers of those "goods and services," seeing their sales fall, must lay off workers (who thus have less discretionary income to spend).

When processed oil (gasoline) becomes scarce, as happens when refineries are unable to keep up with demand (inadequate capacity, or shut-downs for maintenance), the result is much the same. If the increase is gradual over a number of years, we have inflation but not serious disruptions to our economy. If the increase is precipitous, we face economic disaster.

Yet, as important as energy is to this country's wellbeing, we fail to give it the attention it deserves. Certainly we do little to insure its continued availability, relying more on the past than the future, more on oil than new energy concepts. We practice and even encourage denial regarding the future of oil—It is available today and if tomorrow it is less available or if the cost gets too high, we will deal with it then. We have been encouraged in this practice of apathy by both Republican and Democratic leaders who, being smart enough to know what it takes to get re-elected, are careful to tell us what we want to hear rather than what we need to know.

But oil is rapidly becoming a thing of the past. The path to a viable economic future lies not in more of it but an alternative to it. With China and India coming on line and demanding more and more energy to support their growth (as we did to support our growth), the world economies (and perhaps our atmosphere) do not have a prayer of surviving should we rely on more drilling as anything but a short-term solution. There has been much said about further drilling in Alaska, but even if we were successful, it would not provide the long-term assurance we seek. In addition, the oil would, for economic reasons be diverted to Japan (Alaskan oil cannot easily or efficiently be shipped to our Gulf Coast refineries). The benefit to us would come from freeing demand from Venezuela and the Middle East. Restated, Japan would have a more stable supply of oil while we would still have to face the uncertainty of Chavez and Middle Eastern politics.

It has also been said that we should build more refineries, that because of objections to the unsightly and environmentally unsound nature of such facilities, we have too few of them, that as a result we are vulnerable should one or more suffer damage, either by man or by nature. Certainly, that vulnerability exists, but it must be considered whether the billions required for additional refineries are the best use of such investment dollars considering the inevitable loss of petroleum as an energy source. Our people and our economy are not best served by promoting short-range energy "solutions."

The unfortunate fact is we are trapped between dwindling supplies of oil and an explosive demand for it. The United States is only one eighth the population of India and China, yet we consume almost twice as much as the two combined.[17] It does not take a super intellect to project what India and China will consume once they progress from a catch-up economy to even half of what America is today. In 2006, China had only a quarter of the cars we had at that time. They are expected to have <u>more</u> cars than America by 2030. They and their giant neighbor to the south will by then consume exponentially more oil than we, and if we do not have some other place to go to satisfy our energy needs, the price of what oil then remains in the world will expand to a level that will destroy world economies and breed international strife.

"We have met the enemy, and them is us."[18]

We Americans are embroiled in a dependency that has the potential of stopping the heart of our nation. And, as proven by the Iraq experience, it has a frightening effect on how we interact with the rest of the world in <u>military</u> as well as economic matters. If our nation is to survive, we must curb our enormous appetite for oil.

Yet, encouraged by our leaders, we are going full speed in the wrong direction, chasing increasingly illusive deposits, even though the most optimistic predictions are that the world will suffer crippling shortages by mid century. Some forecasters argue that global oil production will peak no later than 2010, with shortages, price spikes and economic decline to follow. Only a few short decades from disaster, yet we show

---

[17] CIA World Factbook, 14 June, 2007
[18] "Pogo," Walt Kelly's political cartoon character

little respect for the hardships this country (and the world) will face when the inevitable happens. Consider the following:

We continue to rebel against conservation, even when this is strongly indicated by more and more credible voices.

We reject the very idea of sacrifice, and search for reasons why we can safely disbelieve those who advocate it.

We stop and start incentives to conserve or produce energy based on the price of oil at any given time— mileage standards, subsidies for developing fuel saving measures (windmills, solar panels, electric vehicles). If the price of oil goes up, we push the incentives. If it goes down, we cancel or "relax" them. (American automakers have known for years how to make more efficient vehicles but had to beg our government for relaxation of average fuel economy standards because Americans did not buy them in sufficient quantities.)

We turn a blind eye to those who say we must put more of our time and hard-earned money into ensuring that a renewable source of energy arrives in time to prevent what would arguably be the worst economic collapse in our world's long and troubled history.

We smile with relief when the oil industry and its supporters assure us that we are being misled by false prognosticators, that the solution lies in more and more drilling and more and more oil, that a by-product of the burning of oil, global warming, is a fraud perpetrated by people who, unlike the oil companies, do not have our best interests in mind.

We argue that other countries are more guilty than we in the pollution they release to the atmosphere, and that it is thus unfair that we Americans should have to cut back our pursuit of pleasure.

The sad fact, however, is that we are years, even decades, away from developing either an economically-viable alternative to oil or a cost-effective substitute for the oil-consuming vehicles we drive today. But we had those decades, and through both Democratic and Republican administrations alike, we did nothing. In 1973, when correction of the problem would have been far less expensive in both dollars and human inconvenience, we were alerted to the fact that energy as we knew it could no longer be regarded as secure, that increasingly we would have to rely on uncertain others to satisfy our energy needs. At that time we imported 35% of our oil (that figure is now above 60% and growing).[19] More than thirty years have passed since then, and rather than being that much further down the road to a solution, we have yet

---

[19] U.S. Department of Energy estimates

to come to accept that there is a real problem. Even now, with the cost of oil soaring and with the certainty that we are financing Middle Eastern extremists through our purchase of their oil, we show little willingness to so much as cut back on our gas-guzzling SUV's.

Are we that much in denial, or do we truly fail to see the apocalyptic arrows aimed at our nation? We speak of Iraq, of democracy, of the war on terror, of gasoline prices, but seldom do we speak of what it is that truly threatens our future, our unconquerable complacency.

The fact that we have wasted away more than thirty years cannot be blamed totally on the politicians. To keep themselves in office, they give us what we want and avoid what we do not want ("sacrifice" is not a good campaign slogan). No amount of finger-pointing, protest or tears can wash out the worst of what might yet be coming as we stubbornly refuse to lift our collective heads out of the sand. Thirty-plus years to solve the problem, yet we are nowhere.

"There are very few notable instances of nations that had the ability to eliminate such a vulnerability but didn't. America's current energy condition, however, is a spectacular example of such a failure."
Frank G. Zarb, former assistant to President Ford for energy affairs.

Whether Democrat or Republican, government officials placed in charge of energy affairs have gone wanting for years. We have no long-range planning regarding energy needs, and no alternative fuel plan should matters go rapidly downhill through price spikes and/or disruptions in supply. Our response is always short-term and tentative (and political), and is generally relaxed when oil becomes momentarily cheaper and more available. The embargo of 1973 engendered unity and resolve on the part of a people alerted to a frightening scenario lingering on their horizon, unity and resolve that was not encouraged by our leaders and subsequently did not last.

At first, those in control established programs designed to nudge us in the right direction: a 55 mph speed limit, year-round daylight saving time and a requirement for steadily improving miles-per-gallon in future automobiles. And, at first, we accepted this. But then we began to tire of the problem. We voiced resentment of the price we were expected to pay: higher vehicle costs, greater inconvenience, limitations on our freedom to do as we wish when we wish. Elected officials, reading the tea leaves, were encouraged to take the easy way out rather than demand sacrifice from reluctant constituents; they relaxed the most objectionable of the 1973 edicts. It was like giving in to a silly child who sees only the immediate benefits of his request. "If you really want a gas-guzzling SUV, mommy will get one for you. And if you do not want to spend your comic book money on gas taxes, mommy and daddy will vote out the bad man who suggested it."

Since then, through Democratic and Republican administrations alike, we have permitted ourselves to ignore the seriousness of a crisis that stands no chance of fading away.

"We can't continue to throw empty rhetoric at the issue, using the oil companies as political punching bags and relying on our troops to keep the oil flowing."
Frank G. Zarb, former assistant to President Ford for energy affairs.

There were events during those 30 years that got our attention. We had a hiccup in the oil supply during the 1989 Iranian revolution and another in 1990 with the Iraq invasion of Kuwait. Then, in September, 2001, terrorists struck the Twin Towers in New York, which not only got every American's attention but instilled in each of us a genuine willingness to surrender comforts to ensure survival. But in each case, our leaders (with our subsequent acquiescence) let the moment pass. They diverted their efforts and our resources toward revenge and protecting existing oil supplies, but gave little thought to beginning a concentrated effort toward really solving the problem. Thus it is still with us today.

We as a people need a stronger will. We need to recognize the harm we do in continuing to eat candy when what our body really needs is spinach. We need to rid ourselves of denial and accept the notion of sacrifice for a greater good. We need to reassure our leaders that they will not put their political seat in jeopardy if they lead us to this sacrifice. We are the problem, not the prostitutes who presume to lead us even as they assume all the desired positions to keep themselves in power.

When we next have an opportunity to select a government, we need to consider that we are not helping ourselves when we base our choice on "family values," "gays in the military," "burning of the flag," "same-sex marriage" or "God in the classroom." That is acting on emotion when what is needed is reason. We need to be less shallow and myopic, less demanding of instant gratification, less of the "one-issue" voters we have become.

In short, we need to accept that our country is facing a clear and present danger, and that this calls for competence above personality in our politicians. We need to make it known to all candidates, right or left, that we will consider those who would encourage us to focus on the irrelevant to be, not good and honest patriots, but connivers of the worst kind.

"Is there anything more depressing than yet another promise of energy independence in yet another State of the Union address?"
Charles Krauthammer, Pulitzer Prize columnist

We turned our collective heads from reality as the unstable Middle East of 1973 became even more unstable. And even as the possibility increased that what happened then could happen again, we pulled back on the subsidizing of oil alternatives, feeling comfortable with placing the burden on the oil industry to come up with a way of hastening their own demise.

"I'd put my money on the sun and solar energy. What a source of power! I hope we don't have to wait until oil and coal run out before we tackle that."
Thomas Edison, 1931

THE INEVITABILITY OF SACRIFICE

World population is expected to increase by some 2.5 billion by 2050,[20] most of this from emerging countries (e.g. China and India) anxious to enjoy the energy-demanding products the richer nations have enjoyed for so long. The potential for turmoil this brings with it is multi-faceted. With sources of oil shrinking and energy demands increasing, not only will the world economy be thrown into disarray, but as alluded to earlier, we face a strong possibility of international strife as countries become more desperate in their search for energy. In addition, as we

[20] World Population Prospects, 2006 Revision, United Nations Population Division

aggressively seek out and consume the remaining pools of world oil, we exacerbate the problem of global warming.

"It isn't pollution that's harming the environment. It's the impurities in our air and water that are doing it."
Former Vice President, Dan Quayle (mistakenly attributed to George W. Bush)

One of the biggest pitfalls to reaching an agreement on a next energy step is the fact that it and global warming each have the potential of doing us serious economic harm, and this is whether we ignore the problem or attempt a solution. Even at best, the people can expect disruptions in their lives, both financial and vocational.

Even if a politician were courageous enough to suggest it, a call to sacrifice does not quickly engender soldiers to the cause. Pain is something humans naturally avoid, and sacrifice equates to pain. And it will be painful if we attempt to make oil so expensive that it forces conservation upon people and innovation upon industry. Few will want to do this; not oil companies who fear the reduction of profits and not people facing disruptions in their lives. Yet if we do not act, even worse will befall us in the future. The problem is simply not going to go away on its own.

"It is difficult to get a man to understand something when his salary depends upon his not understanding it."
Upton Sinclair

We fool ourselves if we think we can have both a good living today and a painless path to a similar future. The price of oil will continue to rise, demanding more and more of our discretionary income and leaving less and less for the other goods and services we have learned to enjoy (and which keep our economy moving). There is no offsetting benefit to a rise in crude oil, such as would be the case if that money stayed within our shores to help stimulate the economy. Quite the contrary; it travels overseas to people who vow our destruction, who use much of this money to purchase weapons to use against us. We are, in effect, financing our own demise.

THE TERRORIST FACTOR

There has been much talk about battling Islamic extremism, but we appear not to understand how this relates to oil. Or if we do understand, we show an unwillingness to effectively combat it, spinning our wheels in costly and unproductive directions such as Iraq.

The Islamic nations are not known for their creativity. They are not educating their people beyond a basic level, and they are not building competitive modern economies. Indeed, because of the intractability of their beliefs—strict religious laws effectively preventing almost any kind of progress—these people can only enjoy the fruits of invention if they purchase them from someone else. They do this now; they buy TVs, telephones, cars, aircraft and computers, none of which are a product of their own intellect. They also buy weapons, the finest their money can buy, weapons that will soon include nuclear.

They are able to buy all these things because we give them the money. Through no exercise of intellect, they discovered oil under their feet, which they now sell to us. This in turn enables them to support their favorite passion, assaulting "infidels," which is anyone who does not believe as they do. If they did not have this oil, they would have no ability to purchase weapons, and Islamic extremism would be a curiosity rather than a mortal danger.

But Islamic extremism is a mortal danger, and we deride this at our certain peril (see section on Fanatical Islam, Chapter 9-2). Muslim extremists will be visiting our shores in ever increasing numbers, this because we have our eye on the wrong ball, Iraq rather than al Qaeda and their ilk. Such extremists harbor an attitude that is both primitive and unyielding. They are a danger to the entire civilized world.

Our addiction to oil makes the extremists very happy. They rush to satisfy our "God-given right" to consume energy in any way we please whenever we please, asking in return only that we give them the money they need to buy the means to destroy us. A perfect symbiotic relationship.

Our current efforts to "tame" the Middle East are not only lessons in futility but the wrong approach. We have spent hundreds of billions of dollars in Iraq, ostensibly as part of a war on terror. What if that money, rather than leading us into an endless quagmire that recruits terrorists rather than crushes them, had been used to finance a crash campaign to develop an alternative to oil (somewhat like the man-on-the-moon program of the 1960's)? There would no longer be money flowing to Islamic fanatics determined to replace civilization with barbarism and backwardness. Once their income is lost, they will be lost as well. As mentioned previously, they are not a people prone to invention.

This might force the price of gasoline permanently above $3.00 a gallon, but we are spending this money and more at the moment trying to protect ourselves against terrorists. Helping to offset our disgruntlement would be a reduction of fossil fuel discharge into an increasingly vulnerable atmosphere.

We need leaders who can think outside the box, see the full picture. Leaders willing and able to get the people of the United States oriented toward achieving this reasoned and terribly necessary goal. Only in this way will the illusive "victory" the Bush Administration is looking for in all the wrong places be found.

It is argued that even if the United States decreased its consumption of oil, the price would not go down, that what we no longer consume would be more than made up by what the emerging economies of India and China consume (and thus the Islamic fanatics would continue to be well-funded). This argument fails when taking into consideration the economics a discovery of an oil alternative would hold for the company (and the country) responsible for its discovery. What kind of logic would suggest we (if it is indeed we who do this) not share our "product" with other countries? We would in a stroke improve our broken balance of payments (covered in Chapter 5-1), contribute to the cleaning up an increasingly-poisoned atmosphere, and dry up the fanatics' source of weapons funding.

"There's no shock absorber left. That leaves us with zero options when it comes to leverage against these oil producers."
Gal Luft, Institute for the Analysis of Global Security

NARROWING ENERGY SOURCES - SUMMARY

"We are too dependent on foreign sources of oil. Too much of it comes from troubled parts of the world. And this will still be true if gas prices decline."

Henry Paulson, Secretary of the Treasury, August 1, 2006 [21]

Our country is heading for bad times, seriously bad times, and all our leaders appear willing to do is talk about it. It is as if the major parties either lack strategic reasoning or believe they can pass through their political lives before the dominoes begin to fall. No president in the last 30-plus years, however much he blustered, has asked his party, the Congress, the people, or United States industry to do a single hard thing to reduce our dependence on foreign oil. During that time the energy crisis has gotten worse, not better, and that means another 1973 is inevitable. With our economy so dependent on energy, this can flip us from prosperity to depression in a flash.

As we continue to wallow in denial, we risk stagnation, depression and war. The modern economies of the world are digging themselves into a very serious hole, and the longer it takes for us to recognize this, the deeper that hole will be. If we are forced to face the end of oil without careful preparation, the collection of advanced societies we call civilization will take a giant step backward.

Even in the unlikely event the price of oil remains stable, it is only a matter of a short while before we will no longer be able to rely on this as an energy source. Oil is finite whereas our demand for it is infinite.

What we need are leaders willing to ask of us, "not what the country can do for [us], but what [we] can do for the country."[22] Leaders willing to establish an alternative fuel plan then battle the inevitable voices against it. Leaders willing to stick to a plan, even when

---

[21] Speech given at Columbia University, August 1, 2006.

[22] President John F. Kennedy, Inaugural speech, January 20, 1961

the price of oil momentarily dips to a less stressful level.

Protesting the length of time to success has no relevance. If it takes 30 years to secure for ourselves a viable alternative to oil, then our shame is that we did not start earlier. And if it takes another ten years before we finally agree it is time to take the problem seriously, then at this moment we are <u>forty</u> years away.

"It is too easy — and too partisan — to simply place the blame on the policies of [President] Bush. We are all responsible for the decisions our country makes."
Al Gore, 'The Assault on Reason'

CHAPTER 4-2
GLOBAL WARMING

"Truth might eventually penetrate denial,
but what good is it if it arrives late?"
John Barr

As pointed out in the previous chapter, we show naïveté in our expectation that the energy we need will be there when we need it and for as long as we need it. Our nation is in denial, and we tenaciously hold on to this denial even as another negative has reared its ugly head, the likelihood that emissions from the oil we consume are bringing about an environmental disaster that could swell to biblical proportions.

More and more there is rational scientific argument that the Earth's temperature is rising, and that this is not only getting worse but has likely passed the point of no return, that no matter what we do now, we are going to suffer a serious climate change that will negatively affect humanity. The preponderance of this and other credible opinion suggests the most obvious cause of this temperature rise is the excessive burning of fossil fuels.

It concedes, however, that there are other factors we should be aware of, and that these other factors are at least partly to blame for the rising temperature. Methane, for example, is a more serious pollutant than CO_2[23]. Much of this comes from landfills and manure management, but also having an effect are the animals we nurture to feed an out-of-control world population (primarily cattle). They release flatulence (methane) that threatens to disturb our breathing in more than the obvious way.

"Bush is willing to jump into a war using information that's faulty at best, but he refuses to do anything about global warming despite all the documentation on its gravity."
Bill Moyers, Journalist and Baptist minister

On the one side we have an administration that likely believes but does not want to do anything about the problem if it will inconvenience them or their friends. On the other side we have opinions that too often reflect ideology more than science and in doing so lose whatever scientific argument their message carries.

One of the more credible reports, commissioned by the United Nations and involving 2,500 scientists, states that there is more than a 90 percent chance that

[23] Methane is from 21 to 26 times more powerful a greenhouse gas than CO2. And millions of tons of methane, at the moment in solid form, are lying at the bottom of the ocean. If the ocean warms, it will begin to convert to gas.

human activities, led by the burning of fossil fuels, are to blame for warming since 1950. Further they assert that greenhouse gases (water vapor, carbon dioxide, methane, nitrous oxide and ozone) are at the highest level they have been for some 650,000 years, and that given the global growth in energy demand, there is no way we can avert a doubling or more of atmospheric concentrations of carbon dioxide in this twenty-first century (assuming technology as it exists today). Exacerbating the problem, there is the deforestation taking place on a large scale in Brazil's Amazon rain forest and other parts of the world where desperate farmers are seeking to feed their families. This will have dire consequences regarding the Earth's ability to remove carbon dioxide from the air.

In a separate study by the North American Space Agency (NASA), the amount of global warming since 1975, as monitored by terrestrial weather stations around the world, has been determined to be greater than that between 1900 and 1940. NASA agrees that the phenomenon is both recent and accelerating and that the climate system is nearing or perhaps has already exceeded a critical threshold (this is the "point of no return" mentioned earlier). They point to the retreat of glaciers all over the world, including the critical north and south poles.

Supporting these findings, the National Academy of Sciences has shown through ice samples that Earth's climate has gone through rapid cooling and heating periods in the past but that something was definitely different about the end of the 20th century.

"The system is telling us an internally consistent story — you can't explain the observed changes ... in the climate system over the second half of the 20th century by invoking natural causes."
Benjamin Santer, climate scientist, Lawrence Livermore National Laboratory

Thus the thinking of mainstream scientists is that the burning of fossil fuels is the primary cause of the current warming trend. They present credible data to show a sharp rise in global temperatures in recent decades and receive strong support in their findings from other researchers taking separate analytical paths. Other scientists, even conservative ones, are shifting in the direction of alarm, many suggesting we should err on the side of caution, that it would cost less to cut emissions now than suffer the consequences later on. They even suggest that there could be a huge market for low-carbon energy products by mid-century, products that produce more energy with less pollution.

"Firms that recognize the challenge early will create opportunities for themselves and thereby prosper."
John Llewellyn, senior economic-policy adviser at Lehman Brothers.

Whatever problem we face with respect to global warming, it is distorted by emotionally-stimulated argument. It is possible that we humans may no longer have the luxury of adapting to slow change, yet we surrender valuable time in unproductive debate, often with weak arguments stretched to the limit and taken out of context to support a desired result. In so doing, we abrogate our responsibility to our grandchildren, leave to them what will likely be an even worse problem. As they struggle to save what is left of the world we passed on to them, they will likely not look kindly at the generations that preceded them. They will wonder how, with so much evidence at our command, we could so easily flee to ideology. What could we possibly say that would penetrate their disappointment?

There is a solution to global warming, but permitting ourselves to reason in an unbiased atmosphere seems all but impossible. We have an economic bias or a religious one or a political one, yet even while a part of us is aware of this, we are unable to brush it aside long enough to get a real handle on the problem. What the world needs at this moment is a better understanding of exactly what is happening to our Earth and what we can and cannot do about it. For the analysis, we need people of good will, people able to hold their bias in check, people who will call what they see rather than what they would like to see. Our biggest fear should be that we will not surrender our ideological bias and reach consensus while there is still time to do something about it.

One thing is certain: if we decide to do nothing to curb greenhouse gases and they later prove to be the cause of this accelerated warming, we will not get a second chance to get it right. Civilization as we know it will change, and not for the better.[24]

The world faced a similar controversy late in the twentieth century, when the Earth's protective ozone layer was found to be retreating, thus threatening us all with greater doses of deadly radiation from the Sun.

---

[24] *Author's note:* There are many of good conscience trying to decide for themselves what to believe and what to doubt about global warming (as opposed to consulting the ideological bible of their party to see what is proper to believe). I admit to sharing that ambivalence. Where I am now, however, is doubting the doubters more than the advocates, and as more and more evidence appears to slide to their side of the equation, I become more and more concerned. Not for myself, since my years will protect me from the worst of our environmental abuses, but for those I leave behind. And I have increasingly fewer doubts that those left behind will someday look back at us with "how could you" contempt.

Scientists learned that a popular refrigerant (Freon) was likely responsible for the ozone destruction, and this prompted governments and industry alike to cooperate in devising a solution. What is needed now is another such cooperative effort.

> *"We're good at rushing in with white hats.*
> *This is not a problem where you can do that."*
> Bobi Garrett, National Renewable Energy Laboratory

What we <u>can</u> all agree on is that CO_2 <u>is</u> being produced at a rate greater than Earth's atmosphere can absorb. Aware as we are that humans are producing CO_2 in prodigious amounts, logic suggests we cut back on that which we can control and which is known to be exacerbating an already dangerous situation. To effectuate such a cutback in CO_2, however, we are (as usual) faced with an unpopular choice:

To sacrifice now:
> *Place stringent requirements on CO_2 emitters, including our cars. Pay to have environmentally-friendly appliances in our homes. Change our driving habits and reduce our selection of cars to those deemed fuel efficient.*

Or sacrifice later:
> *Suffer the disruption of shifting crop yields, withering droughts, lost land due to the rising sea levels, and damage to our lungs as we are forced to ingest more and more damaging chemicals.*

It is a poor commentary on human nature that such serious matters as energy and global warming can be treated as political rather than human issues. Science advisors in the Bush Administration had to go public to voice their resentment of ideologues bending the advisors' opinions on global warming to suit their preconceived notions—ideologues unable to escape the confines of deeply-held beliefs.[25] Not surprisingly, the abuse continued.

The Bush Administration has attempted to maneuver to the sidelines all scientists who might interfere with their political agenda. Instead of soliciting the advice of independent outside scientists, the government now relies on a combination of political appointees and staff scientists who are to advise only on "policy relevant" science; i.e. science that backs predetermined policy. They intimidate scientists rather than learn from them, which effectively diminishes the role of science in policy making. One wonders whether this same "policy relevant" approach is used in deciding which of our food and drugs (and toys) are safe for American consumption. When ideology replaces science, we all suffer.

Mounting evidence suggests a need for more aggressive research, supported by government, into climate-friendly energy options. But this is unlikely to happen unless the public becomes convinced that it is a necessary hedge against future calamity—and there are more government voices denying this than are testifying for it.

Our government has not been an advocate of action now. Earlier plans to regulate carbon dioxide emissions in automobiles have been relaxed again and

---

[25] *Restoring Scientific Integrity in Policy Making,* a report by 62 preeminent scientists, February 18, 2004

again by both Republican and Democratic regimes. Our Environmental Protection Agency in 2006 protested that CO_2 was not considered by it to be an air pollutant, and thus they do not have authority to regulate it under the Clean Air Act. (The Supreme Court later ruled (unanimously) that the EPA <u>does</u> have the authority to regulate carbon dioxide from automobile emissions and that <u>it has shirked its duty in not doing so</u>.)

"We will pay for this one way or the other, either now, to control the emission of greenhouse gases, or later, in military engagements and "human lives."
Anthony Zinni, U.S. Marine Corp (retired)

The effect on world economies and the possibility of international strife from a disruption of energy supplies or from population dislocations as seas and temperature rise should not be underestimated. (Ironically, China, even as their use of energy is soaring, may be beginning to grasp that climate change poses a danger to <u>itself</u> as well as to everyone else, that their air is becoming a serious health risk. They are about to surpass the U.S. as the world's biggest emitter of greenhouse gases.) And we cannot expect conservation and restraint to produce anything more than temporary relief. As with a solution to our energy problem, what is needed here are alternative fuels that do not have as a consequence of their consumption a negative effect on the environment we depend upon to service other human needs.

Once again we must think outside the box, develop such things as drought-tolerant crops, methods of blocking sunlight over melting ice caps, capture CO_2 from power plants and pump it underground, and capture and store energy for later use. We must also improve the efficiency and cost of solar panels and develop ways to generate more fuels from crops (without negatively impacting our food supply). We must establish economic incentives to conserve (as began to happen when gasoline first hit $3 a gallon), even if this means deliberately increasing the price of fuel through taxation. Tied into this can be tax deductions to those who choose more fuel-efficient products, both in the home and on the road.

> *"We just need to build the damn things on a billion-dollar scale."*
> David Keith, an energy expert at the University of Calgary

Not surprisingly, the oil producing nations are against this. More advantageous to them is to let the price of oil fall just long enough to kill our incentive to find energy alternatives, at which time they can safely raise it to new highs. They employ this strategy for a simple reason: it works.

In our blind push for the good life, we people of Earth, whether we come from industrial or emerging countries, are tampering with nature's cycles. We must force upon our reluctant minds a need to limit such freedoms as threaten the critical goal of reaching energy security within a stable atmospheric environment. The concern about economic disruptions if we launched a major campaign to lessen the impact of global warming may be a good one, but like some business executives who concentrate too much on the short-term, it focuses too much on avoiding sacrifice now at the expense of greater sacrifice later. We had this attitude of "too-expensive" and "too-inconvenient" during the 1973 energy crisis, and giving in to it did not serve us well. Project this approach 30 years into the future, and what might we (or our grandchildren) face then?

When the fires of global warming begin to be felt, we lose some of our complacency, but when they momentarily dampen, we sigh with relief then quickly turn our attention to less demanding pursuits.

"Our actions now and over the coming decades could create risks of major disruption to economic and social activity on a scale similar to those associated with the great wars and the economic depression of the first half of the 20th century. And it will be difficult or impossible to reverse these changes."
From The Economics of Climate Change by Sir Nicholas Stern

Adding to our problems, there is a question of whether global warming is having a negative effect on the common honey bee, not only here in the United States, but around the world. A quarter of the world's honey bees have disappeared in recent years, and they appear to be dying at such a rate that, should this continue, crops will no longer be sufficiently pollinated to produce the food the world needs to feed its citizens. And there is currently no satisfactory substitute for the honey bee in pollinating plants.

The problem might be caused, at least in part, by a disease recently discovered,[26] or it might be another human "pollutant," pesticides, microwave devices or cell phones (the latter might disturb the bee's sense of homing, which causes it to be unable to return to its hive). But such an alarm coming at a time of already high concern over global warming is unwelcome indeed.

---

[26] Israeli acute paralysis virus.

"If bees were to disappear,
Man would follow only a few years later."
Albert Einstein

SUMMARY.

"When politicians take a research result out of
context to prove a
preexisting ideal, that is when the lying begins."
Mel Ray, Op-Ed contributor, Spruce Creek, Florida

Swinging the pendulum of power back and forth between Republicans and Democrats has not made much of a difference. What our country needs at the moment is some ideas from "column A" (party in power) and some from "column B" (party in opposition). These should include a focus on the energy crisis plus recognition that while our planet is constant, our use of it is not. The world's population is expanding rapidly, and with this comes more demand for space, food and energy. Rather than political ideology, we need a sensible approach to coping with it all. The discovery of more oil will not do it, nor will increasing our effectiveness in scraping the oceans for more fish and the land for more corn.

Argued by some, there is too much concern for snail darters and other endangered species. Perhaps the pendulum does swing too far in that direction at times, but that does excuse a careless disregard for the delicate nature of our planet, which even those critical of the "greenies" are beginning to acknowledge is happening. For sure we should not feel comfortable with assurances from government that "we will worry about it when and if it happens."

It might yet be indicated to us that human contribution to global warming is not significant, that although we continue to pour CO_2 into the atmosphere at enormous rates, the real culprit lies elsewhere. But we <u>do</u> have an <u>energy</u> crisis that few doubt must be solved in the near future, and however much of the global warming problem can be laid at mankind's door, we have an opportunity to attack this and our energy concern simultaneously.

Denial is hazardous to one's health. That it fits one's political bent does not make it less so. A few decades ago, a number of tobacco executives appeared in front of congress and swore under oath that they did not believe tobacco was harmful to humans. The heavy smokers (or investors in tobacco stocks) of the day seized on this argument to show there was "legitimate" reason why they should not have to modify their behavior as suggested by the "alarmists." Those who have not since died a horrible death have become believers. Twenty years from now, the deniers of global warming might look as foolish to what is left of their peers as those tobacco executives look to us today.

CHAPTER 5-1
SOCIAL CONSCIOUSNESS

In 1982, CEO pay was 42 times that of the average worker. By the turn of the century, that figure had become 411 times that of the average worker—a one-hundred-fold increase.[27] In 1979, the top 1% of Americans controlled slightly over 20% of their nation's wealth. By the year 2000, that figure had

---

[27] *Executive Excess 2000*, Institute for Policy Studies

grown to 38%.[28] While great wealth has been accumulating at the top, we have been steadily losing our middle class, arguably the backbone of our economy.

"You can have wealth concentrated in the hands of a few, or democracy, but you cannot have both.".
Louis Brandeis, former Supreme Court Justice

When wealth concentrates in the hands of a few, democracy is doomed. No republic in the history of mankind has survived this. Yet, even though there were signs that this was happening, and even with the warning they raised (at least to those attuned to history), there was little recognition on the part of the newly-installed Bush administration that it was exacerbating the problem by pushing for a tax cut that concentrated its benefits on an already-wealthy few and was applied at a time when the economy did not need a stimulating tax cut.[29] Its enactment worsened the situation in two ways. It further reduced in numbers and purchasing power America's middle class (as more wealth flowed to those having less of a stimulating effect on our economic engine), and it contributed heavily to a ballooning national deficit.

"The United States risks calcifying into a European-style, class-based society."
Bill Moyers[30]

---

[28] Ibid

[29] Later, as the economy began to sour, the reason for the cut was switched to "to stimulate the economy."

[30] CommonDreams.org, February 24, 2006

We are slipping toward a have and have-not nation, and it is not serving our nation well. Jobs are going overseas. Wages are not what they used to be, at least in relation to what those wages will buy. The good life our parents enjoyed, and which we have come to expect as our right, is slipping.

When our country began, we had such revulsion of the class systems prevalent in the "old country" that establishing equality for all (slaves and women excepted) became somewhat of a religion. Each man was instilled with the idea that he could accomplish anything his aptitude and determination led him to. America was built by people taking advantage of this, common people possessed of an attitude that moved mountains for the rest of us—the Rockefellers, the Morgans, the Vanderbilts, and so on. As their dreams grew, so did their need for workers, whose earnings went on to feed other aspects of U.S. commerce, which in turn resulted in more products being produced and more workers being hired. Henry Ford, for example, began by producing cars for the wealthy, but then found a way of bringing the price of his cars within the reach of the average man, who then began demanding more of Ford's cars—a win-win for all.

As more money found its way into the pockets of the people, our country grew rapidly. The average man was both the beneficiary of this and the engine that made it work. The great heights our country reached since then may thus be credited to elementary economics: put money into the hands of the masses and these masses will spend their way to success. Even the rich understand this, since their businesses depend on the purchasing power of the average man.

At least the rich used to understand. As indicated above, there appears to be a slackening of attention given this economic axiom. Too much middle class purchasing power is being siphoned off by the already-wealthy, leaving less to keep the engine of our economy going. Should this unhealthy trend continue, it is only a matter of time before that engine is no longer able to pull its weight. And that will affect both poor and rich.

There are signs that it will continue. While the average wage continues to climb (although somewhat more modestly), and while unemployment is still at acceptable levels, jobs continue to disappear. What jobs remain require more and more skill, demanding of a laid-off worker that he retrain himself even to take a lesser job with lower pay, lower pay that translates into fewer dollars available to fuel the economy.

It is not, however, an easy fix. The hard truth is that the nature of employment in the United States is changing, and much of it is beyond our control. Hard-goods manufacturing is becoming less and less economically feasible, the price of labor in such jobs no longer manageable for a firm needing to compete globally to stay alive. Of itself, that is not a bad thing, since it frees American labor to fill higher-level jobs, but with the Internet and the almost instantaneous exchange of information around the world, employers can ship even these higher-level jobs to wherever it makes economic sense to do so. As I can work at home here in America, someone in India in touch with the Internet can work at home and instantaneously communicate the product of his work to the United States. On the surface, this is good for employers, cheaper labor permitting more competitive pricing of an employer's product. Less good for the employer is that, as each job leaves, there is that much less purchasing power in the hands of an American consumer who might otherwise be one of his customers.

Thus the shrinking of America's middle class has many causes—poorly thought out government policy, the transfer of production and services overseas and changing world dynamics (not only the technology mentioned above but emerging powerhouse competitors such as China and India). Also to be considered is what we did to ourselves. Both labor and management abused success when they had it, labor demanding wages and benefits above productivity increases and management quick to give in to avoid a strike and production losses, both sides laboring under the arrogant assumption that they could stick the public with the bill by either passing on the cost or reducing the quality of the product. The decline of key unions and key industries has been the result. In a sense, unions are the victims of their own success. They obtained better wage and benefit packages for their members, but it has placed them at a level where the price of their services is no longer competitive. As management must now compete on a global level, so must labor.

In the late 1950's during the worst of such consumer-abuse excesses, the board chairman of General Motors responded to concerns about shoddy work and rapidly rising car prices with, "Americans are NOT going to buy Japanese cars!" The rest, as they say, is history.

> *"Who would have believed that there could ever be a time when the Big Three referred to Japanese car companies?"[31]*
> Lee Iacocca

There are nations engaged in much the same rapid development that America experienced in its youth: China, India, South Korea, Brazil. As it was our right

---

[31] In July, 2007, for the first time, foreign auto companies owned more than 50% of the American automobile market.

to do this in the past, it is their right to do this now. Their growth, however, can present us with tremendous opportunity (exports to China are steadily increasing), even as it suggests problems (worker re-training and dislocations). Unlike any other time in our nation's past, we must study both, the opportunities to emulate and the problems to manage or avoid. There is no reason other than attitude why we cannot do this, why we cannot adapt as the Fords and Rockefellers and those who worked beside them did so successfully in a difficult past. The not-so-simple fact is that we depend on the rest of the world more than we ever have in the past, and we cannot simply issue a decree that will keep jobs in the United States or prevent cheaper materials and products from coming here to compete with home-grown goods.

The acceptance of hard work and sacrifice will have to be better ingrained into our national psyche if we are to have any chance of rejoining our previous life. Sacrifice such as life-long education, flexibility in career choices and willingness to retrain on our own time and at our own cost, as doctors, lawyers and other professionals are required to do.

That said, it is equally important that we guard against misguided government policies that exacerbate an already difficult middle class situation. We must require of our leaders that they think through policies that serve their private ideology more than they do the people. And, in this case, more than they do the country.

POOR SENSE OF ECONOMICS

Arguing against the economic changes taking place in the world makes no sense and wastes whatever time we have left to adjust. Those who understand this and adapt will ride the waves of what can be a favorable future. Those who lie on their couches bemoaning their losses and pointing fingers at everyone except themselves will not.

The fact is, to remain in business, a firm has no practical choice but to seek out materials and labor that will enable it to produce a product that people will be willing to buy at a price that will insure for that firm a profit—without a suitable return on capital (profit), there is no incentive to keep a business and the jobs it supports going. Most of us are in some way invested in profit-making concerns, whether that is through direct purchases of stocks and bonds or participation in mutual funds and pension funds. Yet we show ambivalence in this, on the one hand demanding profits to justify risking our hard-earned money and on the other resenting the greedy businesses that produce those profits.

Profits finance our economic future, and we must not be so resentful of those who produce them that we discourage investment, innovation and entrepreneurship. Disruption in our lives may be as regrettable as it is inevitable, but the alternative— stagnation leading to a second-class status for America—is something we are not used to and will not appreciate.

We have little choice but to demand of ourselves and our fellow citizens, that we and they reject the "arrogance of convenient assumption," the assumption that where we are now is where we <u>deserve</u> to be and where we expect we will <u>always</u> be. If we do less, we might someday learn what "second-class status" really means.

UNFAVORABLE BALANCE OF PAYMENTS

Spending more than we make is a policy that can be defended only by politicians and the disingenuous. (But then, stealing a line from Mark Twain, "I repeat myself.") Our <u>internal</u> national debt shows a naïve disregard for what economic hardships we bring to our children and grandchildren, but that at least, is under our control; i.e. it is America's debt to itself. What we owe to other countries, including those who do not wish us well, is more of a concern.

Although not all that familiar to the average American, "Balance of Payments" is not simply a matter of high-level bookkeeping. With a strong dollar, foreign goods are easier on our pocketbooks, and reacting to this, we Americans buy more from foreign nations than we sell to them. (Oil is in a category by itself, it being something we cannot do without regardless of the price.) For the present we pay for our excess of purchases over income with IOU's in the form of American dollars, in effect asking foreign nations to bear the burden of our spending excesses. This is a policy that is doomed to failure, just as in our personal lives buying more than our credit card can handle is doomed to failure. Along with our addiction to oil, this endless borrowing is our nation's Achilles' heel. The situation worsens dramatically when the economy weakens and interest rates drop, making foreign lenders more reluctant to carry our debt (more on this later). It also worsens when we become embroiled in an overseas military engagement.

For years we have shown little concern for what is now trillions of dollars owed to other nations, some of them not our friends. We appear not to recognize the leverage we give these countries, fail to recognize that collectively (or severally in the case of China)[32] they can do serious damage to our economy through the decisions they make regarding retaining dollars or "dumping" them into another currency. If they lose patience with us or see better investment opportunities elsewhere, they will "dump" and in so doing bring about a precipitous fall in the dollar. This will result in

---

[32] China's dollar reserves rose above a trillion in 2007

a sharp change in American life styles, with foreign goods costing more, domestic goods rising in price in response to less competition from abroad, and a revamping of businesses as consumer spending habits react to a changing marketplace.

There are signs that this is happening, that the rest of the world is tiring of our excesses, that they fear a loss of value should they fail to shift their holdings from dollars to a "safer" currency. The principal sign is that the dollar has been dropping in value, a good thing for exports but bad for inflation. Another sign is that our debt holders have dabbled in reinvesting those dollars in ways that threaten the security of the United States (as in the 2006 Dubai plan to control vital sea ports). Having China (for example) own American pharmaceutical firm(s) could give them leverage over prescription drug plans or make it more difficult to regulate new drugs.

[The large US deficit] "cannot persist indefinitely because the ability of the United States to make debt service payments and the willingness of foreigners to hold US assets in their portfolios are both limited. "
Federal Reserve chairman Ben Bernanke[33]

It has been argued that our national net worth is increasing faster than our domestic and foreign debts, and that this permits us to continue our spendthrift ways indefinitely. But this was the logic used by home owners who took equity out of their homes only to see the value of those homes fall below the mortgage they carried. Domestic or foreign, we cannot justify a rapidly growing debt by pointing to the inflationary

---

[33] Speech given in Berlin, Germany, September 11, 2007

growth of our assets; i.e. by making the assumption that our toys will inflate in value to back our spending excesses. Markets change, and assumptions of convenience made today have a way of evaporating tomorrow.

Successful investors are those who understand this, understand that positive situations do not last forever. Governments, however, act not on sound investment principals but on ideological agenda. There was a surplus generated near the end of the Clinton Presidency. The argument by the incoming president was to give it back to the people rather than save it for a possible "seven years of famine."[34] The result of this decision was a huge contribution to an already staggering national debt.

There is a reckoning to all this, and the possible magnitude of it should frighten us all: widespread dislocation and hardship. Our economy could decline so rapidly that financial chaos will fall upon, not only us, but the entire world—this is used as an argument that it will not happen, that the creditor nation would suffer along with us, that they recognize the harm that would strike their economy should our dollar fall and we become less able to buy their products.

But there are signs that this is happening.

"Beijing's dollar reserves should be used as a 'bargaining chip' in talks with the US."
Xia Bin, Finance Chief at China's Development Research Center[35]

"The Chinese central bank will be forced to sell dollars once the yuan appreciated dramatically,

---

[34] Bible, Genesis 41, *Pharaoh's Dreams*
[35] As reported in the Pakistan Daily Times, August, 2007

which might lead to a mass depreciation of the dollar.
He Fan, Economist at the Chinese Academy of Social Sciences

The market punishes heavy indebtedness with less support of that country's currency; this is a fact we have ignored for too long. Restated, a weaker currency is inevitable for a country as indebted as we. We might protect ourselves from the worst of this by making domestic capital more available for America's needs; i.e. by increasing our savings rate, but without a public understanding of the problem and of the complex solutions to it (and without encouragement by our leaders), this is not likely to happen.

There is at least a fair chance that the fall of the dollar will be gradual rather than precipitous, that it will lead to "only" a mild recession. But even this bleak picture presupposes that governments, ours included, will not exacerbate the problem through ill-conceived action (tariffs, artificial support of this or that currency or a new war). More likely is that we will continue to "max out" our national credit card, and that we will find no rich relative waiting in the wings willing and able to bail us out when creditors come knocking at our shores. Sooner or later, our excesses are going to come back to haunt us, whatever that means and whatever pain it brings with it.

"For the developing world to be lending large sums on net to the mature industrial economies is quite undesirable as a long-run proposition."
Ben S. Bernake, Federal Reserve Board Chairman

"If ... the pernicious drift toward fiscal instability in the United States and elsewhere is not arrested and is compounded by a protectionist reversal of globalization, the adjustment process could be quite painful for the world economy."

Alan Greenspan, former Federal Reserve Board Chairman

This does not mean we should give up. As our ancestors were similarly faced with an uncertain world, we can gather ourselves to conquer <u>our</u> problems as they conquered theirs. For sure, we must improve our ability to select leaders. Whatever other qualities they have that we admire, we must see to it that they also possess skills in managing an economy as large as ours, including the increasingly negative balance of payments. It does not make economic sense, for example, to reduce taxes for a class (high-income individuals) who do not need it and whose use of it does not stimulate the economy. Once again, ideology is gaining ground over reason.

One other thing we must <u>not</u> do. We must not shoot ourselves in the foot by establishing an atmosphere whereby we become less capable of economic success than before. By lowering educational standards at a time when the rest of the world is elevating theirs, we are doing exactly that.

CHAPTER 5-2
POOR SELF DISCIPLINE

We have become weak and ineffective parents. We spoil our young and we spoil ourselves. We are loath to accept responsibility for our transgressions, believing it acceptable to blame others: an abusing parent, an intolerant society, the influence of alcohol sold to us by wrong-thinking bartenders or drugs forced upon us by manipulative dealers. We permit, and even encourage, the "dumbing down" of America, lowering standards below that needed to maintain the United States as a country that can successfully compete in this rapidly changing world. We demand for our country the good life enjoyed by others, yet ignore the need to put forth the same effort as do those others.

> *"Forrest Gump made it because he was lucky, not*
> *because he was stupid."*
> Frank Heasley, Ph.D. FSG Online

EDUCATION

Countries such as China and India are investing heavily in educational facilities and talent, their aim being to attract more of the world's best and brightest. There is an expectation that such students bring with them new ideas, new energy and entrepreneurship that promise economic robustness for the host country. Europe, which can no longer count on their past history to attract international students, is trying to accomplish the same thing by making improvements to their institutions.

The U.S. is still ahead of the pack, but the attraction we once held is waning. International student enrollment either dropped or was flat for the last three years.[36] One problem is we are not building enough new institutions (or expanding old) to accommodate a growing population. Whatever the reason, we no longer dominate scientific discovery, innovation or exploration.[37] The "brain drain," the attracting of talented foreigners that so benefited our nation in the past, is in danger of reversing, with American scientists and engineers finding other nations more promising than their own. Restated, we have lost our edge.

---

[36] Institute of International Education
[37] Michael M. Crow; president of Arizona State University

Exacerbating the "brain drain" concern is our current policy of granting visas. At a time when we are cavalier about low-skilled workers pouring over our borders without documentation, we block the entry of people who would be a definite plus to this country. We deny visas to thousands of the world's most sought-after scientists and engineers, even those who were educated in American universities. Immigrants account for a quarter of the nation's doctorates and a third of its engineering professors, and have founded large new businesses, like Google and Sun Microsystems. We do not act in our best interests when we deny such people access to our country.

"America will find it infinitely more difficult to maintain its technological leadership if it shuts out the very people who are most able to help us compete."
Bill Gates, chairman of Microsoft Corporation

For sure we have a problem with the bureaucracy that controls immigration, but our waning regard for education does not help. The schooling of our young is both critical to our nation's survival and badly lacking. Millions of American youth are not even making it through high school at a time when a four-year college degree is becoming a prerequisite for achieving (and maintaining) a middle-class lifestyle. And too many of those who do make it through have not taken the kind of rigorous courses that adequately prepare them for college. Plus, there is a dearth of students well-versed in science and engineering, and this is of itself putting the nation's economic future in jeopardy.

"It is very likely that hundreds of thousands of students will have

*a disconnect between their plans for college and the
cold reality of their readiness for college,"*
Richard L. Ferguson, chief executive of ACT,

Some children receive (and treat kindly) a good education and go on to contribute to the common good. Others are either offered substandard schooling or fail to take advantage of that which *is* offered, good or bad. This latter category is growing, and it is the fault of all of us, rich and poor alike. Rather than stand up to the forces that weaken our system, we lower the bar of expectation with regard to educational achievement. We offer "Ebonics" to disadvantaged black students rather than force them to learn proper English. When a scholastic test uncovers a weakness in one area or another, we hasten to make it more "fair" to the culturally deprived (i.e. make it easier). Such "kindness" shows little regard for what this does to those so tested, how it condemns an entire group of people to second class (and substantially unemployed) status, probably for the rest of their lives. It also shows little regard for the drain it places on the rest of us— welfare, Medicaid, antisocial and even criminal behavior. Whatever we are doing with respect to educating those most in danger of falling behind, it is not working and should be changed, not with more of the same (i.e. throwing money at it) but by changing tactics.

In lowering the educational bar, we weaken the country as a whole. Rather than devising ways of making it easier on students, we must demand more of them. We cannot, for example, continue to equate study with stress and believe we are "kinder and gentler" when we protect our children from the latter. It is irresponsible and even cruel to pass them on to the next grade without their having mastered the basic skills in reading and math needed to succeed there. Such children need to be pushed not coddled. They must be made to reach, to expand, to excel even when they would rather not and even when they do not think they can. If we do less, if we "bless" them with a willingness to cheapen their education, they will likely ride the coattails of those better equipped than they to succeed.

"We do ourselves no meaningful good to permit the underprivileged an easier ride to the skills they will depend upon in their pursuit of a good life."
Marilyn Edelstein, Ph.D

So lost are we in visions of national invincibility that we fail to notice that the rest of the world views our shortcomings as an opportunity for them, a way of gaining their moment in the sun as we lose grip on ours. As education overseas rises to U.S. levels and beyond, the barriers to shipping white-collar jobs abroad will fall even further and the incentives to do so will rise. High-salaried Americans will either lose their jobs, have to accept lower pay or become part-timers without health insurance.

There are plenty of poorly-educated workers in the world ready and able to do manufacturing jobs at a lower price. These jobs and more will continue to leave our shores and our middle class will continue to decline unless we reverse this stubborn unwillingness to prepare our young to compete.

"We cannot hope to fight jobs lost to international competition without a well trained and educated work force."
Congressman Vern Ehlers

Not long ago, Microsoft Chairman Bill Gates gave a speech at a High School outlining eleven things the students did not learn in school. He talked about how feel-good, politically correct teachings created a generation of kids with no concept of reality. And how such a failure of concept sets them up for failure in the real world. It might not be <u>politically</u> correct, but it <u>is</u> correct.

Rule 1: Life is not fair - get used to it!

Rule 2: The world won't care about your self-esteem. The world will expect you to accomplish something BEFORE you feel good about yourself.

Rule 3: You will NOT make $60,000 a year right out of high school. You WON'T be a vice-president with a car phone until you earn both.

Rule 4: If you think your teacher is tough, wait till you get a boss.

Rule 5: Flipping burgers is not beneath your dignity. Your grandparents had a different word for burger flipping: they called it opportunity.

Rule 6: If you mess up, it's not your parents' fault, so don't whine about your mistakes, learn from them.

Rule 7: Before you were born, your parents weren't as boring as they are now. They got that way from paying your bills, cleaning your clothes and listening to you talk about how cool you thought you were. So before you save the rain forest from the parasites of your parent's generation, try delousing the closet in your own room.

Rule 8: Your school may have done away with winners and losers, but life HAS NOT. In some schools, they have abolished failing grades and they'll give you as MANY TIMES as you want to get the right answer. This doesn't bear the slightest resemblance to ANYTHING in real life.

Rule 9: *Life is not divided into semesters. You don't get summers off and very few employers are interested in helping you FIND YOURSELF. Do that on your own time.*

Rule 10: *Television is NOT real life. In real life people actually have to leave the coffee shop and go to jobs.*

Rule 11: *Be nice to nerds. Chances are you'll end up working for one.*

We have experienced a decline in the percentage of students planning to major in engineering, computer science and education. In fact, many school districts within the United States are reluctant to teach algebra before high school. This is later than in European schools[38]. Margaret Spellings, Education Secretary under President George W. Bush points to this as an illustration of the nation's problem with science and math, "If children are not taking [algebra] until the ninth grade or ever, we are in a world of hurt."

"Many states are not yet serious about teaching science.
'The first step is to set higher expectations, and too many states have low or a lack of expectations to respond
to the new global competitiveness."
Michael Petrilli, Thomas B. Fordham Institute

---

[38] Principles of Secondary Education By Paul Monroe p. 536.

OUR CURRENT SCORE

An alarmingly large number of American teenagers leave school without a high school diploma—only two-thirds of all students graduate from high school (one-half for blacks or Hispanics). This is one of the highest dropout rates in the industrialized world. It should surprise no one that such people are likely to be a life-long drag on society. We watch their numbers continue to swell with the only plan being to shove money in their direction to keep them in their place.

The National Assessment of Educational Progress (NAEP), in a study of 12th grade achievement in 2005, found that the share of students lacking even basic reading skills has risen by a third. In addition:

> *Only 35 percent of high school seniors were proficient (achieved a certain NAEP level) in **reading**,*
> *Only 16 percent of black and 20 percent of Hispanic students were proficient in **reading**,*
> *Only 29 percent of whites, 10 percent of Hispanic students and 6 percent of black students were proficient in **math,***

"Parents and communities in too many states are being told not to worry, all is well, when their students are far behind,"
Michael J. Petrilli, Thomas B. Fordham Foundation

The No Child Left Behind Act (January, 2002) requires that all students be brought to proficiency by 2014 in reading and math. It permits the states to set their own standards and choose their own tests. But because there are sanctions imposed if schools fail to reach proficiency, there is little incentive for states to add challenge to these exams.

One irony to come out of what has become a great disparity of testing, is that a state being honest in its testing shows fewer students reaching proficiency than a state watering down its test. **Massachusetts** and **South Carolina** are two states that set their standards <u>high</u> and thus suffer when compared to **Oklahoma** which sets it standards <u>low</u>.

At first the Act seemed to indicate an improvement across the board. But after matching state progress against tests given by the National Assessment of Educational Progress (the nation's "report card"), it soon became clear that it was the state <u>reporting</u> system that had improved and not the students. It was the "smoking gun" that <u>some state's tests had simply become easier</u>.

> *"They're telling the public in their states that huge numbers of students are proficient, but the NAEP results show that's not the case,"*
> Michael J. Petrilli, Thomas B. Fordham Foundation

Five years after passage of the Act, **Oklahoma**, **North Carolina**, **Alabama**, **Georgia**, **Alaska**, **Mississippi**, **Texas** and more than a dozen other states all showed students doing <u>far</u> better on their own reading and math tests than on the federal one (proving the state tests were too easy). **Tennessee's** proficiency standard did not even meet the <u>basic</u> level on the federal test, and **New York** ranked well in reading but did poorly in math. All this happened at a time when the taxpayer was steadily increasing his contribution to education (in real dollars).

"The achievement level that many states called proficient was closer to what the national test rated as just basic."
Grover J. Whitehurst, Institute of Education Sciences at the Education Department

Thus, although some improvement has occurred as a result of the Act, millions of our young are still being passed along, grade to grade, without mastering basic language and reading skills. Certainly they are not being challenged at the same level as students of other industrial nations. All this is happening at a time when available jobs are demanding <u>more</u> skills as a price of employment.

Not only are our students poorly prepared but they are less teachable as well (poor attitude toward learning), and this translates into young adults unable to survive in the real world. The United States will become a second-rate economic power unless a greater percentage of our young become contributors to our society rather than a drain on it.

"The fundamental question we have to ask as a society is what do we do about it? For starters, we're going to have to get serious about some of the things we just gab about — job training, life-long learning, wage insurance."
Robert Reich, the former labor secretary.

As with our problem with energy, we need a man-on-the-moon-size campaign to combat our nation's deteriorating mental condition. Fortunately, the solution to one problem (oil) assists in solving another (education). As we emphasize the science skills required for a crash campaign to develop an alternative to oil, we emphasize education per se, the latter insuring another generation of skilled individuals able to serve our country in a difficult world. One only has to examine the good that came out of the 1960s man-on-the-moon project to understand the possibilities in another such effort, the miniaturization that brought on personal computers, cell phones and so many other useful products in our homes, businesses and cars.

But none of this will happen if we continue business as usual with regard to education. The unfortunate truth is that we are failing to prepare our children to meet what is rapidly becoming a global future.

> *"A word to the wise ain't necessary.*
> *It's the stupid ones who need the advice."*
> *Bill Cosby*

CHAPTER 5-3
DISTORTED PRIORITIES

CRIME AND PUNISHMENT

A group of mean-spirited teenagers run amuck at a sports event in Decatur, Illinois, brutally attacking innocent bystanders[39]. Jesse Jackson (the perpetrators happen to be black) hurries to the scene to plead against the discipline such conduct deserves. After getting the penalty reduced, Jackson advises three of the students to sue school officials on the grounds that they violated privacy laws by disclosing how many days of school these students had missed (exceptionally high) and that they were "third-year freshmen."

---

[39] 1999

A man (Bernard Goetz) is attacked by four muggers on a subway train in New York[40], and responds by shooting and wounding them all. One of the muggers, permanently paralyzed, sues and a jury awards him $43 million dollars.

Cases such as these lend evidence to the suggestion that we are like a bad parent dealing with a spoiled child, showering him with positive stimuli to negative behavior, comforting him with assurances that he is not to blame when he is. We like to consider ourselves civilized and compassionate, but often our choices are difficult to defend. Rather than civilized and compassionate, we often show ourselves to be gullible and naïve, too quick to surrender ground to evil while giving too little attention to those victimized by this evil.

And we seem to regard accidental errors made by officials as carrying more weight than deliberate crimes against people. In the O. J. Simpson trial, for example, the verdict more reflected resentment of police errors (and bigotry) than revulsion at the brutal slaughter of two human beings. And in the trial of Terry Nichols, accessory to the Oklahoma Federal Court bombing, one juror's reason for letting Nichols escape the death penalty was errors committed by the FBI, errors that to her appeared to outweigh the cruel deaths of 168 of her fellow citizens.

In many of these cases, the _criminal_ is offered book deals by publishers whose instinct tells them the public _will_ buy the end product. Some states have tried to prevent this through what is referred to as "Son-of-Sam laws," but the constitutionality of such laws has been successfully challenged. Regardless, Son-of-Sam laws point fingers at the wrong villain. The real culprit

---

[40] 1984

is us, our devotion to rewarding evil, even as we will not extend the same level of generosity to the victim.

CONFLICTS

Our everyday lives are replete with conflicting priorities; i.e. we seldom evaluate a scene or a situation with logic and careful reasoning but decide one way or another based on shifting prejudices, private agendas and emotion. Regarding the latter, the major news sources, whether oriented toward the right or the left, seem to enjoy promoting the emotional over the substantive. And we the public succumb to this with the outrage the display of emotions is intended to provoke, as if one person's hardship should outweigh all other arguments regarding the subject at hand. A picture of an old woman cruelly treated by a new government policy; the camera zooms in to catch her tears; millions form an opinion based on this one scene. Human nature, perhaps, but what if that new government policy aids thousands, or even millions? Or attempts to correct a past error that has negatively affected so many for so long? Are we to delay or abandon the policy, thus putting the welfare of one ahead of many? (How many tears might that provoke?) Is there any new policy in this nation of 300 million that does not negatively affect at least one person?

"Enterprises of great pith and moment, with this regard their currents turn awry and lose the name of action."
William Shakespeare, Hamlet

This is not so much reporting as it is deliberate (and unwise) shaping of opinion, yet we the people not only let it happen but appear to invite it—if we did not, those controlling the news would move on to something that stood a better chance of capturing our interest. We allow ourselves to be swayed by the emotional rather than insist on the substantive, even as the intellect within us admits that we "lose the name of action" as we do so.

How we regard celebrities defies all logic and reason. We throw prodigious sums of money at movie stars and athletes and almost nothing at those who find new cures for disease or in other heroic ways provide true benefits to our society. (The <u>lifetime</u> income of the man who eliminated Polio compares unfavorably to the <u>monthly</u> salary of a top basketball player.) We are unnaturally influenced by faces seen on television or on the big screen or on the playing field, showering such people with devotion beyond all reason or value to society. We place as much importance on following the Anna Nicole Smith saga as we do the war on terrorism, and pay more attention to the dating affairs of movie stars than to the selection of the people we chose to lead us.

"We are amusing ourselves to death."
Neil Postman, media theorist and cultural critic, 1985

News has become entertainment. The serious problems facing our country have to compete for the public's attention with Britney Spears cutting off her hair or Paris Hilton going to jail. And heaven forbid any of it would get in the way of our worship of the Sopranos, a storybook mobster in whose murderous lifestyle we find, not revulsion, but fascination.

"Great minds discuss ideas;
Average minds discuss events;
Small minds discuss people."
Eleanor Roosevelt

We have a tendency to retreat from reality, withdrawing into a feel-good world as the real world becomes increasingly disappointing to us. We find solace in blow-up-the-world movies that show us as more important than we know ourselves to be, or that bring about a different result than that which haunts our conscience. We watch Sylvester Stallone vanquish the Vietnamese single-handed then comfortably retreat to our beds reassured that America is still in control.

In all of this we show little appreciation for the likelihood that the terrible events happening daily in the world will someday find their way to our shores (and possibly our doors). This is simply not amusing. Besides, we hire politicians to worry about things like that, even if we do select them on the basis of "family values" rather than a demonstrated ability to tackle such problems.

A deplorable example of what our society has become is revealed in how easily we feed children violent electronic video games with no regard to how their immature psyche might respond to it. Our society considers exposure of the human body a more corrupting influence to children than people being mutilated and murdered.

Another example is the relative importance we place on sports. The National Collegiate Athletic Association was asked by Rep. Bill Thomas (R-Calif.), to justify its federal tax exemption, specifically how win-at-all-costs athletics departments served educational purposes. "Why," he asked, "should the federal government subsidize the athletic activities of educational institutions when that subsidy is being used to help pay for escalating coaches' salaries, costly chartered travel, and state-of-the-art facilities?" The feeling in congress was that the NCAA practices undermine the purpose of education, that they encourage grade-padding and preferential treatment all in the name of sports.

"Myles Brand's[41] assertion that college athletes are not professional and that the enterprise is not professional flies in the face of mountains of empirical research and facts."
Richard Southall, The Drake Group (advocates of academic integrity)

The question we should all ask of ourselves is whether the American taxpayer should be footing the bill for this, whether our eye is on the wrong ball as we examine the purpose of higher education.

AFFIRMATIVE ACTION

Passions rise on both sides of the argument when the subject touches on racial preference. Affirmative Action has been around long enough to have picked up a cornucopia of such passions. The policy was intended to redress the racist and sexist insensitivities of the past, allowing a "catch-up" vehicle for minorities and women who suffered from a less than fair distribution of justice. There is little protest to the suggestion that it has done a great deal of good.

Unfortunately, it also has a bad side. It permits discrimination in the name of fighting discrimination. By definition it says that decisions regarding opportunities in education and vocation may be based, at least in part, on race, sex or color, which is precisely the kind of evil we as an enlightened society are trying to eradicate. A more qualified person may, under this law, be denied entry to an institute of higher learning to make room for one less qualified. Restated, we allow

---

[41] President of NCAA

an injustice to the talented child turned away because his skin is white. We also ignore the harm we do to a talented <u>black</u> child who works his or her way to a worthy profession only to be viewed with skeptical eyes that wonder whether the talent is real or "assisted." Such a child will long suffer the taint of our clumsy attempts to ease his path.

> *"The way to stop discrimination on the basis of race is to stop discriminating on the basis of race."*
> Chief Justice, John Roberts

Even as affirmative action helps level the playing field of opportunity for some, it does not quell bigotry. Indeed, it often breeds such resentment that the liberal mind shifts perceptively to the right. The situation is made worse when one's reputation is put at stake through voicing an objection to affirmative action per se, objection that could be viewed with distrust by a downtrodden minority and/or liberal colleagues— easier to give in to a flawed policy than to risk accusations of bigotry that might be difficult or impossible to live down.

Thus, in addition to permitting bias in the selection process, we encourage less than complete honesty in our discussion of the program's validity. Good-faith debate suffers as each side reads more between the lines than what is actually said or written. There is a pattern of doubt followed by an assumption of hidden prejudice, with more attention given to suspicion than to the argument presented.

Yet it is vital that we encourage open and honest discussion on such a matter as this. Failure to do so would see the good inherent in it lost to a tumor of spurious argument. We must resist the urge to search a proponent's soul rather than weigh the merit of his proposal based on the good and bad it appears to offer.

Restated, we should not get so wrapped up in suspicion or in political correctness that we will not consider what might work better than what we have.

To demonstrate this point, as you read this passage, is your first thought to wonder at the author's background and bias, what leads him to write what he writes about this and similar sociological subjects? Or are you able to focus <u>only</u> on the argument, its merits or lack thereof? (The coming section *Author's Bias* might help you decide whether your perceptions are correct.)

WELFARE

Much of what we have discussed in the last few chapters enters the realm of "Politically Correct." We say one should not be measured by high standards in education if one is "culturally deprived," and we impose absurd rules upon our speech when interacting with the "downtrodden" or "underprivileged." We also brand as "intolerant" or "lacking understanding" anyone who suggests those on welfare should work harder to improve themselves.

Such political correctness brings us to shy away from altering the welfare system to make it more workable and less permanent—as with Affirmative Action, others will question our motives if we push too hard. Even those genuinely pained by the hopelessness they see around them wallow in fear of being branded politically incorrect should they go too far in what they suggest as a remedy. Such fear brings us to throw money at welfare rather than exert the same level of control a responsible parent would exert on a child (emphasis on the word "responsible"). We permit children on welfare to conceive children while they themselves are still children (which, of course, puts more children on welfare).

The welfare system of the Great Depression became "engrained and intergenerational among the 'underclass'[42] which was predominantly black and poor. Welfare dependency, crime, illegitimacy, school dropout and non-work skyrocketed. This had less to do with a breakdown of morals than the rewards and penalties of the system. Getting married, for example, was considered dumb, since it resulted in less welfare money (or none) for the family. And often more income could be had from welfare than from a minimum wage job. The results could have been predicted. They were all rational responses to the changing rules of the game.

"The city's welfare-state philosophy was racist and 'enslaved' black New Yorkers."
Rudolf Giuliani, former mayor of New York City

Now we see life-long dependence upon a system meant to be temporary, with little chance that any but a small fraction of this underclass will find their way off welfare and onto the American dream. We watch from the sidelines and write checks, as if in so doing we excuse the misery our "political correctness" allows, young people losing all chance of dodging a painful future. In all of this, we are supported by apologists and would-be leaders quick to counsel understanding rather than responsibility.

There is very little real support from black leaders, most of whom appear more disposed toward building their own popularity than providing badly needed guidance to their people. They are the bad parent, so unwilling to risk a child's love that they would permit that child to assume habits that

---

[42] Charles Murray, Ph.D., author of Losing Ground

ultimately bring misery into its life. Notable exceptions include Bill Cosby, Barak Obama and Juan Williams.

Bill Cosby surprised many during a speech he gave at a NAACP meeting in 2004, haranguing inner-city parents for not doing enough to educate their children and for their bad spending and speaking habits. He cautioned his audience, which went well beyond the walls of the hall in which he was speaking, not to blame all minority failure on the majority but assume some responsibility of their own.

There is so much more to what Bill Cosby was saying than picking on poor people. Unlike so many black leaders, Cosby was choosing to lead rather than deliver feel-good rhetoric. His people needed (and still need) help, and "leaders" such as Jesse Jackson are to inclined to give them reasons why they should hold everyone else accountable except themselves. Bill Cosby, unlike Jesse Jackson, et al, is pointing his people in a more constructive direction, bypassing feel-good rhetoric and suggesting they look not to the stars for a solution but to themselves.

Barack Obama, while bemoaning the inequity between schools in wealthy districts vs. poor districts, said during his Keynote Address at the 2004 Democratic National Convention that black parents need to become more involved in the education of their children, including improving their attitude about educational achievement.

> *"I don't know who taught them that reading and writing and conjugating your verbs was something white. ... Don't tell me it doesn't have a little to do with the fact that we got too many daddies not acting like daddies. ... Don't tell me that we ... can't take more responsibility for making sure we're instilling in [our children] the values and the ideals that the Moses*

> *generation taught us about sacrifice
> and dignity and honesty and hard
> work and discipline and self-sacrifice.
> ... The civil rights movement wasn't
> just a fight against the oppressor; it
> was also a fight against the oppressor
> in each of us."*

Juan Williams, a political commentator and a senior correspondent for National Public Radio, feels it is way past time for black Americans to open their eyes to what he calls "the culture of failure." Although black himself, he feels black Americans per se have lost direction, that they are no longer concentrating on equality through black excellence and achievement. He is not impressed by what is offered by prominent black leaders such as Al Sharpton, Jesse Jackson and Marion Barry.

"You should be the change that you want to see in the world."
Mahatma Gandhi

There is more good than bad in insisting on a doctrine of personal responsibility, one that says the primary person responsible for what one is in life is one's self. A compassionate society should look after those who truly cannot manage, but this should not translate into a free lunch or a lifestyle of free lunches. Our welfare system does not work and smacks too much of political convenience—do only what is required to keep the drums from beating so loudly that they disturb the political landscape. As said earlier, black leaders are, for the most part, apologists, and thus exacerbate rather than help.

And the government cannot by itself teach children to learn, nor create for them an atmosphere where they want to learn. That has to come from their parents and most importantly, from within themselves. A child growing up in a household amid parents who speak poor English will have a difficult time overcoming a grammar and speech deficiency even if he or she has an opportunity to attend a top-rated school. Parents must raise their own expectations (turn off the TV, impose a reading assignment on their children, insist on follow-through on homework assignments, rebuke them for thinking good grades equates to "acting white"). And parents must join rather than battle a <u>strict</u> school system that increases demands on students rather than coddles them, raises standards rather than lowers them in the name of "stress reduction.

AUTHOR'S BIAS

As is unfortunately necessary when discussing race, in particular when the argument does not follow "politically correct" opinion, the speaker (or writer, in this case) must defend himself against suspicions of bigotry. In that regard, I offer the following:

My father was a strong supporter of civil rights, even in the 1940's when it was unpopular to be so, when it more reflected conscience than conformity to a trendy movement. I was thus immersed in the concept of civil rights from birth, at times becoming a reverse bigot, too willing to forgive errant behavior once I discovered the perpetrator's dark skin. My final maturity came after the O.J. Simpson trial, but it had begun long before that.

I loved and respected my father and wanted to follow his lead. He died before I was old enough to have a discussion between equals, but I often wonder how it might have gone. My fear is that he would disagree with what I have come to believe about the disproportionate number of black people on welfare, that our fear of attaching nasty brands to ourselves is making us ineffective in how we tackle the poverty/welfare problem.

Racism of any kind is wrong. When someone makes a decision, good or bad, based on the color of one's skin rather than the content of one's character[43], they are racist. I would add that this applies to all races, not just to those suffering more than their share of injustice. If a black person is in pain and he places the blame for this on white people per se, then he is a racist. More important, he wastes time creating excuses for his pain rather than doing something constructive to alleviate it. Should he feel himself justified in this hatred because of some wrong done to him, he is inadvertently justifying a similar invention made by a more overt (white) bigot.

I was thus taught to hate racism, but to me that meant hating it wherever I found it and regardless of the race, religion or color of the person espousing it. I once heard an influential black man say on television, "It is impossible for a black to be a racist." I was appalled at the ignorance behind this remark, and could not understand why the commentator did not challenge him (likely it was fear of being branded politically incorrect). If you excuse a person's improper remarks because of the color of his skin, you are a racist.

Senator Barack Obama said, *"[the people of New Orleans] were abandoned long ago—to murder and mayhem in the streets, to substandard schools, to dilapidated housing, to inadequate health care, to a pervasive sense of hopelessness."* Unpleasant truths, all of them, but does this mean the indigent are absolved of all responsibility for what they do or fail to do? Have these people less of a moral obligation to try than we? When a fellow citizen is truly in need, most of us would flock to his rescue, but when we sense a

---

[43] Martin Luther King

reluctance to help oneself to one's full capacity, our reaction is different, even resentful.

Nothing is free; someone somewhere has to work harder to pay for what we pass on as welfare, and it would be money better spent if constructive strings were attached to each dollar (i.e. a "negative stimulus"). Money gives momentary satisfaction, but requiring that one earn it attacks the "pervasive sense of hopelessness." As discussed earlier, there is a strong tint of conscience money about welfare as it exists today. Throw in a few dollars and we may all engage in denial until the next election.

We have in place a system that is not only lacking but may even exacerbate the problem of poverty. If a lazy/irresponsible parent feeds his child on convenient, fast-foods and permits him to lie around all day and watch television, it is not difficult to place blame should this child become lazy and obese. But even as we identify the cause, is the remedy to make it easy on the child, this in recognition that it is you the parent who brought about his condition? Is it morally correct to steadily increase the fast-food dinners, bringing each meal to where he rests on a larger and larger couch? Or would a more productive tack be to let him know that his world is about to change, that he has a miserable year or two ahead of him: heavy diet, no television and strenuous exercise, that although he will not appreciate what you are trying to do (and may even hate you for it), he will stand a better chance of a real future? Is that not what responsible parentage is all about?

Permitting anyone, black or white, to get something for nothing, even as it eases the conscience of those paying the bills, provides a positive stimulus to sticking close to the couch and accepting the Big Mac one has learned to expect as one's right. Spend what we have to, but on exercise and diet, not on fast food and more comfortable couches. Attach a negative stimulus (meaningful education, work of some sort, distribution of <u>food</u> rather than <u>money</u>) to every dollar spent, thus *forcing* incentive upon a recipient to work toward a better life.

Black people were dealt a raw deal in the past, but those populating the United States today were not the cause of this. My father should not be blamed for his white skin, but praised for the "content of his character." Black people must come to understand that, regardless of the omissions and poor treatment that got them where they are, the solution lies not in more "conscience money" but in accepting responsibility for their lives, including the failures they invite into those lives. As with our obese child, this will not be easy, but also as with our obese child, the alternative is to be a couch potato resting on society for the remainder of one's life.

Black leaders need to walk a more responsible path, not do or say what is popular or what their people want to hear—Bill Cosby and Barak Obama should be commended for tackling the *un*popular and saying what their people *need* to hear. We, including black leaders worthy of the title, must work in good faith to come up with an austerity program for welfare recipients that stands a chance of producing results. And then, as with the obese child, the responsible parent in us must *impose* it upon those who need it most.

Politically incorrect? Quite likely there will be accusations of such. But to continue as we are is cowardly and *morally* incorrect.

JUSTICE

In the arena of justice we often show more naiveté than humanity. It is good counsel to suppress emotions in the name of humanism, but should this be carried to the point of erring so much on the side of a criminal, staunchly defending his rights even if this leaves him free to steal or kill again? Consider the ACLU, who recently blocked the decision of prison officials to restrict books available to incarcerated criminals (according to the officials, certain books inflame the criminals to violence). Usually an effective watchdog against governmental excesses, the ACLU was concerned that such a policy abridged the rights of a group of individuals who have proven to care little about our rights. Is it truly in the interests of the public, whose trust these criminals have violated, to make it more difficult for prison officials to keep them under control?

In judging the criminal element among us, we often insist on more than we are able to give; i.e. perfection. The police and the courts are permitted to show no human weakness in regard to how they prosecute a case. Evidence tainted by human error is thrown out, even if such evidence points unquestionably to a person's guilt, and even when it is likely that some innocent will suffer or die as a result of that criminal's release.

We go too far in demonstrating our civility to people who have no intent to respond in kind. For many, prison is less a burden than a badge of courage to one's peers. When finally we manage to incarcerate a felon, we bend over backward to be "fair," awarding him privileges beyond what he might experience at home. We even permit him to continue to prey upon the public through telephones and/or computer email. This is not a deterrent to crime; it is not even punishment to some who live worse lives on the street.

Though we appear to encourage the worst of it, many of us have grown weary of a legal system that too often appears broken, so weary that we become susceptible to outrages of the other extreme in the name of national defense: abuse of Habeas Corpus and of privacy laws. This is neither commendable nor healthy for a country that prides itself as governed by the rule of law. When the pendulum swings too far in either direction, the people lose.

CHAPTER 6
BROKEN BORDERS

As a successful nation born of immigrants, it is difficult to argue that immigration has not been good for the United States over its two-and-a-third centuries of existence. People from all over the world have come here, and though they were not always made to feel at home and did not necessarily find their new path free of painful obstacles, they eventually became part of a uniquely-American culture. As we began to mature as a nation, however, we saw the wisdom of qualifying one's entry into eventual citizenship, requiring of immigrants that they bring with them a commitment to assimilate, to learn our language and culture. We also took a harder look at what we needed, what would benefit our society and what would detract from it, and from this came quotas and skill requirements. We had come to realize that, with so much poverty in the world, poverty influenced by politics we Americans could not control, we could not allow our success to be jeopardized by a flood of immigrants who, rather than contribute to the American economy would be more likely to require assistance from the public beyond that needed to assimilate.

The rules governing entry continued to be tightened, with closer and closer examination being given a candidate before issuing the invitation—a useful skill, an encouraging attitude, something that would say this person would fit into the American psyche not long after arriving on our shores. By definition, this labeled us as less than altruistically oriented, more a case of looking out for ourselves than offering a helping hand to a neighbor in need (although we have demonstrated a willingness to do that numerous times in our history). We had become cautious shepherds watching out for our sheep and ourselves, recognizing that while we could not change the world, neither did we want the untamed portion of it to change us—if you came to America you did it our way; you did not bring "baggage" with you, your politics, your prejudices, your incompetence and your poor attitude. Not to our credit, this policy sometimes reflected the prejudices of American officials (and the American public), who based quotas on which country and what people (race) were deemed "desirable" and which were less so.

In 1942, as a result of a shortage of labor going into World War II, a workers plan was agreed to between the United States and Mexico. Called the Bracero Program (Spanish for *unskilled laborer*), its intent was to bring a few hundred trained agricultural workers in to harvest sugar beets in California. With the war draining more and more of our workers, this soon spread to agriculture per se and to most of the U.S. (It became an early "guest worker" program.) Later this was expanded to supply unskilled workers for railroad track maintenance and other labor jobs within the U.S. By the end of the war, the program included some 50 thousand farm workers and 75 thousand railroad workers. The railroad program ended suddenly with the end of WWII, but the agricultural program continued on until 1964. It was ended then by mutual agreement between the U.S. and Mexico because of suggestions of human rights abuses. It benefited U.S. agriculture even in its demise, in that it led to more mechanized farming (to replace the "guest workers"), but the program still gets bad marks from a humanitarian point of view.

The Bracero Program was a controlled situation and meant to be temporary. And indeed, we had never in our history passed on to immigrants the right to construct their own policy; i.e. to decide for themselves who should be permitted entry into the United States, what skills (or lack thereof) they should bring with them and whether they should first demonstrate a willingness to assimilate into American society—learn the language, obey the rules and laws and understand American culture and history.

Things changed in 1986 with the passage of the Immigration Reform and Control Act (called the "Simpson-Mazzoli Act"). Immigrants had been sneaking across our southern border by the millions, and like the poor parent discussed in the previous chapter, we decided to apply a positive stimulus to this negative behavior. We granted amnesty and a path to citizenship to all those who had entered our country illegally. That was when de jure law began giving ground to de facto law, when our immigration policy became irrelevant to Americans and Mexicans alike.

"This problem was created by corporate America, which wants to keep the low-wage labor already here and bring in more through a temporary-worker program,"
Louis S. Hunter, pollster and political analyst

Even with its recognized benefits, we cannot make a blanket statement that since immigration has been good for America, it must always be good. We are in the process of testing its limitations now.

The Simpson-Mazzoli Act was the first major granting of amnesty as a way of "solving" an immigration problem[44]. There was a feeling then (as now) that immigration was "out of control," and that the incentive for entering the U.S. illegally could be

---

[44] 2.7 million illegal aliens were granted amnesty, but this number swelled to well beyond that as these new citizens successfully petitioned to include their relatives.

taken away by keeping such immigrants from gainful employment and by excluding them from all government benefits. While it allowed those already here to remain, the act provided sanctions for employers who knowingly hired new illegals, requiring of them that they check the documents of all prospective employees. The act also provided for a "guest worker" program, a way for seasonal agricultural workers to enter on a temporary basis as long as employers could show there were not enough legal workers able and willing to do the work.

It must be pointed out that the law required everyone, citizen and immigrant alike, to show proof of citizen status before being accepted for a new job. This, however, led to protests of potential discrimination against legal minorities, and perhaps for this reason, was seldom followed.

Since the passage of the act the situation has worsened. Encouraged by the good fortune of their comrades-in-misery, twelve million new illegal immigrants have since flooded the United States[45].

"The fact that these new INS figures show that the last amnesty actually attracted more illegal immigration should give serious pause to those now advocating another amnesty,"
Steven A. Camarota, Center for Immigration Studies

Although part of the Simpson-Mazzoli Act, enforcement has never been tried in this country whereas amnesty has been tried (1986) and failed. Not only did we fail to stem the tide of illegals, but we demonstrated to those staying behind in Mexico that

---

[45] As of 2007

our laws are not to be feared, that there is a promise of reward if one ignores them.

> *"Insanity is doing the same thing over and over again and expecting different results."*
> Albert Einstein

It helps to put one's self into another's mindset when considering what that person may or may not do. If we were desperately poor in a country that finds it close to impossible to assist us or our family, and we saw our brothers and sisters bypass a slow-to-impossible visa application process by sneaking into the United States, and we then saw these people get jobs they might otherwise not be offered at a wage that exceeded what they could get at home and where they not only did not face criminal prosecution but eventually benefited from their crime, would we not be encouraged to do the same? It should thus surprise no one that we have more illegals and a bigger problem two decades after the passage of legislation that was intended to cure our illegal-immigrants problem.

Yet we propose as a solution the same plan that did not work then.

The proposed new solution (now defunct) was to finally enforce the provisions that were put into law in 1986 and never enforced, principal of which was to block further violations of our borders. In support of this we would spend $5 billion to tighten up our borders (also promised in 1986 and also never brought about), and require that state National Guards fill in at times for border agents (even Senator Kennedy, a sponsor of this legislation, voiced a concern that the National Guard was already spread too thin). Enforcement was to be further aided by the creation of an identification card system for foreign workers that would include digitized fingerprints. All of this presupposed a willingness to enforce compliance, which past history suggests is a naïve assumption indeed.

"Congress and the president are completely out of touch with how people here feel about illegal immigration."
Louis S. Hunter, pollster and political analyst

The question bothering so many Americans is whether this new government proposal is in truth another granting of amnesty. The proponents of the new law give an emphatic "no" that matches in intensity the emphatic "yes" offered by the other side. But whatever label is attached to this, it does offer incentive to illegal behavior; i.e. it encourages other would-be illegals to invade our country in pursuit of the same success gained by the law breakers who preceded them. They, with our help, are taking decisions on immigration out of the hands of the American people and awarding it to themselves.

ALICE IN WONDERLAND LOGIC

"War is peace, Freedom is slavery, Ignorance is strength."
George Orwell's "1984," engraved on the Ministry of Truth building:

One argument given by proponents of the proposed act is that by not giving such illegals amnesty we are driving them further underground. But that is like saying that if we interfere with an al Qaeda attempt to kill one of us, we will drive them to kill more of us. If we succumb to such logic, should we be surprised to find al Qaeda demanding the death of two next time? Then four? One does not cure crime by giving in to some of it. Illegal is illegal, and if we are to take our laws seriously we must either remove those laws currently in effect or enforce them in a less hypocritical manner.

Another argument is that these twelve million illegals are too enmeshed in the U.S. economy to be extracted. This presupposes that an invasion of our country is acceptable if the number of invaders is sufficiently large.

The fact is that by doing nothing we demonstrate that we are not in control of our own country, that our laws may be ignored with impunity. And what does that say to new immigrants whom we hope will be assimilated into our culture; how should they observe our laws in the future? Also, what does it say to terrorists who want nothing from our economy except its destruction and who view such weakness as an opportunity? If illegals were law-abiding, they would not be here. They would be in line like everyone else in the world who wants a better life.

"The president is putting the onus on border governors to work out the details and resolve the problems with this plan."
New Mexico Governor, Bill Richardson

"A Band-Aid solution"
California Governor, Arnold Schwarzenegger

THE EFFECT ON OUR COUNTRY

At a time when we are slowing down acceptance of highly-skilled foreign workers (see "Education" in Chapter 5-2), and at a time when we are driving some of the best and the brightest scientists to foreign shores where they can pursue research without government interference (stem cell research), we are permitting unskilled, poorly educated workers to crash our country without invitation in whatever numbers they wish. As proven by the demonstrations of 2006, where illegal immigrants openly protested their "rights" while waving <u>Mexican</u> flags, we also allow them to bring their politics and prejudice along with them.

As more and more uninvited workers enter the United States on their own terms, there is more and more of a danger of their forcing a change in our economy, our culture and our politics. It may be argued that this has always been the case, that new Americans have always had an influence on such matters and that this is as likely to be good as bad. But any change in economics, culture or politics, should it come about too rapidly (and without real and psychological preparation), could bring hardship to all three areas.

We worsen the potential for hardship when we permit illegals access to welfare and other services. Were we discussing a few thousand Haitians, such a concern would be without merit, but by official estimates, the influx of illegal immigrants from across the Mexican border ranges from 12 to 20 million people (including family members who would, as happened in 1986, soon follow). <u>That is a number certain to have a significant impact on our economics, our culture and our politics</u>. Couple a porous border with a strong incentive to cross it and the result is predicable to all but a politician.

The argument begins to change from "tradition and compassion" to "self-inflicted wound," self-inflicted because it is we who are ignoring existing laws designed to prevent illegals from being hired. Illegals invade our country in search of work, and if we were to make the search difficult for them, fewer would come and some already here would leave.

"Nobody thinks you can round them all up and send them home. Nor would we want to. But if we enforce the laws, the job market will diminish somewhat. And for every job that's lost, somebody is going home."
Louis S. Hunter, pollster and political analyst

"Illegal immigrants will not come to Oklahoma if there are no jobs waiting for them. They will not stay here if there are no government subsidies, and they certainly will not stay here if they know that if they come in contact with one of our officers, they will be physically detained until they are deported."
State Rep. Randy Terrill (R)[46]

Ignoring a competing bill put forth by his own party in the House of Representatives, which bill makes it a <u>felony</u> to be in this country illegally, Bush pleaded that the question of immigration reform be addressed in a way that maintains the nation's "tradition of openness." This is a reasonable request, if sincere. But there is so much spin attached to administration arguments that it is difficult to see sincerity in what is being offered now. Knowing Bush hopes to attract the increasingly powerful Hispanic voters to his party, imports additional reason for doubt.

The hard fact is we have a border that is "broken"—even our government does not deny this. And if the attempt to "fix" it in 1986 did not work, what logic says applying the same "magic" we applied then will do any better?

---

[46] Oklahoma restricts access to all forms of official identification, bars illegal immigrants from receiving public assistance and fines employers who hire them.

*"I have maintained that securing our borders and
enforcing current law must come first –
and unfortunately this bill puts amnesty first,"*
Senator Elizabeth Dole

We have in place an immigration policy that is reminiscent of that practiced by seventeenth century American Indians. Like those original Americans, we are giving our country away by failing to control the numbers entering it. Undocumented immigrants from Mexico are coming faster than they can be assimilated into our culture, which is proven by the infiltration of the Spanish language in our signs, our businesses and our schools. Change that we did not want and do not appreciate is being thrust upon us, and it appears we do not have the will to do something about it.

There is a point where America's natural tendency to offer compassion must give way to common sense. Opening our doors to everyone in South America in need of compassion is simply not possible. Not unless we are willing to lower our standard of living to more closely approximate theirs. There could come a flooding of our borders in such numbers that decisions on the direction of America's future will lie more and more with them and less and less with us. We are naïve when we close our eyes to this?

We also show naiveté when we think such people will agree to be our "servants" forever, that they will assume the lesser jobs in our society at bargain prices and "stay in their place" as long as we wish these jobs done—in the past, this was called slavery.[47] Given their general lack of education and skills, the result will be a

---

[47] Labor unions brand this "an underclass of cheap laborers.

new underclass, unassimilated, undereducated, and antagonistic to our population, an underclass that will eventually begin feeding off the public dole as more and more argue for improved positions, pay and status, and are refused this due to insufficient education and skills. As we permit more and more <u>millions</u> of such people amnesty leading to citizenship, they will begin to have the votes to insure for themselves the use of these social services. We will then begin to pay the price for our naiveté.

According to the Immigration and Naturalization Service, the average amnestied illegal, after living in the U.S. for 10 years, had only a 7th grade education and earned less than \$9,000 per year. This places a staggering burden on the U.S. taxpayer who is forced to pick up the slack. Such costs were estimated by the Center for Immigration Studies, to be <u>\$78 billion</u> in the first 10 years following the 1986 amnesty (<u>that would cover only twenty percent of the illegal immigrants cited for amnesty today</u>).

"I frankly see this legislation as assisted suicide … Maybe it is possible to secure the border. Maybe it is possible to establish an employee identification system. But I don't have any confidence that it will be done."
Reagan W. Dean, Georgia state employee and lifelong Republican,

Sooner or later this "cheap labor pool" (or their children) will begin to resent second class status and want to move on. Then the farmers will be forced to invite more underprivileged Mexicans to take their place (and more after that as the cycle repeats itself). It is similar to the burning of the Amazon rain forests, where a poor farmer burns a section of trees in order to plant crops, only to discover a few short years later that the poor soil will not sustain crops for long. He then abandons that land as worthless and burns another section of trees. Then another after the new one peters out.

Here, however, rather than simply walking away from a worthless piece of land, we will be forced to consider each generation of "second class workers" to be a part of us forever, <u>even as this strains our economic system in a way the employment of these individuals did not take into account</u>. As mentioned in Chapter 5, low-skilled jobs in America are disappearing, with workers currently occupying these jobs finding it difficult or impossible to move on to work which demands more than their education and out-of-date skills will support.

"The toleration of illegal immigration undermines all of our labor; it rips at the social fabric. It's a race to the bottom. The one who plays by the rules is penalized."
Vernon Briggs, Professor of Labor Economics, Cornell University

There is also a question of language, how, unlike those who arrived before them, these new immigrants are forcing their host country to become bilingual. Rather than assimilating themselves into our culture, they are bringing their culture to us, in effect saying if there is assimilating to be done, it will be we who do it, not them. We are replacing a "melting pot" metaphor with a "salad bowl" metaphor. More and more Americans are resentful of having to select a language on the telephone or otherwise have to struggle with language in their own country. Such resentment is not a healthy sign for the future. One has only to examine the politics of Quebec to appreciate the damage such diversity can do.

"History shows that no nation can survive the tension, conflict, and antagonism of two or more competing languages and cultures. It is a blessing for an <u>individual</u> to be bilingual; however, it is a curse for a <u>society</u> to be bilingual."
Colorado Governor Richard D. Lamm

"The histories of bilingual and bi-cultural societies that do not assimilate are histories of turmoil, tension, and tragedy."
Seymour Lipset, historical scholar,

As with matters discussed in earlier chapters, this touches on the subject of political correctness. But also as before, it is important to consider the problem with an open mind, weighing all comments and counter comments on their own merits. The fact that this issue primarily involves a minority race (Hispanics) tempts accusations of racial bias, and such accusations (unless they are true) lend nothing to an honest, open discussion. Invoking the word "bigotry" does not automatically import reason to an argument that is otherwise flawed. If it is wrong to perpetuate a behavior that is damaging to our country, then it is the wrong we should be discussing.

Are we that unaware of the doctrine of unintended circumstances that we do not see what this will cost America? This is not simply a few unfortunates deserving of our compassion, these are tens of millions of semi-educated, low-skilled people. We can craft a sensible immigration policy, but it must not be permitted to compromise our way of life or undermine our security. Nor can it be permitted to undermine the rule of law.

The immigration "reform" of 1986 had a devastating effect on our nation. It encouraged exponentially more illegals to crash our border than those who had done so earlier. And that earlier group was considered a problem of crisis proportions. The proposed immigration reform bill of 2007 offers nothing more promising than the 1986 bill. For the moment it is sidelined in Congress, but that could change as the mix in Congress changes. The arguments will thus continue, even as undocumented immigrants continue to pour over our unprotected borders.

Our borders are broken. With the proposed new legislation they will still be broken, probably more so as millions of additional illegals are encouraged by our misguided generosity to become the next generation of a never-ending immigration problem. The heart is a wonderful organ, but so is the brain.

CHAPTER 7
LITIGIOUS SOCIETY

There is too much of a get-rich-quick attitude in America: win the lottery, sue someone, whatever will give us wealth beyond our contribution to society. This is not a healthy work ethic. It sends the wrong message to the next generation on whom we must rely to perpetuate our nation's wellbeing. It creates a fairytale atmosphere in which we ache to insinuate ourselves, there to live happily ever after on the products of someone else's labor, a place where all will be provided and nothing will be demanded. The most insidious of these get-rich schemes uses the law to extract wealth from another, not so much on the merits of their case, but on the defendant's ability to pay.

ADDICTED TO LAWSUITS

We suffer constant disruptions to our way of life due to a short-sighted and even suicidal tendency toward litigation. With arguments far reaching but often weak and self-serving, we permit outrages to our society and to our economic wellbeing in the name of "defending the little guy." Lawsuits for every imaginable reason, ranging from the just to the ludicrous, have become a fact of life in America, a "God-given right." Freedom to sue when and for whatever reason one wishes permits the little guy to stick it to the big guy, makes him pay, forces him to acknowledge one's outrage, even if this "outrage" is substantially unfounded. It is legal permission to act on a base resentment of the rich and successful.

Standing apart from every other industrialized nation, we the people of the United States of America have found a quasi-legal way to "redistribute the wealth"—at least to a few individuals and their attorneys. Large sums of money change hands daily as juries manufacturer reasons why the offending litigant should face, not only damages but "penalties." By no small coincidence, most of those found deserving of such penalties happen to have "deep pockets." With such a gold mine of opportunity, it is not surprising that trial lawyers vigorously fight limits on damage awards and meaningful reform.

We have a dysfunctional tort system in the United States, one that creates as much inequity as it dispenses justice. This happens even as it is generally recognized (even by those who benefit from the system) as not good for our country. Penalties are the purview of the law; they work best if devised and supervised by our chosen representatives, not by twelve jurors riding the emotion of the moment and playing with money not their own. This tendency toward a redistribution of wealth creates an atmosphere of paranoia where U.S. citizens live in constant fear of arbitrary and even illogical[48] awards against them. We fear the

---

[48] (Actual case) A driver avoided an accident by stopping just in time. Someone crashed into him from

consequences of what we say or do in our interactions with others; fear that we will lose a lifetime of accumulated wealth due to a momentary misstep and/or the actions of a jury riding a bias or a private agenda.

However bad it is for America, these lawsuits succeed more often than they do not. Attorneys are well aware that big business and big insurance companies are more likely to give in regardless of the merits (or lack thereof) of the case. They know it is considered less costly to cave than to fight, easier to grant out-of-court settlements than face a court battle that could take years to complete and result in an even worse outcome. (This is often referred to as "shakedown lawsuits" and even "legalized extortion"). The client is pleased, his attorney is ecstatic, wealth changes hands and we take another tiny step toward the end of the American dream.

Surprising only to those with a poor understanding of economics, the wealth transferred by such means does not come from big business, wealthy insurance companies or the rich. All of it comes from the public, you and I, including those same jurors whose weak sense of economics (and justice) brings this about. Rich and successful businesses, being smart as well as rich and successful, do not equate jury-imposed penalties to philanthropic offerings. Restated, they get their money back. This to them is a cost of doing business, and like all other costs of doing business, it is passed on to the consumer in the form of higher prices or lower quality products. Insurance companies simply raise their premiums, with you and I paying the difference. Manufacturers either raise prices

behind and drove him into the car he avoided hitting. The jury found him at fault "for stopping too quickly" (he was the only insured driver).

or the value of their stock goes down (and a million small stockholders lose a portion of their 401s).

This is not magic money that we so generously pass on to a select few, smiling as we do so as if one of our number has won a lottery. The money that we so delight in taking away from the big guy, ultimately comes out of the pocket of little guy. Not big business, not the rich, but from the very poor the jury believes it is protecting. Even so, swayed by ignorance, misplaced emotions and what should be transparent arguments by biased parties, we continue the practice. We sue each other for every conceivable complaint, regardless of merit or the common good, employing a tort system that is no longer civil or just. We absolve ourselves of fault for what used to be called clumsiness or neglect, assuming that, if we look closely enough, someone else can be proven to be at least contributory to our error, and that we will thus be entitled to substantial monetary relief. We are encouraged in this by predatory attorneys ready and willing to encourage us as long as this translates into money in their pockets.

While it is true that manufacturers have a responsibility to provide consumers with a safe product and adequate understanding of the use of that product, we tax reasonableness when we extend this to exclude us from all responsibility to apply common sense to our use of it.

TWO SIDES

Like anything of great import, there are two sides to the argument and bias to be sorted out.

Those who claim lawsuits in American are <u>not</u> out of line do not agree with the suggestion that we have a "lawsuit lottery" going in the United States. They deny that there is a get-rich-quick reaction to every misstep by government, business or private citizens, or that the public winds up paying for all jury awards. They also object to the presentation of the most egregious cases as representative of the whole. That and a tendency to underreport mitigating circumstances—degree of true culpability on the part of the defendant or that a verdict was later reduced in appeal. Further, they claim it is as valid for a jury to decide punishment as it is for a legislative body, and that putting a cap on punitive damages in personal injury cases (as proposed by reformers) is poor reasoning.

They defend the latter assertion with the argument that large companies often weigh the cost of potential settlements against the cost of modifying a product to make it safer. A cap of (e.g.) $250,000 means nothing to a Firestone when compared to redesigning problematic tires. It means even less to Big Tobacco as it considers what claims to make regarding the comparison between their product and cancer.

Those on the side of lawsuit reform equate our litigious status to "jackpot justice" and the "hijacking of justice." They cry out that the legal system is clearly broken, that it is negatively impacting upon our economy and the legitimacy of our position in the international community. They say we have a system of laws and interpretations of those laws that rewards abuse to the detriment of consumers, and that there is too much of a sense of entitlement to the wealth of others.

They feel too much law is being practiced and not enough justice is being dispensed, and that extreme awards do not benefit society as much as a concentration on consumer protection, requiring such action (and expenditures) that make products safer. Restated, it is the money that motivates us and not consumer safety.

LAWSUIT ABUSE IN AMERICA

Lawsuit abuse is defined as the plaintiff and his lawyer using the legal system to strike it rich rather than to seek justice and fair compensation. Judging from the frequency in which this abuse takes place, few of us recognize the threat it poses to the American way of life. We also fail to see the flaw so obvious in the arguments of those whose interests lie in continuing the practice; i.e. the trial lawyers who benefit enormously from the system currently in place. Trial lawyers like to claim they are "sending a message," but the real cost of that "message" falls to the public. It is common practice (and profitable) for lawyers to use the media to rally sentiment for large punitive damage awards, and while it might be argued that this is the American way, it must be guarded against by a public interested in, and deserving of, justice.

It is not just the frivolous cases that hurt us as a nation. There are legitimate claims that deserved to reach closure but are badly delayed by a justice system that is terribly clogged. People with legitimate problems are forced to wait in line while the less worthy claims are adjudicated.

"It is less a matter of injustice than of more justice than we can afford, scattered somewhat at random."
Michael Kinsley, editor of "Slate."

Some states are involving themselves in <u>punitive</u> damages, taking a share for state coffers. This makes sense, since a plaintiff has no more right to a public "fine" than does any other citizen. But passing on to the plaintiff <u>any</u> part of the punitive damage money perpetuates the lawsuit abuse problem. The jury will still be swayed by thoughts of taking money from deep pockets and putting it into more shallow ones, and this will still leave us with legislation by lawsuit. If an offense deserves a <u>penalty</u>, it should be the legislature that enacts it not un-elected jurors. This becomes more readily apparent when we substitute jail time for monetary damages—the former is clearly the sole prerogative of legislators.

Jail time, however, might produce better results. If this is not about money but about consumer safety, then why is it not reasonable to incarcerate those responsible for injuring the public through either design or omission? A provision for jail time would get the attention of a corporate executive more quickly than the prospect of sacrificing stockholder equity through a gargantuan fine.

Americans are hit hard by the cost of lawsuits (reported to be $880 per man, woman and child in 2006[49]), more so than citizens of any other major industrialized nation. Some of what this causes us to suffer comes in the form of absurdity, as manufacturers try to cover themselves with overly-obvious warnings on product labels. "This product moves when used" was found on a certain brand scooter, and attached to a toilet brush was, "Do not use for personal hygiene." In addition, we have banned tag at school recesses[50], and removed atmospheric peanut shells from the floors of popular restaurant chains[51].

> *"Lawsuit abuse is one of the greatest threats to Florida's robust business climate."*
> Governor Jeb Bush

---

[49] Reported by Tillinghast-Towers Perrin, a leading provider of risk management services.

[50] Such a ban is becoming increasingly popular around the country. This despite advice from some children's health advocates that limiting free play can inhibit a child's development.

[51] This was the result of many lawsuits against those steakhouses permitting peanut shells to cover the floor (e.g., Lone Star Steakhouse, 1999 and Texas Roadhouse, 2006)

Although in agreement with throwing out the extreme cases on both sides, the following two examples show what can happen when juries are too quick to side with a plaintiff:

1 - All the companies making whopping cough vaccine discontinued operations after the lawsuits of the late 1970s early 1980s. It was claimed then that the vaccine caused Sudden Infant Death Syndrome and mental retardation. Several studies discovered otherwise but, even so, many of the suits were successful. There are now only two companies in the world that make whooping cough vaccine, and the cost of each injection has jumped from $0.17 to $11.00.

2 - At one time, 90% of the flu vaccine used in this country was produced by pharmaceutical companies here in the U.S. There were 12 such companies thirty years ago, but this has since shrunk to 1[52], a French company in Swiftwater, PA. The economics of flu vaccine making was the main factor in subsequent decisions to get out of the vaccine business (the product carried a low profit margin and often operated at a loss), but it did not help when a patient who received the vaccine came down with the flu, sued the vaccine manufacturer and won almost $5 million. One result of this award was a shortage of vaccine a while back, with not enough U.S. companies willing to run the risk of producing it. Although reported to be a $6 billion industry (2006), the scant returns do not justify the vast sums they are forced to spend in defending lawsuits. And the outcome of such lawsuits is seldom dependent upon scientific evidence.

---

[52] 2004

Defense of the little guy? How many "little guys" have since gone wanting for flu shots as a result of an ill-thought-out decision by twelve of our "peers?" The public suffers because of a shortsighted approach to litigation.

These are but two of many examples testifying to why we need tort reform in this country. On the one hand we complain about health care deficiencies and how terrible it is that the poor or marginally employed have such limited access to it. On the other, we protest the right of everyone (and their attorneys) to profit wildly by physician, et al medical missteps.

CLASS ACTION SUITS

Class Action is defined as a civil suit brought by one or more people on behalf of themselves and others similarly affected. Assuming success, the ones who profit most are the attorneys. Nearly all of the remaining award money is shared by thousands and sometimes millions of investors who, if they still hold the stock, suffer a loss of their investment commensurate with the amount of the award paid by their company. The net effect for them is a huge sum of their equity going to attorneys. (As the average victorious plaintiff in a class action suit walks away with a few dollars, the attorneys more often receive millions, sometimes hundreds of millions.)

"Who can be more nearly a fiend than he who habitually overhauls the register of deeds in search of defects in titles, whereon to stir up strife, and put money in his pocket?"
Abraham Lincoln

It is too easy to file such suits, and there is too little opposition from investors coaxed into believing that they are genuinely participating in a payout. The mere filing of a suit results (on the average) in a 3.5% drop in the stock value of the company being sued, value that often falls to the current owners of that stock rather than to the parties who owned it when the "misstep" occurred. This 3.5 percent drop equated to more than $25 billion in stockholder equity lost in 2005, loss suffered by people who, except for a few individuals, had no responsibility for the alleged "misstep."

What sense does it make to take equity from innocent investors? Millions of stockholders, most nowhere near the status of "deep pockets," are routinely penalized for something they knew nothing about. The alleged offense might even have occurred before their 401 bought into the stock. When the super rich arose in the past, they at least created jobs for Americans. Attorneys who grab chunks of their genius (company equity in the form of damages) do not. Nor are jobs created when we permit the dwindling of business to feed the appetites of a few.

MEDICAL MALPRACTICE SUITS

When a medical specialty is required to spend hundreds of thousands of dollars per year for malpractice insurance, it suggests rather strongly that we are either expecting too much of the medical profession or are too set on this back-door way of redistributing the wealth. Life-saving products are kept off the market and doctors are cutting back their practice or leaving communities due to steadily-increasing malpractice insurance premiums. Healthcare costs are skyrocketing with little of this money going to treat patients.

The cost of medical malpractice insurance since 1975 increased at a rate of almost 12%, this compared to an increase of a little over 9% for all other tort costs.[53] Compounded this comes to a 23-fold increase in malpractice premiums versus a 12-fold increase for other tort costs[54]. This situation was precipitated by a combination of a growing frequency of claims and larger and larger awards. Making the situation worse, a number of insurance companies bowed out of the malpractice business due to the difficulty of making a profit, leaving those remaining in business facing less competition and thus able to increase prices. According to the American Medical Association, there were in 2006 seventeen states in a full-blown medical liability crisis.

Faced with high malpractice awards, insurance companies have no choice but to increase their premiums to doctors (who then have no choice but to pass them on to patients). Some insurance companies, if not withdrawing from the malpractice business completely, are reducing coverage in some areas. This means selected high-risk specialties (obstetrics, orthopedics, neurosurgery) either face inordinately high insurance premiums (above $200 thousand per year) or are unable to find insurance at all. Some abandon the high-risk portion of their practice or cut back on procedures that are beneficial but, as they do not always work, are fodder for a lawsuit. In so doing they insure a lower standard of health care for people most in need, including pregnant women facing difficult deliveries (obstetrics is a particularly hard-hit specialty). Others are forced to change their career choice or move to a state with more reasonable personal liability laws. Yet others retire prematurely or practice without malpractice insurance, forcing hospitals and nursing homes to close or cut back on

---

[53] Tillinghast Update, 2004
[54] ibid

services offered. Excessive jury awards drive doctors to practice defensive medicine, the prescribing of tests and medication whose main purpose is to protect them from future litigation. In 2006 <u>Price-Waterhouse-Coopers estimated medical liability and defensive medicine costs account for ten percent of the total U.S. health care bill.</u> Those supplying the medical industry are forced to make tough choices in order to stay in business, choices that almost always work to the disadvantage of those most in need of what they produce.

"Our runaway tort system is a genuine problem that is causing economic harm and, far more important, is distorting the cause of justice."
Wall Street Journal

Fingers are being pointed everywhere, with doctors pointing at predatory trial attorneys, frivolous law suits, and out of control juries, and trial attorneys pointing to an exorbitant rate of medical errors. Although as with many such debates, the truth lies somewhere in-between, there is clearly "lawsuit abuse" in the arena of medical malpractice. And, as shown above, the ramifications are far-reaching.

PROPOSED SOLUTIONS TO LAWSUIT ABUSE

States that have enacted caps on damage awards have seen a growth in their ranks of practicing physicians. The unfortunate opposite of this is less access to care in states unable to retain physicians who feel forced to leave for liability reasons. Addressing the problem, a number of modifications to existing law have been proposed, some of which have already been enacted by a number of states. This has slowed the current of lawsuit abuse, both medical and non-medical.

Eliminate Joint and Several Liability - Require reduction of damage awards by percentage of defendant responsibility. Currently the law permits going after the deepest pockets regardless of that entity's proportional culpability (thus making this more about money than justice).

Product Liability – Holding the <u>maker</u> of a defective product responsible and not the retailer, wholesaler, distributor, or whoever else a defense attorney would like to include for reasons of deep pockets.

Premises Liability – Not going after a property owner when a third party intentionally hurts someone on his property.

Vicarious Liability – Not going after the owner of a vehicle when it is lent to someone who subsequently becomes involved in an accident that is no fault of the owner.

Limit Class Action Lawsuits - Allowing a defendant to take corrective action if that benefits plaintiffs more than a lawsuit would. Imposing sanctions on those who bring lawsuits that subsequently fail or are dismissed, including the <u>defendant's</u> legal fees.

Reform class action lawsuits - Place limits on product liability actions and caps on punitive damages. (The average malpractice premiums in California are only half that of states that do not have such a cap.)

Asbestos Litigation – Limiting compensation to those truly injured by exposure to asbestos (According to the RAND Institute, 65 percent of total dollars paid to plaintiffs have gone to people who are not ill.)

Limit Venue Shopping – Prevent shopping for regions with a reputation for awarding excessive judgments. Limit civil filings to the county in which the damage occurred, the county in which the company has its principal place of business or where the property in litigation is located. (The American Bar Association argues that this would undermine the legitimacy of such courts and may disrupt the effective functioning of state court systems.)

Limit attorney fees – See that damage awards get to the injured rather than to the lawyers. (Make it illegal for attorneys to ask to waive this right.)

Provide liability protection for teachers and school officials.

Draw attention to the role junk science plays in propping up junk lawsuits.

Create a climate of confidence. - Businesses will locate where the reward is greater than the risk.

Elect lawmakers who support sensible legal reforms

Mandate mediation or arbitration

Standardize the definition of mental anguish

Establish fair rates on post-judgment interest

Create special courts to handle medical malpractice cases

Design a no-fault compensation system similar to workers compensation

Establish a standard of avoidability or preventability rather than of negligence

SUMMARY

The proportion of lawyers to population is higher in the United States than in any other industrial country. In 2005 the ratio was 320 U.S. citizens per lawyer, compared to 694 Englishmen, 2,461 Frenchmen and 8,195 Japanese. We do, however, have fewer physicians per capita. In 2001 the counts were 2.4 per thousand in the U.S. vs. 3.3 in France and Germany. Whether there is a correlation here will be left to the reader.

There is a feeling among Americans that they deserve great riches for perceived injury to their person, their property or their piece of mind. Attorneys aware of this feeling (which translates into juries ready and willing to give someone else's money away, a large portion of which goes to lawyers) pay too little regard for whether or not a case has merit, whether the fault lies more on the part of the litigant than those from whom money is being demanded. Hoping to address this problem, there is a bill in congress (H. R. 420: The Lawsuit Abuse Reduction Act), first proposed in 2005 and now being brought up year after year. Among other things, it places more controls on personal injury lawyers, forces them to end the process of "venue shopping," searching for regions sympathetic to large rewards. It also provides penalties for concealing or destroying documents. So far it has gotten nowhere.

The bill is divided along partisan lines, with Republicans wholly for it and Democrats wholly opposed to it. Not surprisingly, since a substantial part of lawsuit awards goes to lawyers, the American Bar Association is opposed as well.

According to the Wall Street Journal (2004), democrats have blocked almost every tort reform attempt since 1994. Restated, this is another matter that depends, not so much on reason as it does party affiliation.

This is difficult to understand. If something does not work, if in the aggregate it does harm to our country and its people, if it has been tried repeatedly and failed, then it would seem even to those with a minimal level of common sense to be a bad idea that should not be supported. This is but another example of a politician checking his party's "holy" book" to see what he believes. Once again the quote from Poincare:

"To doubt everything or to believe everything are two equally convenient solutions; both dispense with the necessity of reflection."[55]

It is crystal clear that our country is being harmed by current tort policies. Also crystal clear that private interests (trial attorneys) are working at cross purposes to our nation's wellbeing and insuring their right to continue to do so by infusing politician coffers with large sums of money. Crystal clear, yet we continue to allow it to happen in the name of "protecting the little guy," who, as the above examples suggest, is the one who suffers <u>most</u> from this practice.

There is nothing commendable about supporting something of such import without first applying reason to it, in this case whether it provides more benefit than harm or whether it is more "feel good" than "real good." Or whether it contributes one more tiny step toward America's decay.

CHAPTER 8
SELECTION OF POLITICAL LEADERS

"Those who are too smart to engage in politics are punished by being governed by those who are dumber."
Plato (427 BC - 347 BC)

A good leader can "make" a country; a bad leader can harm it. Ignoring the truth in this, we seem to gravitate toward the latter in pondering who should represent us, spending as little time as possible in the

---

[55] Poincare, ibid

choosing and basing our selection on one or two favored issues rather than on a balance of many. We give more emphasis to a belief shared with the candidate than to a demonstration of that candidate's competence. It is said that the people get the leaders they deserve. If true, we are not very deserving of late.

To be fair, there is little possibility of any modern-day politician succeeding in the eyes of the public. To be elected, he or she (I will continue with only one gender for brevity) has to excite so many varied and sometimes diametrically opposed passions that to really be sincere he would have to be schizophrenic. Certainly he has little chance of satisfying both sides of a passionate argument (abortion, for example). The blame for his having to <u>pretend</u> to be interested in every matter known to his constituents lies with those constituents. They have a need to feel he is in their corner, even as part of them has to know that what they ask is not only unrealistic but impossible considering the diversity of positions a politician is required to take in order to succeed. The politicians are playing us, but it is we who are allowing ourselves to be played.

> *"It has been said that politics is the second oldest profession. I have learned that it bears a striking resemblance to the first."*
> Former president Ronald Reagan

A fair example of overemphasizing one issue is our insistence that a candidate be first and foremost a "good family man," even when history proves that some of our best leaders were lacking in that regard. Further, of what relevance is kissing a baby, or wearing a special hat or smiling approval while sampling a local dish? These are "photo-ops" nothing more, and photo-ops more reflect an intention to deceive than to show character. Yet, if the candidate fails to show us this side of himself, we aim our vote elsewhere (which, of course, the politician is aware of as he works the crowds). When this baby-kissing, hat-wearing, smiling politician takes office then enacts an unpopular law or sends our military into war, surprise generally precedes indignation.

We also reason illogically when a disaster occurs, such as Hurricane Katrina in New Orleans in 2005. We place as much if not more importance in the President coming down to inspect the area personally than his sending competent specialists trained to handle a disaster (perhaps Katrina is a bad example, since we did not respond properly). The point is that we confuse photo-ops with substance, and as such encourage our politicians to take less productive paths—our fault, not theirs. Having the President (or a governor or a mayor) visit a troubled area may aid the morale of suffering people, but from a managerial point of view, it only slows things down. The president, governor or whatever will still have to pass the problem down the line to the experts. Choosing <u>and managing</u> such people will better assist a recovery than a personal appearance.

Yet we would criticize without mercy a politician who fails to take a personal tour of a human tragedy.

But even as we give inadequate thought to what makes a good leader, we cannot excuse those candidates who promote themselves as able but later prove to be less so. In winning for themselves the "prize" of leadership, they must accept the inspection and judgment that too often comes only after they are safely ensconced in office. Restated, if they say they can do the job then show less than the competence we expect, they have no right to resent our criticism. Criticism can also be fairly meted out to members of Congress, who have no direct responsibility yet are quick to criticize from the sidelines those who do. Sometimes this criticism is fair, sometimes it is not, but too often it reflects a desire to make headlines rather than import logic, fairness or solution to a problem.

In such a way we choose our leaders, and in such a way we find them lacking. It is said that disappointment is the second thing the electorate feels after a major election is over. The first is that it is over.

"No, I was looking for a southerner."
John Ehrlichman, Nixon's domestic advisor, when asked whether his search for a candidate to fill an important foreign post had produced someone with knowledge of the country and its language.

The pages to come will highlight President George W. Bush, this for two reasons: He is more of a recent memory, and he has arguably proven himself less capable than many of those who preceded him into the Presidency. But this in no way suggests that mistakes and incompetence belong to one man or one party. The evil is in the doing, not the party affiliation of those involved in the doing. Although this is likely to provoke instant objection from zealots on both sides, one party is not inherently pure and the other inherently corrupt. President Bush might have deceived Congress and the public (inadvertently or though ideological blindness) over reasons to enter Iraq, but President Johnson did much the same regarding the Tonkin Bay incident off Viet Nam.

The Democrats, embarrassed at being caught conducting U.S. attorney firings during the Clinton years (the same firings they later criticized), tried to differentiate "then" from "now." This was less than a commendable exercise, even as they tried to divert attention by pointing out that the authority their Republican counterparts sneaked into the Patriot Act, the one that allowed President Bush to bypass Senate confirmation for "interim appointments" (e.g. U.S. attorneys) was an evil step above their evil step. They protested that Republican choices regularly place political bent above competence and suitability to the public need (inferring that their choices did not). In a perfect world, which neither party seems anxious to achieve, the practice of trying to shape law through the manipulation of prosecutors would be regarded as both indefensible and unconscionable.

The Patriot Act is a good example of politics dominating reason. Certainly there is a need for greater tools to use against the growing armies of Islamic fanatics who would do us great harm, but there is also a need to protect ourselves from ourselves. It is said that only enemies of the state will be subject to administration wire taps, but what is far less clear is who will make that determination. Will it be Karl Rove or other ideologues of the Bush administration saying who is and who is not a threat to all right-thinking people of America, perhaps aided in this decision by evangelical firebrands?

"The pigs are beginning to resemble the farmer."
George Orwell's classical novel *Animal Farm,*

This is but another example of convenient reasoning, where a carefully coifed, perennially smiling politician (left or right) waves the American banner of freedom even while contemplating abridging that freedom however it best suits his or her ideological purpose. Regardless of one's opinion of President Bush, this is our freedom being tampered with. Today it is right-wing ideologues, but tomorrow it can as easily be left-wing ideologues. The smile of today might retreat to a frown tomorrow. Better for both sides that our freedom not be tampered with by either.

INFLUENCE PEDDLING

In 1996 some $1.6 billion was spent on Congressional and Presidential elections. By 2004 that figure had more than doubled[56]. During roughly the same time period, the number of lobbyists in Washington, D.C. also doubled (to almost 33,000 in 2005[57]). These lobbyists employed over 100,000 people and spent over $2 billion that year, which comes to almost 62 lobbyists and $4 million per member of Congress. The following comes from a testimony before congress in 2006 by James A. Thurber, Director of the Center for Congressional and Presidential Studies at American University in Washington, DC.[58].

> *"The most recent lobbying reform, the Lobbying Disclosure Act of 1995 (as amended in 1998) was passed with the belief that representative government requires public awareness of what paid lobbyists do to influence the public policy making process in both the legislative and executive branches of the federal government. The assumption was that public disclosure of the identity and extent of efforts by lobbyists to influence government action would serve to increase confidence in the integrity in government. The Act limits gifts to Members of Congress, requires a one year cooling off period before a*

---

[56] A study of campaign finance figures by the nonpartisan Center for Responsive Politics
[57] Senate Office of Public Records as of September 30, 2005
[58] March 2, 2006

Member or senior congressional staff may lobby Congress, and includes some restrictions on privately sponsored travel for members and staff.

"The act has failed badly to meet the objectives of disclosure and increased integrity in government, thus Congress is considering new lobbying reforms. The failures are highlighted by the illegalities noted above, but the actual problems are more prevalent and endemic. The foundation of the ethical problems is the combination of huge sums of money injected into the process by lobbyists and interest groups, the norm of reciprocity that exists between those advocating public policy outside of government and those making policy in government, and the lack of enforcement and non-transparency with respect to lobbying activities."

The pharmaceutical industry, the gun lobby, trial lawyers, the oil industry, farmers and so many other private interests have benefited enormously over the years by financially backing members of Congress. They have spent lavishly to woo support for their various positions and have received as a result preferential treatment far exceeding that available to the public at large. This is corruption on a grand scale, legal but not even close to moral. It is Congress responding to money rather than voters, and sending the bill for what they do to reciprocate for their legal "bribes" on to the people. <u>We may cast the votes, but it is others who shape the agenda</u>, an agenda where the views of the taxpayer are but a secondary concern.

Yet, do we have a right to be surprised? Our American way of running for office is expensive, more so than in any other democracy. It costs an absurd amount of money to introduce oneself to the American public, and even more to combat one's opponent, and this is whether the battle is successful or unsuccessful. That money has to come from somewhere, and knowing this, businesses and private causes are more than willing to jump in with a donation when the public is slow to do so. Not a donation that has to do with philanthropy or with a patriotic desire to promote good government, but a donation that is expected to produce a return well above its cost. Translated, all donations come with strings attached, and none of these strings are connected to the taxpayers.

This is a problem with government per se, not with Democrats and not with Republicans. Our government is corrupted and becoming more so (the incident with lobbyist Jack Abramoff was but an example), and there appears to be no one able or willing to correct the evil we let prey upon us with greater and greater impact each year. Our policies on energy, education, government, military and so much else are governed by the opinions and objections of those who paid to put our leaders in office. If we let this continue, as it appears we will, the United States will belong more and more, not to the people, but to an elite few. And this elite few will get the money they need to "bribe" Members of Congress from the tax advantages or special treatment the Member secures on their behalf. Restated, we the people are indirectly financing, not only the "bribes" but the profits gained from them.

Some states have banned campaign contributions from lobbyists and contractors in favor of public funding, or have in other ways legislated to "clean up" the money passed on to candidates. But it is difficult under our laws to prevent special interest groups from practicing "free speech" on behalf of a favored candidate, taking out personal ads of support and thus depositing the same "hook" as had the money been passed directly. Even so, to some degree this is working, with more diverse candidates running on their own ideas rather than the ideas of special interests.

On a national level, there was an attempt in early 2006 (prior to the Democrats taking control of Congress) to enact a lobbying reform bill, but it fell far short of expectations and was even insulting to the public. Referred to as "a watered-down sham[59]," it did not <u>ban</u> privately-funded "fact-finding" trips but merely <u>suspended</u> them until (by no coincidence) just after the election of that year. Further the law did not change the gift limits or ban lobbyists from coming along on fact-finding trips, and it dropped provisions that would require lobbyists to reveal the fundraisers they host on behalf of candidates.

It is not reasonable to expect that a recipient of a large donation feels no obligation toward the giver. Yet from politicians we receive passionate expressions of indignation at any suggestion of impropriety, and from the abused electorate a nod of acceptance if not blind trust. Both sides pretend it is either not happening or is not a serious problem.

Truth is that there is <u>always</u> an expectation of return, whether that be from business, from the gun lobby, trial lawyers lobby, farmers lobby or from the ACLU. It is naïve to expect otherwise. The donor will want something for his money, and chances are he will get it. Influencing our elected representatives has become a growth industry in this country, effectively pricing the average citizen out of meaningful participation in the selection of his government—this in what we continue to believe is the greatest

---

[59] Citizens Against Government Waste, 2005, an on-line expose of wasteful spending by members of congress.

democracy in the world. This is not how democracy is
supposed to work. It is not representative government.
It is a government of favors, of mutually-excused graft
and corruption.

PORK SPENDING AND SUBSIDIES

The 2006 Pig Book[60] identified almost ten
thousand "pork" (also called "earmarks") projects in
the discretionary portion of the federal budget for that
year, the cost of which came to almost $30 billion.
This came at a time when the deficit for the year was
$371 billion and the national debt $8.5 trillion. (For
2007, the dollar cost of earmarks was somewhat less,
perhaps reflecting a shift in Congressional leadership)

The 2006 "pork" included large payments for the
World Toilet Summit, for wood-utilization research,
for the Waterfree Urinal Conservation Initiative and for
the Sparta Teapot Museum in Sparta, N.C. We pay for
all such earmarks through government "credit cards,"
not income, each such expenditure adding further to
our national debt.

Earmarks are commonplace and rarely reflect the
needs of more than a few people. For the most part,
they are granted to assist a particular member of
Congress in his quest to continue in office—the
Congressman gets to show his constituents back home
that he can "bring home the bacon" (grab the public's
money) as well as the next guy. It is very difficult to
stop. We all know that other Congressmen's pet
projects are frivolous and wasteful, but rarely do we
condemn our own Congressman when dollars come
our way, even dollars that the rest of the United States
believes are frivolous and wasteful. Unless we live in

---

[60] ibid.

Alaska, we cry foul when Representative Don Young of Alaska receives money for a "bridge to nowhere."[61] And unless we live in West Virginia, we cry foul when Senator Byrd of West Virginia is granted money for Turf Grass Research and an Appalachian Fruit Laboratory.[62] In the same spirit, Senator Schumer of New York, who portrays himself as against selfish "plutocrats" of the Republican party, comes out against a proposed reform in the tax laws that would take a more equitable share of the enormous profits being pulled in by hedge fund executives—the fact that these executives are from his home state taps the strength of his "convictions."

> *"I can't wait to put out a press release to tell people what I have done."*
> Illinois Senator Richard Durbin, boasting of $448 million in earmarks for his state

Because of the willingness of one Congressman to "scratch the back" of another, the people of this country see, not only waste and the expenditure of dollars our country cannot afford, but omissions in areas that could benefit Americans so much better, worthwhile projects that suffer the loss of funds committed elsewhere (exploration of space, or research on disease and energy alternatives, for example). Further, earmarks forced on the military sometimes

---

[61] Congressman Young, former chairman of the House Transportation and Infrastructure Committee, received $230 million to build a bridge from a small town in Alaska to an island with fewer than 50 people.

[62] Citizens Against Government Waste, 2006. Senator Byrd has sat on the Appropriations Committee since 1959, his first year in the Senate.

mean armaments and equipment they do <u>not</u> need nor want (e.g. the Osprey aircraft), and cuts in legitimate projects that affect their ability to protect America and its people.

Earmarks are decisions made for the wrong reasons. Applied to the military, they come at the expense of maintenance and training, of improved salaries and living conditions for military personnel, of weapons research and of equipment that is thus forced to await a future budget. There is also a taste of scandal about it, such as Representative Cunningham's conviction on conspiring to receive millions in bribes from two defense contractors then repaying these contractors with earmarks. In the area of pork, we are clearly working against our national interests, even as a few benefit (in particular Congressmen) enormously.

The Democrats, during their successful attempt to regain control of Congress in 2006, vowed to strip pork from spending bills, a practice they publicly condemned when their opponents were in control. This vow was almost immediately broken due to the need to garner Republican votes for a spending bill on Iraq (in an ideal world, which Congress certainly is not, legislators would support (or reject) such a bill out of conscience, not greed). It was a nod to realism, a recognition of how necessary "back scratching" is to getting what a Member wants for himself.

Congress changed the rules in early 2007 to require that the author of a pork spending request be identified. Ironically, this resulted in <u>more</u> pork rather than less due to the members quickly realizing that this gave them favorable exposure at home; i.e. they were identified as bringing federal dollars back to their state or district—some even competed to have their names attached to individual pork projects, while others rushed to put out press releases boasting about their successful tapping of the public dole. Pork was still recognized as against the national interest and harmful to our country, but if it helped a Member remain in office, needless spending of the public's money was to be regarded as only a secondary concern.

Some earmarks are intended to bring about a desired effect, such as in an area of public concern (e.g. medical research) that might not be adequately financed otherwise, or support for farmers to keep basic crops flowing and fertile land available for possible need in emergencies. But even here there is a danger that cannot be ignored. It is not in our national interest to subsidize products that are later exported to foreign countries. This sets a precedent that could come back to haunt us as foreign entities seek revenge by "dumping" their government-subsidized products on us.

Other attempts to service areas in need can result in working at cross purposes to a changing national interest. At a time when ethanol is being sought after as a gas-substitute, and supplies of corn and other ethanol sources (e.g. high-diversity mixtures of prairie plants) are not yet up to the task, we provide through agriculture subsidies a disincentive for farmers to grow the means of producing ethanol. There is much degraded land capable of supporting such means, but we are not yet sufficiently motivated to put it to productive use. Perhaps when the price of corn (currently the most popular ethanol source) gets so high that the rising price of beef (which are fed corn) begins to get our attention, we might discover this motivation.

"Even when grown on infertile soils, they [prairie plants] can provide a substantial portion of global energy needs,

and leave fertile land for food production,"63
David Tilman, professor of ecology, University of Minnesota

CORRUPTION AND DECEPTION

*"The conservative movement who came to town to
lead a revolution and stayed to run a racket."*
Bill Moyers, Journalist and Baptist minister

In 2003, a Republican-controlled congress put together an energy bill in secrecy (Republican input only). It was the culmination of years of work done by Vice President Cheney's energy task force, the manner in which it was handled now being debated in the courts. It moved directly to a vote with no further hearings or public review.

This is not the way government is supposed to operate in a free democratic society. It is new rules put into effect by only one side and presented as a fait accompli to the other. Congressional Republicans argued that this approach was necessary because they

---

[63] Tilman's study shows that high-diversity mixtures of prairie plants can yield more net energy than either ethanol from corn or "biodiesel" fuel from soybeans, and that its use can even lead to a net decrease in CO_2 emissions whereas ethanol and biodiesel increase it. According to Professor Tilman, "If you take into account the greenhouse gas emissions produced by growing, harvesting, transporting and converting plants into fuel — along with the carbon dioxide produced by eventually burning that fuel — and weigh this against the amount of carbon dioxide sucked up by plants during growth, prairie comes out 6-16 times better than corn grain ethanol or biodiesel."

saw no other way to pass an energy bill in a Congress deeply-divided on the issue. Restated: they wanted to remove opposition (or even input) to their unadulterated viewpoint.

"Audacious and shameless people for whom the very idea of the public trust is a cynical joke."
Bill Moyers, Journalist and Baptist minister

A monumental tax cut was "awarded" the American people early on in the Bush administration. Since a considerable budget surplus was expected and since the economy was doing well (not the time for a tax cut as any reputable economist will state), the only argument the Bush administration could offer was to *"return the surplus to the taxpayers."* Although not outwardly against the tax cut, Federal Reserve Chairman Greenspan cautioned against what he feared was a "drift toward fiscal irresponsibility.[64]"

The administration stuck to this argument even when the economy began to grow a little too fast to suit the Federal Reserve. Only after the economy began to sour was it changed to *"stimulate the economy"*.

In fairness to all, the jury is still out on whether it did or did not stimulate the economy (the cut was skewed toward the upper income levels, and thus would be expected to have less of a stimulating effect). But both Greenspan and Treasury Secretary Paulson testified that the expected grown to the federal coffers

---

[64] The central bank chairman's semi-annual testimony before Congressional, February, 2003. Greenspan said, "such a measure (the tax cut) should only be passed if other revenue could be found to replace the lost tax revenue, so as to keep swelling federal budget deficits under control."

would <u>only</u> occur if the tax cuts were balanced with cuts in government spending, that making the tax cuts permanent would expand the budget deficit which <u>would cause an eventual slowdown of the economy.</u> This issue has been argued since back in President Ronald Reagan's time and is unlikely to be discussed other than along party lines now. The switching of claimed motives for the tax cut, however, suggests that effect on the economy was not as important as simply wanting to do it.

"The secret of life is honesty and fair dealing. If you can fake that, you've got it made."
Groucho Marx

The U.S. dollar is dropping in world markets for the simple reason that we have sent so many of them abroad. Our reckless spending habits both here (much of our <u>domestic</u> debt is held by foreigners) and overseas have made it easier for foreigners, anxious to trade risky dollars for something solid, to purchase more and more of our businesses and property (see Chapter 5-1). Yet we show no willingness to either lessen our appetite for foreign goods (including oil) or pay for the government services we use. Exacerbating the problem, our government, who has access to the top economic minds and thus knows better, refuses to risk political disfavor by telling us we (and they) must reform, that such vices as these have the potential to bring down our country.

"The end of an empire always comes when the currency is destroyed."
Texas Congressman Ron Paul

Rather than focus on lessening the dollar and debt problem, our government makes each worse by enacting a tax cut not coupled with a cut in spending. The result is the piling up of IOUs against our grandchildren's future.

Henry Paulson, Bush's highly-respected (by both sides) Treasure Secretary, was more honest, admitting that these cuts have done harm as well as good, that they had indeed exacerbated the budget deficit that concerns him deeply.[65] However, the administration that he advises, promoting its intention to make the tax cuts permanent and anxious to brand their opponents as "tax and spend," argued that if they (the tax cuts) were permitted to expire at the end of 2010 as scheduled, it would constitute "the largest tax increase in American history." Secretary Paulson did not disagree but admitted in his confirmation hearings before congress that "As a general rule, I don't believe that tax cuts pay for themselves." He softened this by saying they were, however, crucial to boosting the confidence of consumers, investors and top executives alike.

In November of 2006, the Bush administration, anxious to prove it can get things done when it counts, came up with a way of eliminating the disturbing picture of corruption seen so often among contracting firms in Iraq: They got rid of the policeman. A special Inspector General for Iraq had sent a number of occupation officials to jail on bribery and conspiracy charges.[66] He had also exposed shoddy work by Halliburton and others and losses of equipment by the

---

[65] Speech by Treasury Secretary Paulson at Columbia University, August 1, 2006.

[66] Stuart W. Bowen Jr. Special Inspector General for Iraq Reconstruction since 2004

military. The heat growing, he was removed from his federal oversight agency by a military authorization bill that was approved by Congressional Republicans over the objections of Democrats. Some legislators (on both sides) claimed it was "truly a mystery"[67] how the provision removing the "policeman" got into what was essentially a conference report.

A more obvious example of political mischief can be found in how we permit redistricting to absurd levels, as witnessed by the bizarre and overtly bias rearrangement of districts engineered by Republican Congressman Tom Delay of Texas. Both sides recognize the evil in such redistricting, but neither side wishes to tamper with what might benefit them the next time redistricting is permitted. When incumbent politicians sneak such unfair rules into the system, they ensure for themselves a substantial advantage over those challenging their seat, an advantage that does not benefit the voter who is thusly deprived of a freer choice.

"A society run by the powerful, oblivious to the weak, free of any oversight, enjoying a cozy relationship with government, and thriving on crony capitalism."
Al Meyeroff, Los Angeles attorney

Once again, however, the criticism cannot fall to one side alone. When the Republicans seized what they considered to be an opportunity in the Terri Schiavo case[68] in March of 2005, the Democrats appeared to be

---

[67] Republican Senator Susan Collins (Maine).

[68] Florida resident, **Theresa Marie Schiavo**, in a coma for 15 years, was the subject of a bitter battle between her husband and her parents in which the U.S.

more interested in solidifying gains with "red" states than fighting the Republican's ill-conceived legislation. Although voicing disagreement with intervening in a "deeply personal matter," they did not block the bill when they could have (a single senator could have sidelined the vote.) Apparently the morality of the issue was less important to them than showing an uncaring side to conservative voters.

The above examples of corruption and deception are not about one party being more possessed of morality than the other. It is about both parties defining morality as it suits their narrow and often changing purpose. It is also about how easily we the people fall prey to their rhetoric and behavior. Step by tiny step we are surrendering our freedom to a few.

SOCIAL SECURITY

"Practical politics consists in ignoring facts."
Henry Adams American author, historian, and critic (1838-1918)

There is a saying that "figures don't lie, but liars figure." The saga of Social Security "reform" lends testimony to the validity of this.

There has been a long-brewing problem with the U.S. Social Security program, a problem that everyone is aware of but few dare tackle. Simply put, we have increasingly more people taking from the program and increasingly fewer people contributing to it—the number of workers-to-retirees (16-to-1 in 1950) is

---

Congress interjected itself with legislation against removing life support.

expected to shrink to <u>two workers for every retiree</u> by 2032.[69]

The worst of this will happen quickly as the "Baby Boomers" of World War II begin to retire. Their numbers are atypically high and the number of children they produced is atypically low (thus explaining why there are fewer workers to contribute to the system at a time when more retirees are using it). On the surface, it would seem a matter of recruiting our nation's best minds and have them figure out what makes the most sense regarding the continued health of the program, what it would take to keep it going as the "safety net" all Americans have come to expect as their right.

But nothing is easy in this world, especially not when so much political gain can be made out of attacking those brave (or foolish) politicians who dare offer solutions. Since there is no easy fix but rather a certainty of pain of some kind, it is easy to proclaim oneself to be a friend of the system and one's opponent to be a foe of it. Drooling political jackals stand waiting in every wing, ready and willing to jump in and slam the other side should that other side make the mistake of proposing specific reform. To suggest sacrifice of any kind puts a politician at a sharp and likely fatal disadvantage to his opponent regardless of the strength of his arguments.

Yet it is unfair to claim that a politician shows a cowardly regard for his duties when it is we the people who routinely buy into the disingenuous rhetoric from his opponent; i.e. whatever the proposal, whichever side proposes it and however sensible that proposal might be, the opposing politician <u>will</u> find something negative to say about it that we <u>will</u> believe (e.g. *"He is trying to take away your benefits!"*). We have

---

[69] According to statistical tables published annually as part of the Social Security trustees report.

proven this again and again, proven that we <u>will</u> favor the disingenuous politician who saw a political advantage and ran with it.

There is no real danger of Social Security disappearing, if for no other reason than it is a political "hot potato"—what so many Americans want, they will get. But the system is truly weak and getting weaker, and some change in the dynamics of it will be necessary. It needs to be modernized, made to accommodate a new set of population and worker demographics and constraints.

This is not to suggest, however, that we throw the burden upon the electorate to provide for themselves via "Personal Retirement Accounts." That would require that the weak and the vulnerable successfully run the gauntlet of financial opportunists in their pursuit of old-age security, an expectation that is both unrealistic and naïve.

We live longer, thus Social Security is not needed as early as it once was, which would suggest the raising of the retirement age to be both logical and sensible. Further, there are those among us who have less need for old-age assistance, which would suggest a scaling down of benefits for those less dependent upon the income it provides. Then there are questions of increasing payment <u>into</u> the program, including the elimination of the present cap on payments by active workers. The point is that there are suggestions that have merit (some more than others), but the atmosphere is such a political minefield that there is no good-faith discussion of any one of them.

One thing for sure: if we do nothing, if we continue to con ourselves into thinking we can have it all while avoiding pain, we will wind up with less benefit and more pain. We must stop providing a positive stimulus to politicians to continue the destructive practice of using Social Security for self-serving political gain.

SELECTION OF LEADERS

"The progress of Evolution from President Washington to President Grant was alone evidence enough to upset Darwin."
Henry Adams; American author, historian, and critic (1838-1918)

Over the oftentimes troubled reign of President George W. Bush, there have been countless articles and editorials written criticizing, sometimes quite heavily, his ideas, his ideology and his ability to lead. Much of this is related to the military misadventure in Iraq, but some relates to matters discussed earlier in this book:

> 1-Importing religion into government with little understanding of or regard for the consequences,

> 2-Favoring current producers of energy (primarily oil) rather than forcing America onto a new energy track,

> 3-Turning a blind eye of denial toward global warming and the loss of the middle class,

> 4-And failing to secure our borders at a time when America is facing a threat more serious than any it has ever faced before, the threat to civilization itself by radical Islamic fundamentalists.

"An amiable mediocrity."
Historian Arthur Schlesinger Jr. of George W. Bush

It has been suggested that we should respect the office of the presidency, that the office means something to Americans and, in a sense, personifies us all. It has also been suggested that we need to come together as one people with one voice while we fight the war in Iraq. Both of these suggestions make sense.

The problem, though, is that the parts to these dogmas do not so easily fit. In Richard Nixon's day, for example, should we have respected the office of the presidency by lowering our eyes and our rhetoric when confronted with his excesses? And should we now agree to further commit our nation's blood and resources solely to present an illusion of unity? Such are the weighty matters that keep people of conscience up until the wee hours.

The situation that is Iraq will be discussed in the next chapter, but it is worth noting here that it has exposed a leadership flaw in President Bush that warrants examination. There is little evidence that he sees grounds for compromise in any idea not in conformity to his own—not only with Iraq but in other matters as well. It is perhaps further evidence that he sees himself guided by a divine source that, thusly defined, could not be wrong. As any attentive student of history is aware, protestations by leaders of being guided by the hand of God is not only a dangerous assumption but one that is almost always repudiated in time.

> *"History is the best antidote to delusions of omnipotence and omniscience"*
> Historian Arthur Schlesinger Jr.

There is testimony in these 2004 remarks by Bruce Bartlett, domestic policy adviser to Ronald Reagan, that President Bush believes himself to be guided by an unimpeachable source:

"I think a light has gone off for people who've spent time up close to Bush: that this instinct he's always talking about is this sort of weird, Messianic idea of what he thinks God has told him to do. This is why George W. Bush is so clear-eyed about Al Qaeda and the Islamic fundamentalist enemy. He believes you have to kill them all. They can't be persuaded that they're extremists, driven by a dark vision. He understands them, because he's just like them.

"This is why he dispenses with people who confront him with inconvenient facts. He truly believes he's on a mission from God. Absolute faith like that overwhelms a need for analysis. The whole thing about faith is to believe things for which there is no empirical evidence. But you can't run the world on faith."

Supporting the above, there was an incident in the oval office involving Senator Joe Biden a few months after American troops entered Baghdad. Outlining his concerns to the President about the explosive mix of Shiite and Sunni, the disbanded Iraqi army and the poorly defended oil fields, Biden said,

"The President was serene. He told me he was sure that we were on the right course and that all would be well. 'Mr. President,' I finally said, 'how can you be so sure when you don't yet know all the facts?' The President put a hand on

my shoulder and said, 'My instincts.
My instincts.'"

An example of an unwillingness on the part of President Bush to deviate from a chosen path may be found in the Baker-Hamilton report on Iraq (the Iraq Study Group), commissioned after it became clear to people of reason on both sides of the political isle that Iraq was a disaster of monumental proportions, one requiring a dramatic new approach if America was to salvage anything of value from the effort. Even before the conclusions from this learned panel were in, Bush made it clear that he would not be bound by its findings, and indeed, the direction he ultimately took was diametrically opposed to its recommendations. Instead of building a workable political consensus to shift the burden back to the countries in the region and to the Iraqis themselves, Bush decided on an escalation of the military effort.

Whether or not a military standoff of some sort comes out of this struggle in Iraq is close to irrelevant. There is a thousand-year-old Hatfields and McCoys battle going on in the Muslim world, and history has demonstrated again and again that it cannot be controlled, certainly not by introducing American ideas of how these people should govern themselves. The fact that such easily accessible history continues to be ignored does not speak well for the people in control. Not understanding it, our leaders are forcing us to relive it.

As a prelude to taking office, an elected official swears to uphold, among other things, the constitution of the United States. This constitution permits the Legislature to establish laws, and it did so in creating "independent" agencies, regulatory bodies that conduct their work outside the influence of politicians. A commendable thought, but it does not always work.

The Bush administration, long in opposition to a morning-after birth-control pill, put obstacles in the way of an over-the-counter version being approved by the Federal Drug Administration. They managed to secure an official FDA letter of rejection for the product, a letter <u>the heads of several key offices of the FDA *refused* to sign</u>. The rational given for the rejection was that this might encourage adolescents to engage in unsafe sexual behavior.

It was the first time in FDA's history that it permitted ideology to trump science. In making drug decisions that the Legislature intended for medical experts, the politicians thumbed their noses at the very laws they swore to protect. In addition they tarnished the reputation of an agency we look to for reasoned medical decisions.

The Executive branch of our government is putting the interests of the few—indeed, an extreme few—above that of the masses. Step by tiny step they are taking over our lives, requiring that we live it within their strict guidelines, guidelines that reflect their private brand of religion.

And we continue to let them.

We have managed in six years to severely damage international relations that took decades to build. Not only that, but weaken our security at the same time. We are now being viewed by foreigners as arrogant, go-it-alone cowboys who refuse to listen to those who share our world (33 of the 47 countries polled in the 2007 Pew Global Opinion Poll expressed a dislike of American ideas about democracy.[70])

---

[70] Global Attitudes Survey, June 27, 2007

"If at first you don't succeed, skydiving is not for you."
(author unknown)

The situation has not much improved as a result of the Democrats gaining control of both houses in 2007. True, they faced a president who talked compromise but rarely practiced it, one who would veto any attempt at significant change, but the new leaders in Congress appeared disinclined to give it a real try. They spent much of their new-found political fortune attacking the performance of their political opponents, hoping in doing so to score political gains for the next election.

These Democrats do not appear to appreciate what got them there. It was not a public reawakening to the wisdom of Democratic Party ideology but a reaction to Republican Party disasters, including arrogance in office and abuses of power. Rather than acting like a mob going after the spoils of war, they should focus on demonstrating to the public that their ideas, their practices and their morality are superior to those of the opposition. Only then will they truly deserve the power that fell by default into their hands.

Notably a step in the wrong direction was the choice by Democratic leaders to employ early on a procedure they bitterly criticized when the Republicans were in power: locking out the opposition (bypassing the normal committee process then disallowing amendments or alternatives on the floor). Not to their credit, they attempted to justify these actions by a need to fulfill a promise of enacting certain changes by the end of their first 100 legislative hours in control—they sought to assure the public and their Congressional colleagues that they would return to "procedural fairness" once finished with this initial wave of legislation. Beyond showing unfortunate similarity to a banana republic, this sets a bad precedent. Fairness becomes a matter of majority sufferance, of convenience rather than principal.

A balanced two-party system works for America, but a system out of balance does not. Both parties need to understand that a dramatic changing of rules to suit the party of the moment serves neither party well—at least not for long. Republicans (and "new" Democrats) have to understand that their actions during their time in power will eventually come back to haunt (and cost) them, that this is inevitable considering the continually changing preferences (and frustrations) of the American people.

Finally, to restore more of a balance in our two-party system, the Democrats need to wake to the necessity for both organization and change. They must get together and speak with one voice (or at least one theme), and they have to drop that portion of their dogma that no longer sells. There has been an overt shift to the right in this country, and failing to recognize this will doom the Democrats to yet another failure at the polls and the country to yet another election with no viable choice.

MISPLACED LOYALTY

What price loyalty, and who gets the bill? "Loyalty" is often portrayed as a virtue, but is it? Loyalty can be blind; it can excuse laziness; it can defeat our willingness to think or become involved.

Should loyalty to our elected leader have carried the day for Nixon during Watergate? Or Lynden Johnson during the Tonkin Gulf incident? Or Hitler and Stalin who used "loyalty" to promote their destructive aims? Consider how many millions of deaths would have been prevented had more Germans fought to retain their republic in the 1930s rather than loyally following without question their new leader.

If we believe "A" is true and "B" is not, we are not better people for publicly defending "B" out of loyalty to the person who proposed it. We would, in effect, be lying to the many others whom we consider less deserving of our loyalty. In a democracy we do not fall into lock-step behind a leader. When one disappoints us, we voice our objections, with as much discretion as the situation calls for but without reservation. What we do now in questioning our current president and those who advise him is far more healthy and better serves our nation and its concept of democracy than blind loyalty to the concept of "my president, right or wrong."

When a United States president and those employed by him swear to serve the people, they are not keeping with that promise by serving each other at the expense of the people. In early 2004 the then-acting Attorney General, untrusting of the integrity of White House counsel Alberto Gonzales, refused to meet with him without a witness present. When Gonzales moved into the A.G. spot, he soon became embroiled in a controversy that put in doubt both his integrity and his competence. Yet President Bush continued to stand behind him. Supreme Court nominee Harriet Miers and CIA Director George Tenet also met questions of competence, yet Bush stood behind them as well, this even though with Tenet there was the serious question of bad information from his department leading us into a disastrous military adventure in Iraq. On a scale of one to ten, how far below "loyalty" should "competence" be placed?

Donald Rumsfeld, arguably a very competent man, presided over a war awash in serious errors, yet he was permitted to remain in office, offering excuses above corrections for critical years in which American soldiers were dying and our country was being drained of its wealth. He was released after the election of 2006, but this appeared to be less a breach of loyalty than Bush's pique at having lost Congress.

Loyalty can rise above conscience, as when the loyalty of Secretary of State Colin Powell to President

Bush helped lead us into the Iraq war. (He later cited loyalty to the president as "influential" in his regrettable U.N. speech on Iraq.)

There is a disturbing pattern of rewarding loyalty to the president with loyalty from the president, of backing subordinates because they do a president's bidding, not because they do a good job for the people. What does this suggest for the concept of good governance? What does it say about oaths to serve the country when one puts devotion to one's boss above the good of that country? If the cause is wrong why is loyalty to that cause (or to the person perpetuating it) a virtue?

And why do we the people place such value on a concept that is so often used against us? Loyalty while in the employ of the American people should be owned by the people, not by a leader and not by a party. We the electorate should demand recognition of this, and should withhold praise of those who demonstrate the opposite. Owing allegiance to our country, we must back up those we put into office, but we should not carry such backing to a flawed level—no one deserves blind loyalty. We should not, as said above, suspend our right to criticize when criticism seems due. And we should never support wrong simply because it was we who made the mistake of electing the official perceived to be in error. In the matter of Iraq, our current government is deserving of criticism, and it serves no lesson of logic for us to wait thirty years to critique the errors that so pain our country today.

SUMMARY

"What is troubling is the gap between the magnitude of our challenges and the smallness of our politics."
Barak Obama

The certainty that a cleverly-conceived piece of political propaganda will have its intended effect is not good testimony to the intelligence (or attentiveness) of the electorate. Seated in front of the TV, watching a slice of tainted rhetoric clearly designed to provoke emotions beneficial to the politician it represents, we buy into the "message" again and again, thus providing a positive stimulus to a dangerously flawed practice—"dangerous" to the very concept of democracy. We seem particularly vulnerable to the candidate's proffered conceit that we are "smart enough to see the truth." Such messages, often aired at the eleventh hour before an election, change our decisions and thus alter our lives.

> *"For the most powerful nation on Earth to have an election in which Swift Boat veterans versus National Guard papers becomes a major theme verges on insane."*
> Newt Gingrich, former Speaker of the House

Character assassination, defined as much being made of little regarding a politician's past life, is often the purpose of the message. This tactic works well with an electorate searching unrealistically for perfection in their leaders, as if in finding it they atone for sins of their own. One wonders how many good people have been lost to a leadership role because they have been less than godlike during their lifetime. Some of our best leaders have been "morally disappointing." Roosevelt had a mistress, Eisenhower as well, JFK is obvious. But did this demonstrate in any of these leaders a lack of competence? Is a good family man who leads our country into harm's way preferable to a person of questionable family values who has the knowledge and skills to guide us through difficult waters?

"I'm going to find out what brand he drinks and send a case of it to my other generals."
Abraham Lincoln, when pressed by critics about Grant's heavy drinking

Even if it <u>were</u> the role of the electorate to mandate morals in their leaders, it clearly does not work. Democrat and Republican alike find themselves showing their human frailty almost as often as they encounter temptation. Add to that the arrogance of ideologues in power proclaiming the superiority of their morals over ours, and we begin to see the potential for serious friction. Morals relate to opinion, and if my opinion differs from another's then that person is free to ignore me as I am free to ignore him or her. The point here is that the morals of the candidate should be considered but should not dominate one's selection process. Morals alone will not get the job done.

The game of politics is discouraging to many. Not only the requirement of unrealistic morals, but the smear tactics, false smiles and ideas watered down to that level which will offend the least number of people. Our country needs good and competent candidates on both sides, and if we scare such people away, we will gravitate from cautioned reasoning to hip-shooting, with decisions falling more in the realm of the idealistic than the realistic.

"Only two things are infinite, the universe and human stupidity, and I'm not sure about the former."
Albert Einstein

Are we that susceptible to what should be transparent rhetoric (smear messages) or are we simply inattentive? More to the point, are we any more likely in the next election to focus on the competence of the candidates, or will we once again consider gay marriage to be a more relevant issue than a functional energy policy?

Whatever we decide to do, we must live with what comes of it. Good or bad, it will be entirely our fault, even as with both feet planted in denial, we shake our heads at the corrupt cabal of politicians infesting government offices.

"That's unconscionable ... I believe in family values!"
Florida State party chairman Jim Stellings, protesting the accusation that he had been married <u>six</u> times (the correct number was <u>five</u>).

Many believed the presidential election of 2004 offered no real choice. Even as the people were decidedly unhappy with President Bush's record of deficit spending, increase in the size and scope of the federal government, lax immigration policies and his handling of postwar Iraq, Bush's opponent appeared to be no better bet than "the devil we had." There was enough fear of Senator John Kerry's "out-of-touch liberalism" that many disillusioned Republicans were brought back into the Bush camp on Election Day. <u>But this does not excuse the fact that we the people approved the process that led to these two candidates being our only choice.</u>

"It is impossible to underrate human intelligence – beginning with one's own."
Henry Adams American author, historian, and critic (1838-1918)

We the people must take responsibility for our political leaders. We are the "Johns" seduced by what they are selling. There are exceptionally gifted politicians (e.g. Karl Rove) who are listened to by many, in particular those who wish to stay in office and are not particularly disturbed by what it takes to accomplish this. They are only "exceptionally gifted," however, when we are "exceptionally responsive" to their persuasion. Or restated, when we are "exceptionally slow" to recognize devious over responsible argument (somber-faced politicians, wrapped in a flag and waving a Bible, their favored profile turned to the camera as they shoot visual darts at their misguided opponents). The war in Iraq is a good example of the devious over the responsible. On the Republican side we have pathetic denial (voiced as indignation), while the Democrats, taking little stock of the lives and resources sacrificed on the path to this brief political advantage, spend more time pointing out their opponent's missteps than legislating relief from our national disaster.

But then it is naïve to expect any politician to inform the people that they and their country have sunken into a hole from which it will take decades to extricate ourselves. That would take the exceptional, the kind of politician John F. Kennedy wrote about in his *Profiles of Courage*. How likely is this when such people are generally rewarded for their courage with the loss of their career?

But in truth, we are sliding into a "hole." A recent study done by George Stephanopoulos of ABC News showed the people have gravitated toward more extreme views over the last thirty years. They face more "muckraking" (the stirring of passions), even by the "legitimate press." We hear language that is more vitriolic, with more name-calling and exaggeration. Whatever this change represents, it is coupled with (and perhaps related to) an ability to disseminate information and misinformation in ways not imagined thirty years ago.

We have also gravitated toward less compromise. Senator Lindsey Graham, <u>a conservative Republican</u> from South Carolina, once received thousands of emails and telephone calls from <u>conservatives</u> angrily rejecting what they regarded as conciliatory messages on his part. Lindsey and eleven other senators, some from the other side of the isle, had been trying to avoid gridlock by getting together on important issues.

"We're supposed to be the most mature democracy on Earth, but the current climate seems more representative of those warring cliques we all saw in the fifth grade."
Warren Sovereign, Op-Ed contributor, Ponce Inlet, Florida

Part of the problem is our devotion to momentary comfort, a logical goal, as long as it does not preclude responsibility. Too many of us retreat from the latter with dismissive comments such as, "I don't watch news because it's too depressing!" Yet these same people go on to vote, confident as they do that whatever opinions they have formed, they are sound ones.

Our laxity permits political opportunists to solidify their grip on office, thus preying on us that much longer. There are no government positions so small that "inspired" politicians cannot benefit by salting it with people of their leaning, people who see such correctness in their ideology that they let slip the rules that seemed so necessary when the opposition was in power. Hundreds of government positions the filling of which, if they are clever in how they go about it and if they are able to steel themselves against the self examination that tickles the conscience of the weak, can build such a solid political base that all those "right-thinking" individuals to follow will slip right in. Restated, as politicians gain access to the power they crave, they work to consolidate and backfill less this power inadvertently slip back into the hands of the electorate.

The history of failed empires begins with a relaxation of the high standards that put them on top. Not standards of sexual misbehavior but standards held by good and competent people who band together to create and perpetuate good government. As we surrender more and more control of our lives to those who know what to do with the opportunity we carelessly bestow upon them, our nation climbs another step on the ladder of failure.

The principles we citizens call upon in the selection of our leaders need to be reconsidered and revised. It diminishes us all when we so easily fall prey to clever politicians who, like prostitutes, proclaim themselves capable of satisfying our desire of the moment. We listen to their words rather than what those words are saying and punish them should those words come too close to a painful truth. We are in danger of proving ourselves incapable of selecting leaders skillful enough to manage our affairs, not to our absolute liking since that as stated earlier is not likely to happen, but for the good and even the continuance of our nation. Most of all, we must lose this conceit regarding the ability of democracy to endure complacency. There is growing evidence that it will not.

CHAPTER 9-1
IRAQ

The discussion of Iraq will be split into two parts, the first outlining the difficult situation our country has gotten itself into, and the second (Chapter 9-2) touching on the growing danger of Islamic fundamentalism, the latter coming at a time when the United States is steadily weakening itself.

> *"The American people will not support an infinite war whose sole remaining purpose is to prevent the situation in Iraq from becoming worse than it is today."*
> Sen. Joseph Biden

By most accounts, President Lyndon Johnson misled the Congress and the American people in the Tonkin Gulf incident[71] that led to a widening of the Vietnam war. Perhaps this might have gone unnoticed (or had less made of it) had the Vietnam war gone well for the United States, but it did not, and "Tonkin Gulf" became a poster child for government duplicity. This damaged both Johnson and his Democratic party, but a greater tragedy was what it did to our nation. Countless years of fighting, huge wastage of American wealth (our national debt increased enormously) and the loss of more than 58 thousand American soldiers with another 150 thousand suffering wounds of either mind or body.[72] Further, we demonstrated to ourselves and to the world that even a superpower has limited power and resources.

We thought we had learned from that terrible national misstep, but in March, 2003, playing on the

---

[71] The Gulf of Tonkin Incident was an alleged pair of attacks by naval forces of North Vietnam against two American destroyers. The second attack is highly disputed, even today.
[72] Wikipedia encyclopedia - 58,209 killed, 153,303 wounded and 1,948 missing.

emotions of a public still reeling from the terrorist attack on the Twin Towers a year and a half earlier, and offering as justification intelligence that was highly flawed and replete with arguments reflecting ideological bias more than fact, President George W. Bush repeated Johnson's mistake. He took us into another quagmire, this one called "Iraq."

In fairness to Bush, the Clinton administration, the Congress and many Western governments also thought Saddam had weapons that we need fear. Most, however, believed the current policy of containment and inspection was working, that no further action was necessary. We had our no-fly zone policy and implemented it whenever and wherever we wished—the danger Saddam represented was held in check at a cost of jet fuel and pilot time. Regarding Saddam's gassing and murdering and raping and otherwise mutilating his people, that was for the Iraqis to cure, not us—why should we be willing to fight and die for their freedom when they were not? If we were to dash around the world trying to "cure" all the ills we Americans decide need curing, we would not come even close to succeeding. Likely we would not survive the effort.

One candidate for the Senate (Barak Obama, October, 2002) bucked the more popular trend toward entry into Iraq, and the reasons he gave were prophetic:

> *"The threat Saddam posed was not imminent, the Administration's rationales for war were flimsy and ideologically driven and the war in Afghanistan was far from complete. And I was certain that by choosing precipitous, unilateral military action over the hard slog of diplomacy, coercive inspections, and smart sanctions, American was missing an*

opportunity to build a broad base of support for its policies."

"... What I could not support was "a dumb war, a rash war, a war based not on reason but on passion, not on principle but on politics."

"... I know that even a successful war against Iraq will require a U.S. occupation of undetermined length, at undetermined cost, with undetermined consequences. I know that an invasion of Iraq without a clear rationale and without strong international support will only fan the flames of the Middle East, and encourage the worst, rather than the best, impulses of the Arab world, and strengthen the recruitment arm of Al Qaeda."

The weak reasoning leading to our entry into Iraq, coupled with poor supervision of the invasion and of the early attempts at reconstruction, led that nation into chaos. And we became enmeshed in a tragedy of colossal proportions, one which will painfully impact upon us and our neighbors in this increasingly shrinking world for generations to come.

"Anybody who tried to tell them anything that challenged that idea–they simply shut it out,"
British Major General Tim Cross, reflecting on conversation with Rumsfeld addressing insufficient planning for the post invasion period."

INTELLIGENCE

Much has been said about the quality of the intelligence relied upon by the Bush Administration, including how often and to what degree the meaning of that intelligence was twisted to accommodate preconceived ideological opinion[73]. Loath to include judgment that contradicted their own, the administration selected data that would support decisions already made then ran them through the Congress and the American people.

"If you go after Iraq you're gonna lose a lot of allies, but who cares."
Charles Krauthammer (Fox News 9/22/01)

Much of the administration-selected data conflicted with the opinions of experts, those skilled at collecting and analyzing bits and pieces of intelligence. For example, Under Secretary of Defense, Douglas Feith, was sent back to the drawing board to develop "alternative" assessments on Iraq, assessments that drew conclusions that in the opinion of intelligence experts "were not supported by the available intelligence[74]."

Intelligence is meant to make sense of real events around the globe, not to make, or even recommend, policy. When something is uncovered that a leader would rather not hear, he must discipline himself to not only listen but consider fully and fairly what it is telling him. If he does not, the very meaning of

---

[73] See *Foreign Affairs*, by PAUL R. PILLAR, former National Intelligence Officer for the Near East and South Asia from 2000 to 2005.

[74] Report by the Pentagon inspector general, February, 2007.

intelligence-gathering falls apart. What a leader should never do is assume data presented in an objective manner to be invalid simply because his "instincts" tell him so. This is "Cherry Picking," and it politicizes the intelligence effort, encouraging gatherers and analysts to provide only data that the "King" wishes to hear and to which he will respond with rewards rather than pain.

"Many of us are convinced that Saddam will acquire nuclear weapons fairly soon."
Vice President, Dick Cheney, August, 2002
(an opinion not shared by the intelligence community)

Policy makers introduce a bias when they take the lead in deciding which information to consider, and this puts our country in the terribly dangerous position of acting out of ignorance (as is proven by Iraq). We should rely on the sound judgment of professionals not on the overheated leanings of ideologues.

After the war began going badly, an embarrassed Congress tried to reach a bipartisan consensus on the true nature of our pre-war intelligence. They established an Iraq Intelligence Commission (IIC), chaired by Judge Laurence Silberman (conservative Republican) and former U.S. Senator Charles Robb (Democrat). The Commission ultimately concluded that the Intelligence Community had been "dead wrong" in almost all of its pre-war judgments about Iraq's weapons of mass destruction, and that this constituted a major intelligence failure[75]. The error, however, was skewed toward the top of the managerial chain. Lower-level analysts, aware of discrepancies but

---

[75] Report to the President by the Iraq Intelligence Commission, March 31, 2005.

fearful of angering the upper echelon, had made private (and cautious) protest when the use of their data went beyond what they considered credible[76].

"More likely, ... Iraq would become a magnet for extremists from elsewhere in the Middle East."
PAUL R. PILLAR, former National Intelligence Officer for the Near East

The Iraq Intelligence Commission discovered that the intelligence community, on its own initiative and a month <u>before the war began</u>, had assessed the situation in depth. Their findings, however, were <u>not</u> presented to Congress or to the American people[77]. Those findings include:

> *1 - Iraq was a **deeply divided society** that likely would engage in violent conflict unless an occupying power prevented it.*
>
> *2 - A **heightened terrorist threat** would result from a war with Iraq (although the expectation was that, after an initial spike, it would decline slowly over the subsequent three to five years).*
>
> *3 –* **Al Qaeda would** see an **opportunity** to increase terrorist attacks during and after a US-Iraq war.

---

[76] Pillar, *Foreign Affairs*
[77] Report by the Senate Select Committee on Intelligence, February 12, 2004

4 – Establishing a stable democratic government in postwar Iraq would be a **long, difficult and probably turbulent challenge**.

5 – The United States' defeat and occupation of Iraq probably would result in a **surge of political Islam** and increased funding for terrorist groups.

6 – Iraq's neighbors would jockey for influence in Iraq.

7 – Iranian leaders would try to influence the shape of post-Saddam Iraq.

8 – Military action to eliminate Iraqi WMD would <u>not</u> cause other regional states to abandon their WMD programs.

9 – The Iraqi government would have to walk a fine line between dismantling the worst of Saddam's police, security, and intelligence forces and retaining the capability to enforce nationwide peace.

10 – Iraq's large petroleum resources would make economic reconstruction a less difficult challenge than political transformation, but that **postwar Iraq would nonetheless face significant economic challenges.**

11 – Major outside assistance would be required to meet humanitarian needs.

12 – The new Iraqi government would require significant outside assistance to rebuild Iraq's water and sanitation infrastructure.

Much of the above proved to be prophetic, yet, as said earlier, it was not widely broadcast prior to the war. What possible reason can be offered for that omission other than it did not support conclusions and decisions already made by the administration in power?

"There were some people in the intelligence community who knew at that time that some of these sources were not good and shouldn't be relied upon, and they didn't speak up. That devastated me."
Colin Powell, former Secretary of State

There were serious doubts about the information passed on to then Secretary of State Colin Powell, yet these doubts did not reach him when he needed them most, when he was attempting to vet questionable information from his speech to the United Nations. Further, the claim that Iraq had tried to purchase uranium ore in Africa, which had been substantially debunked by our intelligence arm, was left in the President's State of the Union address. The same with the relationship between Saddam Hussein and al Qaeda, put forward by administration officials as if true even though there was never any analysis in support of it offered by the CIA.

Demonstrating its bipartisan makeup, the Iraq Intelligence Commission stated in the opening paragraph of its conclusions, that much of this problem is endemic and not owned by the Bush administration.

> *"We have approached our task mindful of its historical context. In truth, looking to the past, we find cause for discouragement. Many of the ideas and recommendations that we have made in this report were advanced with compelling reasoning by previous commissions. After ceremonious presentations to the President and to Congress, the <u>previous recommendations were ignored or implemented weakly.</u> Most of them failed to take hold. The question is inescapable: why should this Commission be different from the others?"*

They went on to offer opinion on the thinking of the intelligence community just prior to Iraq:

> *"...Iraq was still pursuing its programs for weapons of mass destruction (WMD). Specifically, the NIE [National Intelligence Estimate] assessed that Iraq had reconstituted its nuclear weapons program and could assemble a device by the end of the decade; that Iraq had biological weapons and mobile facilities for producing biological warfare (BW) agent; that Iraq had both renewed production of chemical weapons, and probably had chemical weapons stockpiles of up to 500 metric tons; and that Iraq was developing unmanned aerial vehicles (UAVs)*

> *probably intended to deliver BW agent."*

The Commission then goes on to add: *"These assessments were all wrong."*

> *"This became clear as U.S. forces searched without success for the WMD that the Intelligence Community had predicted. Extensive post-war investigations were carried out by the Iraq Survey Group (ISG). The ISG found no evidence that Iraq had tried to reconstitute its capability to produce nuclear weapons after 1991; no evidence of BW agent stockpiles or of mobile biological weapons production facilities; and no substantial chemical warfare (CW) stockpiles or credible indications that Baghdad had resumed production of CW after 1991. Just about the only thing that the Intelligence Community got right was its pre-war conclusion that Iraq had deployed missiles with ranges exceeding United Nations limitations.*

And by the co-chairman, Charles Robb:

> *"The intelligence community imposed pressure on itself. There was a conventional wisdom and there certainly was a feeling articulated by some that they did not want to go against the conventional wisdom."*

Although the Commission found no evidence that intelligence analysts had shaped reports in response to political pressure, it admitted that <u>analysts worked in an environment that was strongly influenced by intense policymaker interest</u>. It's other findings make interesting reading:

Overall Commission Finding

The Intelligence Community's performance in assessing Iraq's pre-war weapons of mass destruction programs was <u>a major intelligence failure.</u> The failure was not merely that the Intelligence Community's assessments were wrong. There were also <u>serious shortcomings in the way these assessments were made and communicated to policymakers.</u>

Nuclear Weapons Summary Finding

The Intelligence Community seriously misjudged the status of Iraq's alleged nuclear weapons program in the 2002 NIE and other pre-Iraq war intelligence products. This misjudgment stemmed chiefly from <u>the Community's failure to analyze correctly Iraq's reasons for attempting to procure high-strength aluminum tubes.</u>

Biological Warfare Summary Finding

The Intelligence Community seriously misjudged the status of Iraq's biological weapons program in the 2002 NIE and other pre-war intelligence products. The primary reason for this misjudgment was <u>the Intelligence Community's heavy</u>

reliance on a human source—code-named "Curveball"—whose information later proved to be unreliable.

Chemical Warfare Summary Finding
The Intelligence Community erred in its 2002 NIE assessment of Iraq's alleged chemical warfare program. The Community's substantial overestimation of Iraq's chemical warfare program was due chiefly to flaws in analysis and the paucity of quality information collected.

Delivery Systems Summary Finding 1
The Intelligence Community incorrectly assessed that Iraq was developing unmanned aerial vehicles for the purpose of delivering biological weapons strikes against U.S. interests.

Delivery Systems Summary Finding 2
The Intelligence Community correctly judged that Iraq was developing ballistic missile systems that violated United Nations strictures, but was incorrect in assessing that Iraq had preserved its Scud missile force.

Regime Decision-making Summary Finding
The Intelligence Community, because of a lack of analytical imagination, failed even to consider the possibility that Saddam Hussein would decide to destroy his chemical and biological weapons and to halt work on his

nuclear program after the first Gulf War.

Beyond the report on the areas most in question, the committee came up with a number of conclusions, some of which are damning to both the Bush Administration and the intelligence community.

Conclusion 5
In the case of Iraq, collectors of intelligence absorbed the prevailing analytic consensus <u>and tended to reject or ignore contrary information.</u> The result was "tunnel vision" focusing on the Intelligence Community's existing assumptions.

Conclusion 13
Analysts did not question the hypotheses underlying their conclusions, <u>and tended to discount evidence that cut against those hypotheses.</u>

Conclusion 17
The Community <u>did not adequately communicate uncertainties</u> about either its sources or its analytic judgments to policymakers.

Conclusion 22
The President's Daily Brief likely conveyed a greater sense of certainty about analytic judgments than warranted.

Conclusion 26

> *The Intelligence Community did not make or change any analytic judgments in response to political pressure to reach a particular conclusion, but <u>the pervasive conventional wisdom that Saddam retained WMD affected the analytic process</u>.*

Conclusion 27

The CIA took too long to admit error in Iraq, and its Weapons Intelligence, Nonproliferation, and Arms Control Center <u>actively discouraged analysts from investigating errors.</u>

Thus we went to war. And thus our country suffers needlessly and at length.

"They [neoconservatives] had long wanted to transform the Middle East, beginning with the removal of Saddam Hussein. The terrorist attacks [9-11] gave them the chance they wanted. And the media gave them a platform."
Bill Moyers, Journalist and Baptist minister

Whether it is Johnson using intelligence to take us into Vietnam, or Bush using intelligence to take us into Iraq, when we allow the tail to wag the intelligence dog, drawing conclusions ahead of (and in some cases, <u>instead</u> of) findings, intelligence becomes a detriment rather than a solid tool aiding governmental decisions. This problem will likely continue as long as the intelligence function is tightly controlled by the Executive branch of our government, with top department officials serving at the pleasure of the President.

ENTRY INTO IRAQ

Somewhat heated at times, there were discussions before the war in Iraq began which addressed the notion of "nation building" (termed "reconstruction" by an administration loath to admit a similarity to what it so vilified during the election process). On the negative side, the director of the Agency for International Development, Andrew S. Natsios, met with White House and State Department officials and debated the likelihood that they could manage any large-scale reconstruction project in a hostile environment. Natsios argued that 50 years of observing other countries had shown that such an effort in unstable environments is <u>not</u> the best use for aid money.

"We set it up to fail."
Natsios, reflecting his disappointment when the effort began to crumble

Also prior to the invasion, a group of State Department officials put together what they referred to as the "Iraq Working Group," their job to offer an Assessment of post-war Iraq. This Assessment was more than a year in the making, and it detailed many of the problems that eventually developed, including widespread violence and looting.

But the Defense Department, over the objections of the State Department, won control over reconstruction and <u>refused to consider the study</u>, calling it "too superficial." The Assessment had a diplomatic stamp on it and came at a time when Defense and State were engaged in something of a turf war, a prolonged and bitter debate that began in the months leading up to our entry into Iraq. Restated, a critical opinion offered by regional experts that took a year to construct and which was eventually proven correct was tossed aside because of petty rivalries between government departments supposedly working on behalf of the American people. The insurgency that followed brought us to scrap scores of projects and reduce our "nation-building" budget considerably.

These two reports, both warning us of the consequences of throwing money and effort into areas that were not militarily secure, and pointing to fifty years of experience in other countries as proof of this, were ignored. History was trumped by ideology.

Well <u>after</u> the invasion (January, 2006), an internal staff report entitled "Provincial Stability Assessment[78]," offered in draft form by the State Department, suggested that our government had learned a crucial lesson, that in future conflicts they would not immediately begin a major rebuilding program but would first establish a secure, stable environment then begin <u>political</u> reconciliation. They concluded that otherwise they were likely to "suffer major political repercussions by making promises that could not be kept[79]." The draft report, put out by State <u>and also dismissed by Defense</u>, reads like a refutation of everything the U.S. has done in Iraq.

"We certainly have not done as much as we originally had hoped for."

---

[78] Ten pages of briefing points titled "Provincial Stability Assessment." An internal staff report by the United States Embassy and the military command in Baghdad, January 31, 2006.
[79] ibid.

James Jeffrey, State Department's senior coordinator for Iraq.

With the Congress apprehensive but essentially in agreement, and the American people convinced by intelligence assessments and by our leader's assurances of the necessity, our country went to war with Iraq for the second time in twelve years. Few foreign nations agreed with us concerning the necessity to do so, even as we touted the "Coalition of the Willing," a collection of some 30 smaller countries, most sending only token support to our effort in Iraq. The principle nations of Europe and Asia, including traditional allies, sat on the sidelines. In hyping a "Coalition," we seemed to be equating numbers with quality.

In truth, the United States, with substantial help from only one meaningful ally (Great Britain; Australia was a close second) essentially went it alone. Worse, as later admitted by former Secretary of State Colin Powell[80], we went in with insufficient troops to secure the country and failed to see the necessity of retaining enough Iraqi forces to assist in the stabilization effort. The wonder is that we were surprised when, after a short period of what appeared to friend and foe alike to be a spectacular victory, we and the country we invaded quickly retreated into chaos.

"The only people who think this wasn't a victory are Upper Westside liberals, and a few people here in Washington."
Charles Krauthammer, Inside Washington, WUSA-TV, 4/19/03

---

[80] Interview with Barbara Walters of ABC News, September 9, 2005.

One reason for the downturn may be found in our enthusiasm; i.e. we had too much of it. Stimulated by a rapid advance toward Baghdad and unwilling to slow this down, huge caches of weaponry and ordinance were bypassed and left unguarded. Much of this disappeared (as much as 250,000 tons of explosives were unaccounted for by October, 2004[81].). Even Tuwaitha, the Iraqi <u>nuclear</u> center that UN inspectors had been most interested in, was left unguarded and later may have been looted.

Later we discovered that we had lost track of nine billion dollars in <u>cash</u> plus hundreds of thousands of rifles and other weapons. (Ironically, the black market for weapons has become one of the strongest segments of the Iraq economy.) We also lost track of hundreds of thousands of body armor and helmets[82] earmarked for Iraqi soldiers and police. There is a fear that such material and weaponry fell into the hands of Iraqi insurgents and are now being used against us. Restated, we have through carelessness and lack of forethought provided the enemy with the means to construct IEDs (improvised explosive devices) to use against our soldiers.

Soon after the end of our dash to Baghdad, widespread looting began, the effect on the country's infrastructure devastating. The U.S. military had experienced similar looting following the 1989 invasion of Panama, but for some reason did not expect history to repeat itself. When it happened, we found we did not have the manpower to control it. Unlike in the

---

[81] Report by Pentagon spokesman, Lawrence Di Rita, October, 2004.

[82] Report to lawmakers notifying them that the Defense Department cannot account for 135,000 items of body armor and 115,000 helmets reported to be issued to Iraqi forces as of September 22, 2005.

first Iraq war, when over a half million allied troops were deployed, here only 130,000 were committed to the effort[83], enough to overwhelm the Iraqi army but not to secure the peace. Secretary of State Powell, as was alluded to earlier, had argued for "overwhelming force," and the then Army Chief of Staff, General Shinseki, recommended several hundred thousand, the extra to help maintain post-war order[84]. Both recommendations were overruled by Secretary of Defense Rumsfeld. Paul Wolfowitz, Deputy Secretary of Defense, even called General Shinseki's estimate, "wildly off the mark."

"I will bet you the best dinner in the gaslight district of San Diego that military action will not last more than a week."
(Fox News Channel's Bill O'Reilly, 1/29/03)

General Abizaid, former commander of the U.S. Central Command later admitted in front of Congress that Shinseki had been correct[85], that the troops on the ground had not been sufficient to guard all the sites that needed to be guarded, with the result that weaponry was lost and the country's infrastructure fell into instant disrepair.

Lewis (Jerry) Bremer, a competent man with a MBA from Harvard University, was given the

---

[83] The initial invasion force was some 130,000 soldiers and Marines. This was expected to drop quickly (end of 2003) to from 30,000 to 50,000.

[84] Paul Wolfowitz, Deputy Secretary of Defense, testifying in front of congress, February 23, 2003."

[85] General Abizaid, testimony before Congress, November 15, 2006.

monumental job of postwar administrator to Iraq[86].
Appointed in May of 2003, Bremer reported directly to
Rumsfeld. In addition to disbanding the Iraqi army (he
claims there was no army to disband, that they had all
faded away), he fired thousands of school teachers and
removed Ba'ath party members from government. The
combination is said to be instrumental in creating the
vacuum that led to the insurgency.

The fault, however, does not belong to Bremer
alone. Prior to his arrival in Iraq, the Senate Foreign
Relations Committee was told by Under Secretary of
State Marc Grossman that:

> *"Last March the Bush administration
> announced and has stepped out on
> what we call a Future of Iraq
> Project...not to have an academic
> discussion but to consider thoughts
> and plans for what can be done
> immediately."*

It was billed as a "roadmap for Iraq's political
future[87]. Said Grossman:

> *"One of the reasons that we have
> spent so much time and so much effort
> on these Future of Iraq Projects, [is]
> so that we have a way forward, we
> have an idea for a constitution, we
> have an idea for laws."*

---

[86] Bremer's title was Director of Reconstruction and
Humanitarian Assistance for post-war Iraq. He replaced Jay
Garner, May 6, 2003.
[87] Senate Foreign Relations Committee hearing on the future
of Iraq, February 11, 2003

Unfortunately <u>the Future of Iraq Projects was never communicated to the one responsible for carrying it out, Jerry Bremer</u>. Bremer admitted that he learned about it from the press much later.

On the first of May, 2003, while our administrators in Iraq were beginning their struggle with an uncertain future, President Bush landed in a flurry of cameras and admirers on the aircraft carrier Abraham Lincoln. There he gave a speech announcing the end of major combat operations in the Iraq war

"Now liberal commentators must address the victory at hand and confront an ascendant conservative juggernaut that asserts United States might can set the world right."
New York Times reporter David Carr, 4/16/03

Since then many pundits, including those formerly supporting the President's position and strategy, have become openly critical of the way the war was conceived, how the aftermath of the initial invasion was handled and how Iraq has been managed since then. Bush was said to be especially stung by comments made in a 2005 newspaper column by Brent Scowcroft, his father's national security adviser. Scowcroft openly questioned the necessity and wisdom of going to war[88].

As with many examples of misguided efforts outlined within this book, the blame for the decision to enter Iraq can be laid at more than one doorstep. Congress voted to give President Bush the right to begin military actions, and rather than rely on <u>administration</u> intelligence reports and assurances, they

---

[88] Interview with *The New Yorker,* October, 2005.

could have done homework on their own. Certainly they could have obtained the Provincial Stability Assessment mentioned earlier through their various intelligence and defense committees. And they could have steeled themselves against the momentarily-inflamed emotions of constituents that tended to place in jeopardy any politician viewed as weak on fighting terrorism. They could have waited out those emotions rather than play to them in such a counterproductive way. (As we know now, those "momentarily-inflamed emotions" have turned 180 degrees and are now unforgiving of politicians who helped lead our country into this quagmire.) In taking the easier path, Congress demonstrated that, rather than learn from history, they might not even bother to study it.

LEGALITIES

Questions of legality concerning a U.S. President taking his country into a protracted war have been posed since the time of President John Adams (*Quasi War*, 1798-1800[89]). In modern times, it was leveled against Truman (Korea), Eisenhower (Lebanon), Johnson (Vietnam), Reagan (Granada) and Clinton (Yugoslavia). Politics and the electorate being what they are, however, "legality" could be said to be irrelevant. Operation Allied Force, code name for the NATO invasion of Yugoslavia, is thought to have violated the constitution because it created a situation of war that had not been declared by congress and did not defend U.S. territory, U.S. nationals or U.S. interests. Yet that "invasion" continues to this day.

---

[89] An undeclared war between the United States and France (1798-1800). It is sometimes referred to as the "The "Half War.""

If a president mistakenly launches a war, even if he is convinced that he is averting harm to the U.S. in doing so, the question of whether to continue the war is primarily a political one, matching a president's wishes against public opinion. If the war goes well, so does regard for the President and his military adventure. If it does not go well, then we have what we had in Korea, Vietnam and now Iraq: public clamor to end it and loud cries of "illegal war."

"I think in this case international law stood in the way of doing the right thing."
Richard Perle, normally an Iraq "hawk," conceding to an audience in London the possibility that the Iraq war was illegal; November 19, 2003

Similar in opinion to the above, Lord Goldsmith, Tony Blair's Attorney General, said that a reasonable case could be made that U.N. Resolution 1441 authorizing military action did not make the invasion legal, that claims to the contrary could be legally challenged.

Congress has the right under the constitution to deny a declaration of war and/or to remove funding to continue it. In concession to timing concerns regarding modern day warfare, Congress has given the president the right to act spontaneously in the defense of the United States, to respond to an imminent threat with something less than a full declaration of war. In this, however, the president does not have the right to be wrong in the assumptions that led to such action. When evidence of error becomes obvious—and that opinion has been smoldering since the early days of the Iraq war—it is up to Congress to revoke implied authority by eliminating or curbing funding. That Congress has not done so with regard to Iraq would appear to make them culpable, although it could be argued that they had no real choice, that they could not curb funding for fear of making a bad situation worse.

Thus it would seem that Congress gave Bush permission to go to war but with enough caveats that the blame would fall to him rather than to Congress should things go awry. When it became obvious that things had indeed gone awry, politicians on both sides of the isle, some of whom had earlier acted in fear of looking soft in the face of America's enemies, quickly focused on distancing themselves from action they had earlier approved. (One wonders what turn their "conscience" would have taken had the war gone in our favor.)

The question of legality will likely be debated for decades, but history suggests that some future president, regardless of his ideological bent, will not be so impressed with questions of legality that he or she will let it interfere with whatever it is he or she wishes to do. Unless we change the rules, the game of Korea, Vietnam and Iraq will be played again.

One final thought on legality. It has been suggested that the Iraqi Interim Government, which we put into place to govern the country until a more properly constituted "Transitional Government" could be created, was also "illegal." It is ironic, however, that such a distinction could be made in a country that has been ruled by a brutal dictator for 35 years. Arguments such as these do not add credibility to a situation that is already muddied enough.

"It is three-dimensional chess in a dark room."
General Graeme Lamb—former deputy commander of the multi-national force in Iraq

RETREAT INTO CHAOS

We entered Iraq to end Saddam Hussein's program to acquire nuclear weapons, reported to be close to the boiling point for the United States. When no nuclear weapons were found, an acceptable alternative was biological and chemical weapons of mass destruction. When only a few aging bombs previously thought to be discarded were found, the reason for entering Iraq was again revised, this time to rid the area of Saddam Hussein and bring democracy to, not only Iraq, but through the example of Iraq to other Middle Eastern countries. The autocracies in the area, some of them friends (Saudi Arabia, Jordan, Egypt, Kuwait, the United Arab Emirates) did not think much of the idea.

Later, when none of the above could any longer be sold to an increasingly skeptical American public, the reason for being in Iraq was switched to fighting the war on terror: *"We are "fighting them over there so we will not have to fight them here."* As with the other inventions, however, we are coming to understand that the opposite may be true, that our presence in Iraq might be the incentive driving al Qaeda recruitment, and that while we spin wheels trying to put down a destructive insurgency we weaken our ability to fight the real enemy, including those found in Afghanistan.

"To say that Al Qaeda was out of business simply because they have not attacked in the U.S. is whistling past the graveyard,"
Michael Scheuer, former head of the bin Laden tracking unit at the C.I.A.

When the looting ended and the damage was assessed, it became clear that a long and expensive rebuilding effort would be necessary (and we had not yet learned the lesson that such rebuilding is ill-advised in unstable environments). Although we had expected to be able to pay for this rebuilding effort through a restoration of Iraqi oil exports, guerrilla insurgency made that impossible. Oil lines and supporting equipment were attacked then attacked again, with the result that the flow of oil was less than was needed to pay for the rebuilding effort. The bill was thus given to the American taxpayer. And it was a big one.

Unfortunately this came at a time when we had recently given ourselves a big reduction in taxes, which meant there was no surplus American money to rebuild Iraq—it would have to be borrowed. Our national debt, with all the negative it represents to future generations of Americans, increased enormously. The earlier decision to "give the surplus back to the taxpayers" rather than save it for the inevitable "seven years of famine," proved to be short-sighted by far.

The welcome we earlier received from Iraqis suddenly freed from a brutal dictator quickly turned to anger at an infrastructure that no longer worked. In short order, the malfunctioning systems—electricity, water, sewer, transportation, government services—reduced the country to turmoil and its citizens to desperation. And we, in this case justly, received the blame, since it was we who had set the stage whereby looting could occur and we who had fired the Iraqi personnel trained to manage this infrastructure.

While this was happening, resentment began to grow among Sunnis at the thought of surrendering power to "religious fanatics;" i.e. the majority Shiites. An equal amount of resentment was building among Shiites who were looking to get even with Sunnis for having dominated them for so long. From this came an explosion of emotion that metastasized from an insurgency to sectarian violence then to a civil war, the latter made worse by incursions from an opportunistic al Qaeda.

Our real enemy had found a way to rejuvenate himself.

Yet, as if blind to the changes occurring around them, the United States stuck to the plan of fostering upon a people totally foreign to the idea and unimpressed with what they saw unfolding, an American concept of democracy. We had inserted ourselves into the middle of a classic Hatfields and McCoys[90] situation (which we had been warned about by the intelligence community's assessment of January, 2003) yet imagined we would find only smiles and words of welcome.

"To believe that Americans, with an occupying force that long ago outlived its reluctant welcome, can win over a recalcitrant local population and win this counterinsurgency is far-fetched."
"The War As We Saw It," by Buddhika Jayamaha, Wesley D. Smith, Jeremy Roebuck, Omar Mora, Edward Sandmeier, Yance T. Gray and Jeremy A. Murphy[91]

The history of the area, as the British found out before World War II, was such as to strongly suggest that Arabs will not sit still to attempts to impose western concepts upon them, no matter how altruistic we imagine those concepts to be. And winning over religious fanatics with more than a thousand years of demonstrated inability to get along with either their neighbors or each other, is both unrealistic and naïve. For example, one of Iraq's provincial governors (a Shiite,) was killed in August of 2007 by what is thought to be a member of the Mahdi Army militia, which is also Shiite. This is regarded as a political killing among rivals of the same sect, and it was the second such killing in a ten-day period.

---

[90] A deadly rivalry took place in Kentucky between two families, the Hatfields and the McCoy. It began around 1863 and ran off and on for nearly 30 years.
[91] All are combat soldiers fighting in Iraq. Sergeants Mora and Gray died there on September 10, 2007.

The time to worry about the consequences of failure is <u>before</u> committing United States troops to battle. We Americans now find ourselves in a situation that offers no good way out; no path to "victory" and no withdrawal that will not bring additional pain. We have severely damaged our reputation and demonstrated to the world that we are not all-powerful, that in spite of our incredible weapons, technology and wealth, we can be stopped. We have also demonstrated once again that the American public will not long endure a conflict that involves sacrifice and hardship, not unless there is real meaning attached to it. We have shown incompetence and fallibility to the countries of the Middle East on whom we will, through our lack of foresight in providing for our energy needs, depend for the foreseeable future. It should thus not be surprising that these same Middle Eastern countries are now reexamining their relationship with us and with each other, with little of what they decide expected to work to our benefit.

"The current approach is not working, and the ability of the United States to influence events is diminishing."
LEE H. HAMILTON, co-chairman of the Iraq Study Group.

EFFECT ON THE MIDDLE EAST

A common assessment is that Iraq has devolved to a bloody and highly destructive civil war into which both the invaders and neighboring countries have been drawn. It is difficult to say how long this struggle will prevail or what further damage will be done before it ends, but it is a safe bet that we will have to leave short of the "victory" sought after by the Bush administration. And we will not leave behind a pleasant smell.

Rather than fostering the cause of democracy in the Middle East, our incursion into Iraq has had the opposite effect. In some Middle Eastern countries the gap between government and public has widened, with places like Lebanon and Gaza experiencing a weakening of central authority. Important allies have experienced growing unrest among their populous, and there has been a growth of militancy among religious fundamentalists, the destabilizing effects of which have not yet been fully realized. Iran and its neighbors, rather than being cowed by our demonstration of American strength, are emboldened, which means Israel is more threatened than it has ever been before. In short, the Middle East, never stable to begin with, has been turned into a conflagration that may reach all the way to the American shores.

We have shown the world that we are weak and uncertain. Friend and foe alike now believe, as do a majority of Americans, that we are in a poor position to respond to military emergencies, even when it is clearly in our interests to do so. They are thus freer to act as they wish.

Our moral authority has been shattered by our performance in Iraq. Our record there has made the concept of democracy suspect to the very people we are trying to convince, placing it for them somewhere between not-for-us and evil. Russia's Vladimir Putin said it best during a Bush/Putin press conference. Responding to a suggestion by Bush that Russia would do well to study Iraqi democracy, Putin replied with a smile, *"We certainly would not want the same kind of democracy they have in Iraq."*

EFFECT ON THE UNITED STATES

The war has put in jeopardy our nation's security. Continuing it in the hope that something might yet be salvaged gives aid to the terrorists who thus find it easier to recruit and train new troops to fight against us. Iran and Syria, both of whom were treading carefully after our success in Afghanistan, have been emboldened. Also emboldened are the Taliban of Afghanistan, who have regrouped and are now coming against us in force.

We have shown more arrogance than strength. When it came down to the kind of fight where our technology could not effectively be brought into play, where we had to fight house to house and sometimes man to man, we were only slightly more effective than the people we were up against. Perhaps less effective, considering the harsh survival skills their severe lives teach them. Revealed to our enemy is confusion and ineptness regarding how we cope with suicide attacks, a strategy the other side gleaned from the Japanese Kamikaze attacks that so devastated us near the end of World War II. We apparently are slower to learn this lesson—one more example of not understanding history thus being condemned to repeat it.

There is a certain intractability within the Bush administration, a stubborn refusal to admit fault or mistake. Since 2003, knowledgeable people of both political parties have protested that things in Iraq were not as our government was purporting them to be. Such protests have either been dismissed as "defeatist" or have simply not been listened to. Sadly, all too often it has been the latter. Closer to fact is that we are responding to what is arguably the greatest danger our country has ever faced—a full-scale attack against civilization by Islamic fanatics—by throwing the forces of the United States against the wrong target

"If you're looking at it from the cave, or wherever al Qaeda is hiding at the moment, you have to be pretty happy with the way the world is moving."
Michael Scheuer, former head of the bin Laden tracking unit at the C.I.A.

We are fighting the wrong war on the wrong battlefield using outdated tactics (a civilized, technically-oriented country such as ours cannot win in old fashion hand-to-hand, house-to-house fighting against a primitive enemy who has nothing to lose and does not mind dying in the process). We faced a potentially mortal problem with the above-mentioned Kamikazes off Okinawa in WWII? Had the Japanese used that tactic earlier, the outcome of the war might have been different. We have had sixty years to learn how to deal with that tactic, yet there is little evidence that this time was well spent.

Perhaps a sign of our growing disappointment, Americans are coming to realize that boyhood slogans and cheers do not take the place of adult rhetoric and adult reasoning. Administration cries of "surrender monkeys," "cut and run" and "these colors don't run" are having less and less effect over time. We are coming to realize that Iraq is not a sports contest, and if the totality of our thinking is whether or not we take home a figurative silver cup, then we do not deserve to "win." People are dying and we are leaking American treasure at a prodigious rate, treasure that should be used to provide true benefit to our people and to our country. Further, we are exacerbating an already frightening balance of payments situation by financing the Iraq war through borrowing from an increasingly hostile world. There is nothing in any of this to suggest we are making our country more secure.

There is a fear, a common one, that to discontinue the fight would be to say to the families of fallen soldiers that their loved ones died in vain. Upon closer examination, this argument breaks down. It will not make grieving families feel any better to see their neighbors' sons and daughters die as well. A mistake was made, a big one, and we are being irresponsible when we ask more young men and women to climb into the grave to keep us from having to admit it.

Staying the course in Iraq in the name of fighting terrorism is an oxymoron. It is like attacking Granada during World War II and arguing that the battle against fascism justifies our keeping the effort going there even as it diverts men and material from that same battle against fascism. Iraq is the wrong battle. Fanatical Islam is our enemy, and as mentioned previously, we have yet to come up with an effective way to fight it. There are large pockets of fanaticism spread throughout the Middle East and Southeast Asia, all of which wish harm to the United States and a return to the "purity" of Mohammed and Wahhabi. If they could, they would reduce us all to their wretched level of existence (more on this in the following chapter).

SUMMARY

Yale psychologist Irving Janis coined the term *Groupthink* in 1972, which he defined as

> *"A mode of thinking that people engage in when they are deeply involved in a cohesive in-group, when the members' strivings for unanimity override their motivation to realistically appraise alternative courses of action."*

An Oregon State University Web site dealing with communication described *Groupthink* as:

> *"Groupthink members see themselves as part of an in-group working against an out-group opposed to their goals. You can tell if a group suffers from groupthink if it:*

1. Overestimates its invulnerability or high moral stance,

2. Collectively rationalizes the decisions it makes,

3. Demonizes or stereotypes out groups and their leaders,

4. Has a culture of uniformity where individuals censor themselves and others so that the facade of group unanimity is maintained, and

5. Contains members who take it upon themselves to protect the group leader by keeping information, theirs or other group members', from the leader."

The above suggests a pejorative connotation to the term *Groupthink*, but it is difficult to deny that it defines important areas of our lives—in how we pursue our spiritual beliefs, for example. More relevant to this writing is that it also defines the Bush administration. There is a dangerous naiveté in the executive branch of our government that says because something is decent and good that it can be made to work as long as we set our mind and energy to the task.

Middle Eastern cultural is vastly different than ours. It is one with a history of disunity and violent disagreement, state to state and Muslim to Muslim. Our version of "decent and good" is not theirs. Often it is quite the opposite. Going into Iraq, regardless of how many of us approved of it when it began, has helped no one. It was a mistake, and failing to admit this now suggests either incompetence or denial on the part of the *Groupthinkers* we elect to decide such matters for us. If this were a business, we would not hesitate to concede that, not only is our plan not working, but it is making matters worse. Picture the state Ford Motor company would be in if its leaders had stubbornly insisted on "staying the course" with the Edsel. Had they replaced good sense with bravado and patriotic expression and refused to admit that their business plan had failed, the company, its investors and all the people it employed might have gone down the tubes. Any good businessman knows that when you make a mistake, you admit it and take whatever action best repairs the damage it caused. Not to do so is another and even greater mistake, one deserving of more intense criticism.

But this is not a business; this is our country. Automobiles are not at stake here; it is our way of life, perhaps our lives themselves. We need better leaders than we have at the moment, leaders who do not think going full speed in the wrong direction is a virtue, who do not point to a genuine threat to our survival to justify continuing a flawed strategy.

Reflecting on how much we and the world we knew have changed as a result of our entry into Iraq is painful. We have angered our friends, undermined the cause of freedom and democracy, encouraged the fanatics even as we weakened our ability to cope with them on a global scale, and revealed our limitations to the world, which Islamic fanatics and those of our friends who have had enough of our go-it-alone, never-a-doubt arrogance, will now be anxious to exploit. There will be attacks on our soil, of that we should have no doubt. And they have been made easier by the flawed strategy of intractable ideologues.

Consider this excerpt from a 2006 National Intelligence Estimate:[92]

> "United States-led counterterrorism efforts have seriously damaged the

---

[92] National Intelligence Estimate "Trends in Global Terrorism: Implications for the United States," April, 2006

leadership of al-Qa'ida and disrupted its operations; however, we judge that al-Qa'ida will continue to pose the greatest threat to the Homeland and US interests abroad by a single terrorist organization. <u>We also assess that the global jihadist movement—which includes al- Qa'ida, affiliated and independent terrorist groups, and emerging networks and cells—is spreading and adapting to counterterrorism efforts.</u>

"Although we cannot measure the extent of the spread with precision, a large body of all-source reporting indicates that activists identifying themselves as jihadists, although a small percentage of Muslims, are increasing in both number and geographic dispersion.

"If this trend continues, threats to US interests at home and abroad will become more diverse, leading to increasing attacks worldwide."

Lee Hamilton stated after the Iraq Study Group report (discussed in Chapter 8) was released, that we have very little time left before a mess becomes a disaster. *"Not a matter of months, but weeks, perhaps even days."* They also said, *"U.S. forces seem to be caught in a mission that has no foreseeable end. ... Making no changes in policy would simply delay the day of reckoning at a high cost."* (Their recommendations, as was said previously, were <u>not</u> accepted by President Bush, and the situation <u>did</u> continue to deteriorate.)

No one really expected the Iraq Study Group to come up with a solution that would lead to "victory." Rather they were looking to them to apply learned reasoning to an unreasonable situation and derive from their deliberations the best choice from a crop of only bad choices. That they did not offer the solution Bush was looking for was grounds enough for him to, not only reject their recommendation, but to substitute in its place a greater push toward a military solution, in this ignoring the collective opinion of experts that whatever military gains might come out of this, they would be momentary and fleeting. Restated, the ISG failed to convince the President that the tingle he felt in his chest was not God encouraging him to "stay the course" but simply gas.

During World War II, Adolf Hitler reacted to each failure with even more rhetoric. Victory to him, rather than illusive, was a matter of the "right attitude" coupled with a greater willingness to sacrifice. That such intractability contributed to millions of German deaths and to the destruction of Germany appears to be overlooked by those in government today.

During the winter of 1942-43, a German general with almost 300,000 men found himself surrounded outside Stalingrad. Recognizing the need to break out and withdraw to a more defensible position, he pleaded with Hitler for permission to do so. Hitler, his pride engaged, would have none of it:

> *"Sixth Army will hold their positions to the last man and the last round and by their heroic endurance will make an unforgettable contribution towards the establishment of a defensive front and the salvation of the Western world."*

(Sound familiar? Great expression of pride and patriotism, but destructively naive.) As a result of

Hitler's insistence, the 91,000 German soldiers still alive after a period of senseless slaughter (of the original 300,000) surrendered to the Russians. Most of them died in captivity.

Yet even with all the collective wisdom calling for us to get out of Iraq, it is difficult to find anyone who truly believes we can simply "pack up and go home," declare our intention to leave Iraq then withdraw our troops (this includes ISG co-chairs, Lee Hamilton and Jim Baker). And there is validity attached to a go-slow approach to leaving, considering the many facets of withdrawal and what it means to friends and foe alike. Leaving too quickly could upset the balance of power in the Middle East, encourage mischief against the United States and pull the rug of security out from under millions of people our actions have made desperate. Increasingly, however, deciding when and how to leave is becoming less our option. We are holding a tiger by its tail.

If you have a tiger by the tail, you are bound to get hurt in some way. If you let go early, you might retain enough energy to defend yourself against the worst of its anger, but if you wait until you are a step or two beyond fatigue, it will be the same tiger you release, but you will be less able to escape its wrath. Whatever foolishness possessed you to grab the tiger's tail is not so relevant at the moment. Having done so, you now have to decide how best to let it go, for sooner or later, you are going to have to.

What we need is, not expressions of bravado or even patriotism, but solid unbiased thinking, untainted by emotion or pride. We must, for example, come up with realistic aims. The democratic concept of "majority rule" is not going to work in Iraq, especially when the other half of our strategy is to convince the Sunni states in the region to help us contain Iran. Saudi Arabia, Egypt, Jordan, Lebanon, Yemen, Bahrain, Qatar, Oman, UAE, Kuwait, Turkey and even Afghanistan and Pakistan (and al Qaeda) do not want to see a Shia force in control of Iraq, majority or not, and they definitely do not want to see Shiites in alliance with Iran. They fear an Iranian ascendancy, armed with nuclear weapons. Yet we cannot as an alternative put a <u>Sunni</u> force in control of Iraq because the majority Shiites and the Kurds do not want this—and neither does Iran. One of our hands appears to be fighting the other.

All these forces have been put into motion because of our poor strategic thinking, and the continuance of such thinking will only insure that Pandora remains out of her box longer than she should. What we must do now is let the forces in the area play out their ugly game of fear and dominance without us there to stir the pot. There is evidence that this has already begun, perhaps spurred by visions of the United States' ultimate (and inevitable) withdrawal. The Arab League met in Cairo in 2005 and voiced a collective belief that they could guide Iraq's insurgents toward a political rather than a military solution[93]. Restated, reading the handwriting on the wall, they are already planning an Iraq without the presence of United States troops.

"We realized that we have to wake up. Someone rang the bell"
A high-ranking Saudi diplomat

Iraq is in shambles and will likely remain in shambles for many years to come, this whether we stay or leave. In making the decision to go or stay, we must apply realism to our argument, recognize our

---

[93] Arab League conference on the reconciliation of Iraq, November 19-21, Cairo, Egypt.

limitations here, what we are capable of accomplishing and what we clearly are not. As the Senate Select Committee on Intelligence pointed out before the war began, Iraq is a deeply-divided society, one we are ill equipped to understand, let alone manage. And there is considerable argument that, even though we have made a bad situation (Saddam) worse, there is little reason to try. The countries in the area, however their anger at us will grow as a result of our leaving behind a worse situation than we found, must come to grips with the problem of Iraq and solve it in their own way, "an Arab solution," as the late King Hussein of Jordan once put it. Considering the close similarity of cultures, there is promise in an Arab solution, more so than with us arrogantly (and naively) promoting "the American way." We stand little chance of winning the hearts and minds of a populous that sees only their arch enemy, the infidel Crusader. They will shoot solemn glances at us during the day and bullets at night.

Yes, the situation has been made worse for Middle Eastern countries, but every day we remain in Iraq we add to the dangers they face. Iraq breeds terrorists who foster death and destruction, not only to the Western world, but to Middle Eastern countries as well (anyone who disagrees with their ideas of the moment). Terrorists are using Iraq for training then are branching out to do their mischief elsewhere. We have invaded a country that was once an enemy of al Qaeda and turned it into a recruiting and training ground for that same al Qaeda.

The Iraq Study Group made the following assessment:

> *"If the situation continues to deteriorate, the consequences could be severe. A slide toward chaos could trigger the collapse of Iraq's government and a humanitarian*

catastrophe. Neighboring countries could intervene. Sunni-Shia clashes could spread. Al Qaeda could win a propaganda victory and expand its base of operations. The global standing of the United States could be diminished. Americans could become more polarized."

The Bush Administration persists in claiming no one has yet come up with an alternative plan for Iraq. They make this claim because no other plan meets their selected criteria, principal of which is it must lead to "victory." That criteria, however is flawed. It is too limited; it is thinking inside the box when what we need is just the opposite. (This is not to say, however, that the Democrats can claim the high ground. Since taking over Congress in 2007, they have made no serious effort to end this war, their feeling being that to attempt to do so this close to the next presidential election would be risky, offering too much of an opportunity for the other side to show them as weak on terrorism.)

Wanting to meet the Administration's goal of "victory" has no bearing on whether or not we stand a chance of doing so. Iraq, and indeed most of the Middle East, is replete with bad actors who consider only their own ideas. They will fight to the death rather than compromise even a tiny bit on those ideas (When in the last thousand years has this not been so?) The stability that exists in the Middle East today is only because dictatorial regimes are in place to keep their populous in line.

In his pursuit of "victory" at all costs, President Bush persists in the suggestion that Congress should not second guess the experts, that they should leave the war to the generals and the responsibility of the conduct of the war to the Commander in Chief. Apply that logic to the disaster recovery effort after Katrina and Mike Brown, the man who led FEMA during that time, would still be running that show. Closer to reality is that we have left the war to Bush for entirely too long. As with Brown, we should not allow such an important matter to remain in the hands of those who have proven themselves incapable of handling it. Congress should not leave war decisions to our Commander in Chief, but should do whatever is within their power to end what has become a disastrous folly.

Had we insisted on the Bush idea of victory during the Vietnam era, we would still be bleeding badly. Likely "Stay the course" would have devolved to "Would the last American heading for Vietnam please turn out the lights?" We are sitting in a vat of garbage of our own making and protesting that we cannot come out without tracking garbage all over the floor. Unfortunately, this claim is valid—there <u>will</u> be a mess when we leave, but this does not justify staying where we are hoping to find a way of turning garbage back into edible food. None of the options visible to us at the moment look all that good, but we need to do something other than what is clearly not working today. We must pick the option (or combination of options) that do the least harm.

"Stay the course? You've got to be kidding. This is America, not the damned Titanic."
Lee Iacocca

A good first step would be to admit that it is we (the U.S. and Britain) who created this garbage, <u>not</u> the terrorists and <u>not</u> Saddam Hussein. Admit that we made a mistake in starting a war that did not have to be fought. Saddam was unpleasant but manageable and so was Iraq. The Iraqis' "bad" was that they could not find the courage to overthrow their oppressors.

Then we should announce our intention to give this mess back to the Iraqi people, tell them that they have but a short time to decide under what circumstances this will occur. Telling them in a voice that will brook no argument will make it clear to both the Iraqi government and the insurgents that the rules of engagement are about to change, that we will no longer stand in the way of their bad behavior, that whatever they do next, they will be doing it to their own people and to their own country. Leaving would also remove a sore spot with those Muslims who believe we should not be there, that we are "occupiers" or "crusaders."

To protect our troops, withdrawal could take time (although this should not be used as an excuse to slow it down more than is necessary). We might have to leave in stages, the first being the relatively stable north (Kurdish area). That might not sit well with Turkey, who is in conflict with the Kurds, but that is a problem Turkey must deal with themselves. They were not all that supportive of us, and indeed are not now. The Turks did not permit the use of their bases and greatly restricted bomber overflow during the start of the war. They are our friends when it suits their needs and less friendly when it does not. The unpleasant fact for them is that it does not suit our needs at the moment to spend our wealth and our young lives keeping Kurds off Turkish backs.

Regarding our allies in country, there are "tokens" who will leave without creating a noticeable wake. We should, of course, protect them as they exit, recognizing that it was our error that brought them there.

Ironically, Syria and Iran might rather we stay. The longer our display of American democracy is seen by their people as something to be avoided, the greater their ability to stay in power. Beyond that, if we were to leave, Syria (which is Sunni) and Iran (which is Shiite) will have to confront each other rather than us, a sobering thought for both countries and one that might spur them toward cooperation. Finally, our bleeding of national treasure, including human treasure, works to their political and even military advantage.

There is a fear that Iran will come to <u>dominate</u> Iraq, this because they are supporting the militant Shiite cleric Moqtada al-Sadr with weapons and money. Logical, except that Sadr is unlikely to accept domination by anyone, Iran included. Like Saddam before him, he is egotistical and independent-minded. And ruthless—he is said to have assassinated rivals from other <u>Shiite</u> militias, including a provincial Iraqi governor.

However the countries of the area decide to play this out, our presence there (as we demonstrate every day) is only making matters worse. Without a monumental effort that the American people are unwilling to put forth, we cannot win a religious war, and that is what Iraq has become. We are the enemy of both sides, a recruiting poster for religious fanatics. If we get out of the way, these forces will continue their little dance, putting down their brother would-be dictators until only one is left. Likely he will look a lot like Saddam Hussein.

The United States did not sign on for an Iraqi civil war, and if this is the best the Iraqi people can do with their new-found freedom from tyranny and oppression, it is best they do it alone. We should not be held hostage to the resolution of an endless blood feud.

"It is one thing to try to break up a fight between two people who disagree; it is another thing to try to break up a riot. You just get sucked into the middle."
Michael Mandelbaum, foreign policy expert at Johns Hopkins.

What happens after we announce our intention to leave will depend on how much the garbage begins to smell, but under no circumstances should we back down from our commitment to get out of the pit. The odor will only get worse the longer we remain there. As it is, it will linger on our clothes and bodies for decades to come. Maybe longer if some distant President forgets the lessons of Vietnam and Iraq.

"No one can guarantee that <u>any</u> course of action in Iraq at this point will stop sectarian warfare, growing violence or a slide toward chaos,"
Report by the Iraq Study Group, December, 2006

As long as we remain immersed in Hatfield and McCoy passions, there will be Iraqis hating us as well as hating each other. At every opportunity, at every momentary lapse in our attention, at any perceived weakness in the Iraqi government, they will return to what history has suggested to be their favorite sport, warring with anyone not in lockstep to their religious opinion.

"Whenever we depart, Iraq will go right back to mixing religion and government, because they are conditioned from birth that religion <u>is</u> government."
Mel Ray, Op-Ed contributor, Spruce Creek, Florida

Much of Bush's rejection of the Baker-Hamilton report comes from his regard for his "instinct," which he believes is guided by God. To accept the Baker-Hamilton assessment of Iraq would be to admit a failure, which by his parochial definition of "instinct" would be a failure by God. Beyond unhealthy it is frightening to contemplate a person sitting in the most powerful chair in the world and guided by faith rather than by reality—one has only to pick up a history book to see the harm that can come out of this. That our fear might be valid lends emphasis to the earlier discussion of religion in politics, how important it is that we elect government officials who understand the difference between the two.

Whatever our government does or does not decide with respect to Iraq, it is critical that they (and we) become more strategic in our defense against Islamic fanaticism, that we take aim at the people who raise generation after generation of Islamic killers, that we cure our addiction to oil and thus starve Islam-dominated countries of the money they use to buy weapons and methodology. Since they are not a people prone to invention, once their income is lost, they are as well. Restated, spending hundreds of billions of dollars unproductively in Iraq does not protect America as well as spending an equivalent amount on alternative energy. The latter is a sensible strategic approach to victory; firing our guns wildly in Iraq is not.

This world, as is increasingly driven home to us, is becoming daily less safe due to Islamic fanaticism fueled by our misguided adventures in the Middle East. Unless we latch on to a leader (or leaders) who can think outside the box, the threat will grow until too large to effectively counter without a monumental loss of human life. And if we do arrive at that point, rather than admit fault, we will likely see pointing fingers everywhere we look, pointing at everyone but oneself.

ADDITIONAL THOUGHTS

1 - The argument (posed by Administration supporters) that says we should stop agonizing over how we got into Iraq is disingenuous at best. We have been dragged into a conflict whose justification existed in the minds of people too quick to believe and too slow to think, people so submerged in preconceived

and unalterable notions that contrary thought was regarded as a temptation of the devil. Because of such "good," God-fearing people, we once again spilled our nation's blood and resources, and for the Administration to dismiss this as "yesterday's headlines" fills the war-weary public first with disgust then with despair.

New York Times columnist Thomas Friedman posed the question, *"Is Iraq the way it is because Saddam was the way he was? Or was Saddam the way he was because Iraq is the way it is — ungovernable except by an iron fist?"* If there is truth to the inference in this, it would seem to suggest the world is not better off without Saddam. Certainly we are not, and neither is the Middle East. *We The People* did not agree to go to Iraq for the purpose of fighting Saddam's tyranny, and *We The People* should not let the Administration and its supporters get away with such an obvious attempt to divert us, nor excuse the serious errors they made by accepting their spurious arguments. The world would be better off without any of its many tyrants, but should a president come to the American people and ask of them that they go to war to unseat these tyrants, we would hear such a resounding "NO!" that it would not be necessary to publish the results.

One lesson to be learned from Vietnam and Iraq is that we must limit the ability of a president to take us to war. We can permit him or her to act to protect the country and its citizens but we must attach such restrictions to any and all military action that the right to declare war will effectively be returned to the Congress where our founders intended it should be.

2 - There is a fair chance that we will momentarily raise banners of outrage over our experience in Iraq but do little more than that. When our emotions are high, so are our promises to ourselves, but emotions cool as quickly as a libido, and with much the same results regarding follow-up action.

As with an exhausted libido, will we go back to whatever it was we were doing before we became aroused? Or will we truly make an effort to record and remember? We can only hope that competent military minds, mindful of history and what comes to those who carelessly disregard it, will surface to consider our emotional and physical limitations as they plan the future defense of the United States. Hope also that they find a way to arm themselves against presidents possessed with a sense of heroics and an allegiance to World War II tactics. In New Orleans we faced a <u>real</u> need yet responded poorly. In Iraq we faced a <u>false</u> need yet responded poorly. It would seem that the Bush administration, when faced with a serious crisis, responds poorly.

3 - We are too interested in being "The Leader Of The Free World," even when it is obvious that Germany, Japan, South Korea, and other countries in which American troops are housed, only show willingness to feed our ego and our illusions in this regard as long as American taxpayers keep contributing to their defense. We jump through hoops and spend prodigious sums on a world that laughs at what our ego forces us to do. To ourselves we are "the leader of the free world" but to the rest of the world we are "Uncle Sap," a rich uncle whom our "relatives" tolerate as long as we continue to buy them dinner. We accomplish very little for what it is costing us in both cash and reputation.

4 – It is surprising, after all the restoration of good health that has been America's experience since Viet Nam mercifully ended, that anyone would still be lamenting that we could have "won." If President Ford, a conservative Republican, had not had the courage to admit what everyone else in the world already knew, that we had no business in that country to begin with, we would still be there. Iraq is not Viet Nam, but Viet

Nam should have taught us a lesson: that our country should tread carefully in world affairs, certainly much more so than we have of late. We are not saviors, we are not masters of all that is right, and we are not without limits to our power. We cannot and should not insist that our way is the only way. That, to the detriment of civilization at the moment, is the philosophy of the radical Islamists.

Will we remember our mistakes or will we repeat them? Will we consider our limitations, including an intolerance to pain and a crippling lack of patience, or will we once again lead our country into a military and political debacle? Thirty years into the future, when we are again tempted by a Vietnam or Iraq, we will know the answer to that. Denial can be a potentially fatal disorder, in this case for America

CHAPTER 9-2
FANATICAL ISLAM

BACKGROUND

The "monsters" we have discussed thus far are matters over which we exercise at least some degree of control, matters that have either escaped our notice or are not yet considered a sufficient threat. What we discuss now, Islamic extremism, has to a large degree "escaped our notice," but in a very significant way it is different. It is something over which we exercise very <u>little</u> control. Indeed, at present it would appear that others, who do not wish us well, may have a greater influence on our future than we, this in spite of our superior strength and ingenuity.

Since Islam's beginning in 622 AD[94], there have been three "spread the faith" invasions by militant Islamists. The first was the conquering of northern Africa in the seventh century, leading to African Moors taking over most of the Iberian Peninsula in 711 AD and remaining there until driven out by Christian forces around 1200 AD. Although the Muslim culture was at first beneficial to a continent lost in the dark ages, the teaching of Islam, which is strict and uncompromising, eventually fostered violent disagreement, even among others of that faith (Muslim began turning on Muslim). The conflict revolved around an inability to decide who would lead the faithful after Muhammad died (632). One side considered that only direct descendants of Muhammad would qualify (they eventually became known as Shiites). The other side (Sunnis) believed any worthy man could lead. The Sunnis eventually became the dominant force in Islam, but bloody conflict still takes place today over this disagreement. (This is the "Hatfields and McCoys" comparison used in the last few chapters.)

The second Islamic invasion involved the Ottomans (Turks) who began expanding beyond their borders in the middle of the 14th century (this threat to Christendom is what triggered the crusades) and lasted until World War I. They considered themselves an Islamic successor to earlier Mediterranean empires (Greek and Roman).

The third invasion is currently underway. It is the exporting of Islam's excess population to the West. Unlike many western countries that have brought their

---

[94] The start of the Islamic calendar. (Mohammed, the founder of Islam, was born in 570 A.D.).

population growth under control, the birth rate in Islamic countries is growing rapidly. Primarily due to this atypical birth rate, Islam has become the fastest growing religion in the world today.

To understand the Islamists better, we should better understand ourselves. Throughout history religious zealots have committed egregious harm in the name of often twisted interpretations of their faith. No major religion has escaped the shame of this. What is happening within Islam today mirrors the excesses of Christianity, and even as we claim that, for us, that was the past and we would never permit such barbaric behavior today, we allow the chipping away of what keeps us from the worst of those past excesses. (e.g. Christian doctrine working its way into government affairs). It is Islam's destructive side showing at the moment, but we should not think in this that our slight but inexorable shifts in the same direction escape being both hypocritical and a threat to our country's well being. Less evil is still evil.

"Extremism in the defense of liberty is no vice."
Barry Goldwater, Republican convention, 1964

"Extremism" is by definition beyond reason. It is religious "extremism" we are battling against, and religious extremism is wrong, whether it is personified by Osama Bin Laden or Jerry Falwell. The war against terror/extremism currently being fought by America is critical to our survival, and to win this war men and women of good intent must examine their own behavior as well as that of the enemy.

CONFLICT

Centuries of History have demonstrated that Muslims have difficulty getting along with anyone not completely in line with their constricted thinking, even fellow Muslims. Further, the intolerance shown through the years and the intolerance we see in "believers" today rarely limits itself to debate. Rather it quickly devolves to hatred then violence, person to person, sect to sect and nation to nation. In Iraq there are even deadly conflicts between groups of the same sect (e.g. the Shiite Badr Brigade loyal to the Iraqi Supreme Council, fighting the Mahdi Army loyal to the Shiite cleric Moqtada al-Sadr). The dangers this uncompromising dogma presents to the world are growing at a frightening rate. We show a lack of understanding of this when we naively demand Iraqis (Sunnis, Shiites and Kurds) bury the hatchet and just get along.

The problem is in the way the religion is practiced. Mullahs, the religious leaders of Islam, are permitted to preach hate, bigotry, intolerance and murder to impressionable young children then prevent these children from hearing alternative opinion. Not surprisingly, the next generation of Muslims grows up with hate, bigotry, intolerance and murder as an irrepressible part of their makeup.

Muslim children are taught from a very young age to believe strictly in the Qur'an, the Islamic holy book, which assures them that there is a special place in the afterlife for those who aid Allah in ridding the Earth of any who do not accept Islam. Mullahs offer children no other basis for reasoning than this. Indeed, they tell them it is a mortal sin to question what they are being taught, that others before them have proclaimed that no further interpretation of the Qur'an is to be permitted under pain of being branded an apostate deserving of death.[95] They are given no chance to learn how the

---

[95] Teaching of Abdel Wahab (1691-1787), a reformer of Mohammedanism. He believed that all interpretations of the

world turns, no chance to discover that there are opinions that differ sharply from their own and that those in possession of these opinions are as convinced of the truth in them as they are of the truth in Islam. Young and impressionable Muslims thus accept as truth the only input they are permitted to hear.

Fundamental   Islam   is   strong   and uncompromising[96], and it has not weakened its extreme position in the millennium and a half since its inception. Its people (children <u>and</u> adults) are kept ignorant ("Learn only the Qur'an, no more—and men only."), and ignorant people are more easily indoctrinated, less able to discern or accept reason. Since their society is not prone toward improving living standards for its people, they go on to a life of squalor, generally under savage dictatorships, that becomes increasingly desperate to them. One manifestation of this is that they are more easily molded into suicide bombers.

This is not to say, however, that the Islam ideology is not capable of also seducing well educated and highly trained individuals to murder and suicide. Indeed, for reasons that are not yet clear, even healers (physicians) have fallen under this spell. As we have recently seen in Britain, such people are willing to commit acts of violence that their fellow citizens have

---

Qur'an have already been decided, and that further intermediation of Muhammad will be considered an act of polytheism, the worship of multiple gods. This theology is the dominant form found in Saudi Arabia, Kuwait and Qatar, as well as some pockets of Somalia, Algeria, Palestine and Mauritania.

[96] There are Christian et. al sects that have pursued their beliefs in barbarous ways in the past, but diversity has made it difficult for any one religion to grab so much power as to bring out the radical in them once again. Islam has not yet arrived at that stage.

trouble understanding. It has made identifying a potential terrorist that much harder.

Much of the anger in Muslims is said to come from resentment of the successes of the West. Nowhere in the Islamic world is there a modern society they can be proud of, where innovation matches that of Western countries, where the conveniences of life are equal to those produced in the West, where such conveniences are freely available to all of its citizens and not just the privileged. Nowhere is there respect for invention and medical breakthrough. Their religion teaches them to distain such things, even as they enjoy the fruits of what the more industrious countries produce. Why, young Muslims say, if their faith is supreme and the West is morally inferior is the West doing so much better than they?

"There is a deep knowledge gap separating the Arab and Islamic nations from the process and progress of contemporary global civilization. We are no longer keeping pace with the advances of our era."
Abdallah S. Jumah, CEO of Saudi Aramco

The humiliation and loss of dignity this engenders triggers the kind of rage that lends itself to psychotic behavior. Those suffering this rage cannot accept a causal relationship here, cannot accept that their society suffers because they subscribe to intolerance and illiteracy, that their autocratic leaders neglect their economies and squander the wealth found under their soil, that they disenfranchise their women, that they permit and even worship suppression of dissent and inquiry. Rather than learn from the West, they spend their money and intellect showing contempt for a society that would rule from a <u>collection</u> of voices rather than from a single prophet. Their chief domestic product has become hatred of "infidels" and "crusaders," and they seem to prefer pyrrhic victories such as 9/11 to educating their population to the innovation and progress that will help overcome this resentment of others.

The Islamic world is flooded with oil money that does not serve their people well. Mostly it is spent on senseless wars and foolish self-aggrandizement of the wealthy and the powerful. A peaceful end to the threat Islamic fundamentalism represents will come only if Islamic society per se comes to grips with the modern world. Considering that we have had more than a thousand years of experience with this culture, a thousand years where nothing has really changed, this is not expected to happen soon.

"The trouble with Islam is deeply rooted in its teachings. Islam is not only a religion. Islam [is] also a political ideology that preaches violence and applies its agenda by force."
Syrian-American psychiatrist, Wafa Sultan

The expectation of Armageddon is believed by <u>many</u> religions. It is a final climatic battle between God and the Devil, the end of which will see all believers being lifted to Paradise. Although not a concept welcomed as a near-term prospect in the west, in the Islamic world, where life is difficult and unlikely to get better under the constraints their religion imposes upon them, it is not only less feared but in many circles desired. It is this latter attitude that so threatens civilization today. To survive what could be a <u>self-fulfilling</u> Armageddon,[97] it will be necessary for us

---

[97] The current leader of Iran, Mahmoud Ahmadinejad, is thought to believe Armageddon is coming soon. His toying

to counter Muslim rigidity and what comes out of this, the murder of those whose only "crime" is to disagree with the fanatics. As indicated above, Muslim children are not taught, they are brainwashed, and brainwashed children are food for the Devil. They grow up as zombies ready and willing to destroy themselves along with their victims. They become soldiers of evil, automatons under the control of psychopaths. Their numbers are large and growing, and if left unchecked, civilization will give way to barbarism. The tenet of Armageddon will be fulfilled.

Moderate Muslims argue that Islam is a peaceful religion. This would be more believable if they would, as a group, come out strongly against the staining of Islam's reputation by the barbarous behavior of its practitioners. What condemnation they do offer is insincere, obviously ineffective and too often accompanied by a "but"—"See things our way and all will be well." Even as they shake their heads at fundamentalist excesses, they show sympathy for the terrorist's feelings and motives. And even as it is proven that hate and intolerance spill daily from their religious and teaching institutions, they do nothing to curb it, thus giving tacit approval to conduct that breeds barbaric behavior.

The painful fact is that Islam is not a live-and-let-live religion. It permits no room for compromise, no willingness to question the more violent of its dogma, no willingness to put down those who favor death and destruction over debate. There is ample evidence in the Qur'an (Islam's holy book) of intolerance and deadly intent. In the following excerpts the killing of those who do not believe is encouraged:

---

with nuclear weapons could make that a self-fulfilling prophesy.

Q 9:5 "Fight and kill the disbelievers wherever you find them."

Q. 9:73 "Struggle with the unbelievers ... and be thou harsh with them."

Q 8:65 "O Prophet, urge the faithful to fight. If there are twenty among you with determination they will vanquish two hundred; if there are a hundred then they will slaughter a thousand unbelievers, for the infidels are a people devoid of understanding."

Q 47:4 "Thus are you commanded by Allah to continue carrying out Jihad against the unbelieving infidels until they submit to Islam."

Q 8:39 "Fight them until all opposition ends and all submit to Allah."

As the above shows, this is far from an intellectual debate, where each side presents arguments and respects the other side's right to present theirs. To Islamists, debate is considered to have no value since "truth" has already been established[98]. They will accept no other outcome other than our conversion to Islam or our death. Unless the Islamic world defeats the worst of these religious excesses, we are heading for a bloody clash of cultures, perhaps the most costly in terms of human life that the world has ever known. To be sure, the more successful nations, those witnessing a steady improvement in the living standards of its

---

[98] Abdel Wahab, ibid.

people, will not sit still for those who would see them reduced to a primitive level.

CLASH OF OPPOSITES

The following was taken from an al Jazeera interview on a show called *The Opposite Direction* (Qatar, February 21, 2006). The topic is Clash of Civilizations, and the words are those of Syrian-American psychiatrist, Wafa Sultan. Ms. Sultan fled from the Middle East because of atrocities committed by the Muslim Brotherhood. She has since renounced Islam and as a result is a target for Islamic fanatics. She emigrated to the US in 1989, and is now a naturalized U.S. citizen.

> *"The clash we are witnessing around the world is not a clash of religions or a clash of civilizations, it is a clash between two opposites, between two eras. It is a clash between a mentality that belongs to the Middle Ages and another mentality that belongs to the 21st century. It is a clash between civilization and backwardness, between the civilized and the primitive, between barbarity and rationality. It is a clash between freedom and oppression, between democracy and dictatorship. It is a clash between human rights, on the one hand, and the violation of these rights, on the other hand. It is a clash between those who treat women like beasts, and those who treat them like human beings. What we see today is not a clash of civilizations. Civilizations do not clash, but compete.*

"The Muslims are the ones who began using this expression [clash of civilizations]. The Muslims are the ones who <u>began</u> the clash of civilizations. The Prophet of Islam said: "I was ordered to fight the people until they believe in Allah and His Messenger." When the Muslims divided the people into Muslims and non-Muslims, and called to fight the others until they believe in what they themselves believe, they started this clash, and began this war. In order to stop this war, they must reexamine their Islamic books and curricula, which are full of calls for takfir [unbeliever] and fighting the infidels...

"What right do you have to call them [Christians] "people of the book?" They are not "people of the book," they are people of <u>many</u> books. All the useful scientific books that you have today are theirs, the fruit of their free and creative thinking.

"The Jews have come from the tragedy [of the holocaust] and forced the world to respect them, <u>with their knowledge, not with their terror</u>, with their work, not their crying and yelling. Humanity owes most of the discoveries and science of the 19th and 20th centuries to Jewish scientists. Fifteen million people, scattered throughout the world, united and won their rights through work and knowledge. We have not seen a single Jew blow himself up in a German

restaurant. We have not seen a single Jew destroy a church. We have not seen a single Jew protest by killing people [not quite true]. The Muslims have turned three Buddha statues into rubble [Taliban in Afghanistan]. We have not seen a single Buddhist burn down a Mosque, kill a Muslim, or burn down an embassy. Only the Muslims defend their belief by burning down churches, killing people, and destroying embassies. This path will not yield any results.

"The Muslims must ask themselves what they can do for humankind, before they demand that humankind respect them."

Muslims protest that Islamic extremists are motivated by a feeling of injustice, but that is too convenient. This overlooks Islamic doctrine, samples of which will be presented under *The Growing Danger* which follows. The "injustice" is our stubborn refusal to accept the word of God as they see it.

THE GROWING DANGER

"After two thousand years, the Arab world finally agrees on something. They hate America more than they hate each other."
Jack Cafferty, CNN

One of the less obvious dangers we face in the war against terrorism is going too far politically, curtailing cherished liberties in the name of protecting against a threat to our security. There are examples of our having done this in the past (the internment of

Japanese during WWII), and our national conscience is still taking hits on this. Benjamin Franklin once said, *"Those who would give up an essential liberty for temporary security deserve neither liberty nor security."* With fear building over the threat aimed at us by terrorists, we are toying with just that: giving up "essential liberties." The Patriot Act is an example. Perhaps it is necessary, perhaps not, but it is definitely a curtailing of what we have long expected is a right to privacy. And in permitting government this power, we run the risk of its being used for <u>political</u> gains by unscrupulous politicians. The trick, of course, is to allow so much and no more, to establish machinery such that the unscrupulous cannot easily make use of this tool, cannot through an inappropriate use of weakened privacy laws perpetuate themselves, their believers and their agenda to such an extent that it will be difficult to extricate the ideology that imbues within the system. Restated, we cannot leave it up to politicians to decide which of us should be monitored and how the results of such monitoring should be handled. The leaders of what was then a Roman Republic (67 BC) took much the same chance and lost. Because of a growing danger of pirates in the Mediterranean, the Roman leader Pompey asked for and was granted special powers.[99] It was a classic demonstration of the law of unintended consequences. Pompey, even after the danger passed, refused to relinquish this power and the Republic was lost.

That said, even as we must guard against a loss of freedom, we are forced to acknowledge that we need better tools to protect us from dangers such as the armies of Islamic automatons being readied to throw

---

[99] Called the "Lex Gabinia" after the Tribune Gabinius.

against us. Our response to this at present is weak and ineffective, perhaps the price we pay for wanting to show civility in our reaction. We consider it abhorrent, for example, to even think of going after the mullahs who train what becomes our enemy, this because it interferes with <u>our</u> concept of religious freedom. Instead, we try to win the hearts and minds of those who have the power to control the mullahs' excesses, a tactic that so far has not produced results.

"For every individual captured or killed, there are at least five more coming down the assembly line."
Sajjan M. Gohel, director for international security at the London-based Asia-Pacific Foundation.

As unreasonable as the thought appears on the surface, we must question why we should be so "understanding" of people who freely express their desire to murder us. Doing so might put us on a higher moral plane, but it can also lead to our demise. Whether Muslim or Christian or Jewish or whatever, murdering in the name of an unprovable spiritual belief is evil. And filling the minds of the young with expressions of hatred that leaves them no outlet other than to pursue that hatred to the destruction of others is also evil—it makes little difference in what deity's name they do this. Our devotion to civility sometimes exceeds reason.

Consider the following[100]:

1 - Hezbollah fires rockets with no target in mind other than Israeli

---

[100] Regarding Israel's invasion of Lebanon in 2006.

crowds (innocents). Israel strikes targets of military value, hitting innocents but not specifically targeting them.

2 - Hezbollah protects their forces by surrounding them with a human shield (innocents). In attempting to defend themselves against the rockets being fired at them, Israel hits innocents.

Flames of outrage are directed at <u>Israel</u> for the death of civilians at their hands, but where is the same outrage toward Hezbollah for <u>deliberately</u> seeking civilian deaths? Why do we condemn Israel while with Hezbollah we call for "understanding?" It would appear our criticism is as poorly aimed as the occasional Israeli shell.

There were cries for "proportional response," do no more to the aggressor than the aggressor did to you, but is Hezbollah of the same mindset? Hezbollah's intrusion into Israel was proportional to what? What had Israel done that Hezbollah was responding "proportionally" too? "Understanding" is a two-way street, and we err when we give more of it than we receive.

We stand little chance of winning the hearts or minds of those so cloaked in intractable rhetoric that they would attempt to import legitimacy to the following:

In early 2007, a <u>five-year-old </u>boy was doused with gasoline outside his Baghdad home. It is thought that the act was a "message" aimed at the boy's father, a security guard, a dangerous occupation in Iraq. This

> was an act of pure savagery against a
> defenseless child simply because the
> perpetrators disagreed with the politics
> of the child's father.
>
> A savage act against a child who
> had no hope of defending himself
> against grown men. What part of an
> ideology that would permit such an
> atrocity is open in either heart or
> mind?

As public as the above story has been, condemnation among Muslims, even those professing their religion to be a kind and just one, has been minimal, mostly limited to lip-service disapproval. They appear not to see in such barbaric behavior a need to curb the enthusiasm of their religion for hate and violence, even when this hate and violence manifests itself in the killing or maiming of their own[101]. Some Islamic governments even pay the families of homicide bombers upon their death, and perpetuate the notion that such bombers will receive 72 virgins in "paradise." It is precisely this attitude that is so dangerous to the world, the attitude that says anything goes, that God will reward the murderer for his act regardless of how cruel and how cowardly that act might be.

"The Islamic world today is being held prisoner, not by Western but by Islamic captors, who are fighting to keep closed a world that a badly outnumbered few are trying to open."

---

[101] Muslim extremists kill more Muslims than any other group.

Salman Rushdie, Author of *The Satanic Verses*

Those who defend Islam feel no need to be fair and balanced in either argument or action. Words that would offend them they feel free to use against others. They present Jesus any way they wish but are inflamed to riotous behavior should Christians do the same to Muhammad. They blow up other Muslims in mosques on their most holy day of the year, and there is little said about it in the Muslim world. Yet a cartoon or an off-hand papal remark can set off wide-spread violence. They are fanatical about a non-Muslim entering a "holy site," yet do not hesitate to use that same "holy site" to store weapons, plan murder and even conduct battles. They view with indifference (or pleasure) the sawing off of a Westerner's head, yet rise with an inflated sense of indignation when a Westerner forces one of them to appear nude in a photograph.

On May 9, 2005 Newsweek magazine reported that interrogators at Guantanamo Bay desecrated a Koran. The report turned out to be a mistake (for which Newsweek apologized), but it caused wide-spread riots in the Islamic world with great loss of life and property. Newsweek made a mistake, no one argues that, but logic dictates that responsibility be applied to all. There was little outcry in either the Muslim or non-Muslim world about the uncivilized behavior of thousands of people quick to demonstrate the ease at which they can be inflamed. Rather, the actions of these rioters were glossed over, with the blame for the death and destruction they caused passed on to Newsweek.

The intolerance of Islam to criticism is shown even in their own media. All news is to a degree propaganda in that it expresses a newsperson's (or a station's) opinion, but compare what can be said in the United States to what is permitted in countries in which al Jazeera is a primary (or sole) source of news. In the west we are given the opportunity to wade through conflicting opinion and decide for ourselves, but this does not happen where information—in particular religious information—is tightly controlled. The people there have no choice but to accept what they see and hear as "truth." That religious leaders would present deliberate lies to their people tells us much about their morality.

> *"It erases the distinction between legitimate dissent and terrorism, and an open society needs to maintain a clear wall between them."*
> Robert Rubin, Treasury Secretary under President Clinton

What in any of this disproves the notion that Islam is a religion tainted by violence? What is the logic of our calling for "understanding" of such people while failing to insist in an equally loud voice that they try to understand us? And why should we be so willing to excuse intolerance simply because it is the basis of a religious faith?

We need to share with them <u>our</u> outrage, point out to them that responsibility and understanding are two-way streets—the Muslim <u>rioters</u> were responsible for the death and destruction that occurred after the Newsweek error, <u>not</u> Newsweek magazine. If followers of Islam (or any of the world's many religions) are so lacking in control of their emotions and so reluctant to educate their people to other than their own point of view, then it is they who must assume the lion's share of what comes of it. It appears at the moment that they are getting a free ride, that those in the media are fearful of pointing the finger of evenhandedness their way.

> *"Self-censorship does not help us against people who want to practice violence in the name of Islam,"*

German Chancellor Angela Merkel

It is said that Zealots are not amenable to reason, but that does not mean they should suffer less condemnation than those who have grown weary of their excesses. When we weakly condemn Hezbollah and their sponsors for how carelessly they play with human lives, we show a serious fault in ourselves. We grant too much credit to the less civilized, deluding ourselves into believing they will join us as friends if we try harder to show them our civility. In this we gloss over their freely-given opinion that they regard it as a sin even to listen to us, that when we speak, we are the Devil tempting them from the "true path." Such people are not going to swoon into our arms when we expose them to "the American way."

"Don't smile at them, don't wish them well on their holidays, don't address them as "friend."
Part of a 1,265-page souvenir sold in the holy cities of Mecca and Medina

Such is the ideology arming against us, people who believe in their heart of hearts that they are fighting evil infidels, who believe that an apocalyptic war is not only inevitable but to be desired, that such a war will hasten the second coming and that there will emerge from this a utopian (Islamic) society. The many who believe this are certain without a doubt that in what they do to encourage an apocalypse that they are following God's will and thus cannot be wrong. (Sound familiar?)

CIVILITY VS. CIVILIZATION

Americans are, for the most, civilized. We play by the rules and assume by this that we will prevail. But there is no golden rule to assure us that we will win just by being good, that we will prevail even as we refuse to mimic the barbaric behavior that terrorists practice with such abandon (and success). We might yet discover how quickly the uncivilized can tempt our grasp on morality.

The time might come when the rules of engagement are sorely tested, when we can no longer defend sticking to the high road knowing that to do so would place in question the continuation of civilization itself. When and if that happens, will we defend ourselves with unspeakable weapons and unspeakable actions? If the goodness in us prevails, will we be reduced to the point where, with our dying breath, we proclaim pride in the fact that we stuck to our moral guns while they destroyed us with their real ones? A part of us knows it is right to apply civility to barbarism, but such strategy does not always serve us well.

Because of our inability to understand the correlation between Islamic terrorism and our addiction to oil (which finances such people), we are falling more and more into the hands of those who see a fulfilling prophesy in hastening Armageddon. Iran, who is insanely fanatical with regard to "infidels," will soon have nuclear weapons, and there are few who believe they will not use them against the West. Beyond Iran, we are up against a billion people with uncompromising views who feel God has endowed in them the right to impose those views on non-believers by any means at their disposal. It is in every sense of the term, a clash of opposites.

America's approach to this problem has been laced with such caution that we have proven ourselves ineffective and, by this, emboldened our enemies. If nothing changes, if we continue to play by rules that have yet to produce results, we might discover that devotion to morality comes at a high price. There is a serious cancer growing on civilization, personified in the names of Hezbollah, Hamas, al Qaeda, and whatever other name murderous religious extremists use to describe themselves. There is not much cure for this cancer at the moment, but for sure one baby aspirin is not going to do it.

Distrusting of a government that promotes prized programs by invoking the threat of al Qaeda as if they were the evil organization SMERSH in Ian Fleming's James Bond, Americans are reluctant to consider radical Islam as other than a nuisance, deadly at times but more a topic of conversation than a mortal threat against civilization. As time goes by we will come to realize our error, but much preparation time will have been lost. And involving ourselves in such adventurers as Iraq will only make us weaker and less able to cope with the real threat. We need to come to grips with the reality of all this then prepare ourselves to battle it, not in bits and pieces and not by limited actions but through a global effort. Sooner or later, unless we "starve the devil[102]" of his means to war against us—including curing our addiction to oil and letting those who would murder us wither to the primitive state that ignorance and intolerance deserves—we will be drawn into a global catastrophe that civilization itself will have difficulty surviving.

Critical in this is to establish and <u>enforce</u> limits to the behavior of those so willing to be our enemy. They cannot be permitted to continue to commit horrors in the name of their religion. They cannot be permitted to train enemies of civilization, especially as they make it clear that these enemies are to be used against us in murderous ways. Finally, we cannot continue to

---

[102] Starve The Devil, by Noel Carroll, is a fictional approach to Islamic extremism.

proclaim uncivilized behavior to be their right, an exercise in the kind of religious freedom we Americans cherish but which they have no intention of permitting us to enjoy for long.

In this, we cannot count on the voices of moderate Muslims. Their lack of effective response thus far has created the conditions whereby religious extremism can grow, and as it grows, the danger to the world grows in proportion. What we <u>can</u> do requires further discussion, but if left unchecked, Islamic extremism will bring about more senseless slaughter, more hatred and eventually the awakening of a sleeping giant (more on this later).

None of this, however, should be taken as support of the Bush Administration's approach to fighting terrorism. Our president uses fear of terrorism to foster favored goals, not least of which is encouraging more oil exploration. Looking backward for a solution to a problem that requires forward thinking will only exacerbate the problem and postpone the solution. What we face now from terrorists is far from the dangers we faced (or imagined we faced) from Saddam Hussein. There are dictators all over this globe, but even united they would not be as threatening to Western civilization as is unchecked Islamic fundamentalism. Saddam was a dictator not an ideologue.

"Our enemy is easy to finish, but hard to find. Today, we are looking for individuals or small groups planning suicide bombings, running violent Jihadist Web sites."
General Michael V. Hayden, Director of the CIA

A short time before the start of WWII, a top governmental official refused to decrypt secret messages sent by the Japanese. His comment was, "Gentlemen do not read other gentlemen's' mail." In a perfect world, that might make sense, but considering the dangers we faced then (Pearl Harbor was soon to happen) it was nothing short of irresponsible. (It should be noted that enterprising government employees conspired to listen anyway.)

The point is that civility is not necessarily the best tool to assist a bad situation. There are times when gentlemen <u>do</u> have to read other gentlemen's mail, when not to do so is lending aid to the other side at a time (such as the beginning of WWII) when you need all the assistance you can get for your side. A devotion to civility, carried beyond practical reason, could, in the case of global Islamic extremism, prove to be suicidal. Rather than help to preserve civilization, it could lead to civilization's defeat, with the West slowly surrendering the reins of civilization to those who would see it relegated to what existed under the Taliban in Afghanistan (with many of us no longer around to complain). The Dark Ages was not a good time for humanity, and sitting by while it steadily regains a foothold serves only to encourage ignorance and human decay.

"Our leading thinking is that we are closer now to an attempt at a major attack in the United States than at any point since 9/11,"
Ben Venzke, Head of the IntelCenter, a government contractor doing support work for the intelligence community.

No man is an island, and seeing innocents die bothers us all, some quite deeply. It matters little the nationality of these innocents. But there comes a time in any society when lives must be put on the line, ours as well as those who would destroy that society. At such times the best we can hope for is that, in succumbing to whatever tactics our conscience-of-the-moment permits us to employ, we at least hold <u>our</u> losses to a minimum.

IRAN AND NUCLEAR WEAPONS

On Oct. 22, 1962, President John F. Kennedy spoke to the nation about the missile crisis in Cuba. One announcement in particular was difficult for the other side to misinterpret:

> *"It shall be the policy of this Nation to regard any nuclear missile launched from Cuba against any nation in the Western Hemisphere as an attack by the Soviet Union on the United States, requiring a full retaliatory response upon the Soviet Union."*

The man currently leading the Middle Eastern nation of Iran is a fanatic weaned on unchallenged propaganda perpetuated by religious despots. We should harbor no doubt that he is capable (and very willing) of inflicting pain and suffering on all he considers Allah's enemies, which is everyone except fellow Shiite Muslims. The radioactive material he boasts of having developed *will* find its way to America's shores, whether through a nuclear device or a "dirty bomb." Bad timing for us, considering the Iraq quagmire we have permitted ourselves to fall into, but we cannot point to this as a reason for ignoring a very real threat to our future.

Demonstrating a change in the rules of engagement (and perhaps in our hold on civility), it is time for another Kennedyesque promise to an incautious enemy. We should loudly proclaim to the people of Iran that,

> *"It shall be the policy of this nation to regard any nuclear material*

> *determined to originate in Iran and delivered in any manner to the shores of the United States as an attack by Iran on the United States, requiring a full retaliatory nuclear response upon Iran."*

It is not known the extent to which we can identify the signature (fingerprint) of Iran's uranium, but the danger to Iran will only increase if we have to guess. If it quacks like a duck, if it promises monumental harm to our country then "quacks" as if it is in the process of fulfilling this promise, then we are entitled to regard it as a "duck" and act accordingly. We must give these irresponsible fanatics ample warning that the United States has had enough, that, for us, business will *not* be as usual; and that we will react quickly and decisively should they cross so much as one toe over this critical line in the sand.

The Cold War carried with it a very real threat of nuclear war. Patience and reason kept this from happening, the "reason" prompted by the doctrine of MAD (Mutually Assured Destruction), where each side realized the world would come to an end for them as well as for the enemy should nuclear weapons be launched. We cannot, however, treat the future as if it belonged in the past. What we face with Iran is not what we faced with the Soviets.

The MAD concept in all likelihood saved the world, but the circumstances that made it work have changed significantly. We do not have two relatively mature nations applying practicality and reason to the dark side of their behavior. We have a fanatically religious society convinced of the inevitability of Armageddon, the end of the world and the triumph of Islam. As we award them supercilious smiles of understanding, they see weakness waiting to be exploited, weakness that says to them the tide is going their way.

"Appeasing murderers doesn't buy protection. It earns one disrespect and loathing in the enemy's eyes. Yet apathy is the weapon by which the West is committing suicide."
Brigitte Gabriel, speech delivered at the Intelligence Summit in Washington DC, February 18, 2006

We should not award Iran's leaders any more capacity for reason than they show at the moment. President Ahmadinejad has promised the total annihilation of Israel, and as we should have with Hitler in the 30's, we should take him seriously, including making the assumption that he does not expect to accomplish this with aging Iranian tanks. Saddam Hussein had a practical streak; he was motivated by money and power. Ahmadinejad is more moral. His motivation is his religion.

A DANGEROUS DIVERSION

"What's clear is that there is no focus whatsoever in the way we are fighting terrorism"
Veronique de Rugy, of the [conservative] American Enterprise Institute

The tale of Iraq demonstrates all too well our national confusion. Our country faces a mortal danger from terrorists, yet we permit our leaders to delude themselves (and many of us) into believing that tilting at windmills is going to do the trick. Or that, like the horse in George Orwell's *Animal Farm*, all that is needed is for us to work harder (in Iraq) and fanatical Islam will be vanquished.

Proponents of the effort in Iraq ask, where is the "real" battle, if not Iraq?", but one cannot ask a question and think in the absence of an answer that it proves the question. That is saying, "We do not know, therefore we know." The "'real" battle, however, is wherever fanatical fundamentalist religions preach such intense hatred and destruction as to represent a threat to civilization per se. There are pockets of such fanaticism in Pakistan, Saudi Arabia, Indonesia and many other parts of the world of Islam. And, of course, there is the clever but insane leader of Iran. If such people are pledged to destroy us, then they are our enemy and deserve a reaction from us at least equal to what they intend against us. And we should not be misled or impressed with their Muslims brothers who do little to stem the worst of the fanatics' enthusiasm.

When the inevitable happens and we are forced to take action, we must hope that we are not wasting away in senseless conflict more designed to protect our pride than our lives and our way of life. Our poorly conceived and poorly executed actions in the small Middle Eastern country of Iraq, rather than vanquishing terrorism has encouraged and empowered it. We have pushed the enemies ever deeper into psychopathic behavior and added grist to the mill from which suicide bombers are born. Trapped as we are and unable (or unwilling) to attack the extremes of fundamentalism at its roots (where the young are being trained to hate and kill), it is only a matter of time before a new flood of dedicated killers join those already knocking at our shores.

Our government has gotten us into the pickle of the century with its reckless, ideologically-inspired invasion of Iraq, a never-ending and economically-crippling misadventure. But however large this un-confessed error may be, its legacy will be so much more condemning if we take from this the idea that we are battling the real enemy.

There is another unfortunate legacy of Iraq. We are seeing an ever-increasing reluctance to defend our country. We are, as happened after Vietnam, retreating into an isolationist mentality. This attitude could prove to be dangerous to our country's survival.

The loss of a son or daughter in combat is terribly difficult for a parent to bear. More than one life is affected (if not destroyed), not only by the fatality itself, but by the inherent senselessness of the loss. What logic is there in one set of human beings trying so hard to mortally reduce the numbers of an opposing set of human beings? What brass ring of the moment justifies the proud waving of the winner's superior body count? Yet what might our country look like now had the parents of World War II the same access to publicity as is available to a protesting mother of today? Four hundred thousand of our soldiers died in that horrible conflict, exponentially more than we have lost in the current madness in Iraq. Regardless of one's opinion of this most recent war, consider for a moment the effect of so many mothers exposing their anguish in a way that cannot fail to impress all 300 million of us. Consider what the course of events would have been had access to our homes and hearts been so effortless during what was arguably the worst crises our country has ever faced. Absorbing a daily dose of passion from 400,000 mothers in rightful anguish, would we have done what was necessary to protect ourselves from the madmen we faced at the time? Would we have thrown our young people into Tarawa, the Philippines, Iwo Jima and Okinawa? And in North Africa, Normandy and even Germany itself? And in not doing so, would we have lost the war, maybe "compromised" with Hitler, let him kill only half the Jews and keep only half the world?

Will we ever be able to face an enemy again, even a real one such as we faced then? Or will each set of weeping eyes weaken our resolve that much further?

Along with so much else that troubles our conscience these days, this is something we must consider.

SUMMARY- THE SLEEPING GIANT

As mentioned in previous chapters, what is said here is not intended as an attack against any particular religion but an attack against intolerance and intransigent ideology. If our Western civilization has any hope of avoiding a global catastrophe, we had better come up with a means of effectively countering those who have no qualms about bringing Western civilization to an end, people trapped in intolerance and intransigence, people who, from cradle to grave, permit themselves to hear only one side of humankind's many-sided story. Finding an alternative for the oil that feeds their military machinery will help, but even if we finally come to agreement on the need to do this, we have to consider that we might not be granted the time.

"While we have the will and the resources to fight in this context, we are effectively hamstrung because realities on the ground require measures we will always refuse - namely, the widespread use of lethal and brutal force."
"The War As We Saw It," by Buddhika Jayamaha, Wesley D. Smith, Jeremy Roebuck, Omar Mora, Edward Sandmeier, Yance T. Gray and Jeremy A. Murphy[103]

Through the timidity with which we address the problem of terrorism, we lead the barbarians to the gates of Rome and invite another dark ages, one from which we will not so easily emerge. There is an enemy

---

[103] Ibid, Combat soldiers fighting in Iraq

out there who wishes to infect us with all the misery they have endured for more than a thousand years. This enemy is daily attacking us, and our devotion to fairness and justice, however commendable, is not keeping pace with the growth in their ranks. While we politely deal with one, thousands are being cultivated.

Sooner or later, whether involving us or our grandchildren, a battle of monumental proportions will have to be fought against this growing evil. As with the world wars of the previous century, the more we delay before finally coming to grips with the truth of what is aimed against us, the higher the price that we (or our grandchildren) will have to pay

"There is every sign that radicalization in the Muslim world is spreading rather than shrinking."
Council on Global Terrorism, an independent research group of terrorism experts

Our status of "super power" no longer impresses. We have demonstrated quite effectively, through our efforts in Iraq and through careless disregard for foreign opinion in what we do and how we do it, that we are vulnerable, that we can and do make mistakes, and that we are as "human" as the rest of the world in our inability to instantly heal a perceived wrong. In so demonstrating, and in so encouraging the terrorists that they have more of an opening than before, we must expect an escalation of violence.

It is likely that the terrorists view us as more of a "paper tiger" than a "sleeping giant." Also likely that many nations around the globe (and many Americans) see us the same way. But what they (and we) have to realize is that we truly <u>are</u> a giant, and that we <u>will</u> be awakened should the din around us reach such a level that we will finally say "enough." When that happens, the giant will forget his manners; he will react in way the fanatics did not expect. He will abandon baby aspirin for a pain reliever with teeth in it.

A man being smothered beneath a pillow will use any means available to save his life. Such will be the case with us. When faced with no alternative other than surrender to a dark and primitive force, the sleeping giant in us will fight back using whatever is within our reach. Like a bear called out of hibernation early, the dark side in us will emerge with terrible consequences both to the enemy and to our conscience. This might well involve weapons that will live in infamy in our hearts even as we feel relief that the action we took saved us from imminent suffocation.

The ugly fact is that no one thus far, in or out of office, has found a way to employ our limited resources to effectively counter the growing menace of Islamic extremism. And in not having an answer, we gravitate inexorably toward a conflagration (nuclear) as the only means of defeating the insanity that our reluctance has encouraged for so long. If it does come to this, it will not represent a blessing to mankind (the collateral damage will far exceed that taking place today) other than that it will rid the world of a terrible scourge and permit what is left of civilization to continue on.

In the unlikely event we accept the pillow rather than employ so distasteful a defense, the world will devolve to widespread insurgency, with human and material losses on an unimaginable scale. There will also be a total breakdown in the very civility we were trying to protect.

"...After we lose a city, we will adopt rules of engagement that use every technology we can find to break up their capacity to use the Internet, to break

*up their capacity to use free speech, and to go after
people who want to kill us..."*
Newt Gingrich, Former Speaker of the House[104]

The employment of nuclear weapons is something we, at the moment, would rather not consider. Indeed we rebel against even a hint of their use. It is the unthinkable; it is inhuman! Heavy on our conscience are thoughts of the innocents who would fall along with the guilty, as happened during the atomic attack on Hiroshima and Nagasaki. We are not much mollified by the thought that, had we not taken such a 'draconian' approach in 1945, another million American soldiers would have died[105], not to mention countless millions of Japanese. The tactics of WWII no longer apply, but the lessons of that time should not be forgotten. We reacted in a terrible, even cruel way because we were weary of war and its losses and because it was easy to justify the destruction of enemy humanity with thoughts that it was they who "brought this about." There is little doubt that we can (and will) come to this point again, come to where we have had enough, where we see humanity itself being threatened and feel the lesser harm would be to destroy those who "brought this about."

If we are to avoid the unthinkable and the inhuman, then we must otherwise provide a way to attack the problem of Islamic fundamentalism at its core, the wide-spread training of Islamic young to waste themselves in senseless (and endless) battles.

---

[104] Speech given to the Loeb School of Communications, November 27, 2006.

[105] General Douglas MacArthur, Supreme Commander of the Southwest Pacific, estimated American casualties at one million men by the fall of 1946.

Success against the fanatics demands that we cause there to be less of them, that we find a way to deny the Devil his disciples, deny him time to lead us back to our savage past. Events will bring us to realize that we have no choice but to forcibly alter their way of life or surrender ours one 9/11 at a time.

"We are fighting a powerful ideology that is capable of altering basic human instincts."
Brigitte Gabriel, speech delivered at the Intelligence Summit in Washington DC, February 18, 2006

We are skirting the edge of Armageddon because *we the people* are taking too long to recognize the seriousness of what is inviting it (as evidenced by our convenient assumption that the end of oil is far into the future, that we do not have to concern or inconvenience ourselves about it at present).

But that is less true of our leaders. Whatever else we might think of our government, it is composed of men and women bright enough to see the truth, even as they choose to play the issues in ways that more serve the cause of politics and ideological backers (oil and other special interests) than of the citizenry. Further, for reasons known best only to them, they use the threat of terrorism to scare the populous into supporting wasteful military adventurers such as Iraq. Where this careless disregard for reality will lead us, we have yet to see, but it is likely the ones currently applying weak and transient arguments to weak and transient policies are well aware of what they are doing.

As should be clear from the preceding pages, we have little chance of winning the minds of Iraqi insurgents, little chance of convincing them that their poverty and backwardness relates, not to any action on our part, but to their religion and how they practice it. That leaves us few options. The military option, of course, but as was proven in Iraq, we are poorly equipped to fight this kind of battle. Whether or not we hold a military target for a month or so, or even for a year, will not negate the fact that these people are not likely to get along with one another, nor will they ever be receptive to our way of looking at the world. If we expect to succeed where we have thus far failed, we must develop a vastly different approach than that practiced at the moment. We must find a way to "Starve The Devil,"[106] rob him of the means to do mischief. The economies of the Middle East survive only because of the oil they are able to dig out of the ground, oil that, much to our detriment, we cannot live without. It is late in the game, and we have already financed an army of dangerous fanatics, but we must begin such a program ASAP.

In the meantime we will have no choice but to continue to help our enemy purchase the guns and ammunition they need to kill us.

One final note: The nature of religion is such that it breeds a need to be correct which, by definition, prohibits compromise. And being unable to compromise, it is eternally in conflict, sometimes (as with radical Islam) in mortal conflict. What in this suggests that it is wise for any nation hoping to breed harmony among its citizens to legislate even lightly a favored religion? Better for all of us if we take such lesson from the destructive nature of Islamic intractability that we become _less_ inclined to think our uncompromising religion is any more beneficial to humanity than theirs.

---

[106] *Starve The Devil*, ibid.

CHAPTER 10
CONCLUSION

I fear the loss of our country. Through apathy, neglect, and weak guidance from self-serving politicians, our American way has fallen into such disrepair that it might never regain the luster it once had. We have come face to face with a Hydra, the nine-headed monster of Greek mythology that could not be killed and that spewed poisonous breath from each head.

I fear the suicidal excursion of religion into politics. I fear an energy policy that all but guarantees severe economic hardship. I fear the lack of appreciation of national and even international economics and of our substandard approach to educating our young to compete in a global market. I fear our careless disregard for our nation's borders and I fear the tendency of juries to redistribute wealth with careless abandon. I fear Islamic extremists organizing to come against us, and I fear our lack of appreciation of the seriousness of this, which of itself can move civilization backward a thousand or more years.

Most of all I fear because so few other Americans do. So few who recognize that collectively or even severally the "monsters" eating away at our nation do not represent business as usual, routine problems similar to those we have faced down in the past. So few who understand why the fears presented in this book are not, as opportunistic politicians would have us believe, more smoke than substance. The multi-headed Hydra monster is tearing through the fabric of American life, and it is not at all certain that we have it in us to defeat them.

What was presented within this book are not the only Hydra heads tormenting our nation, but they are arguably the most threatening. Almost making the list is our nation's attitude toward "controlling" illegal drugs, which borders on the insane. It is a dichotomy of moral reasoning and denial. We refuse to legalize drugs because it might result in weak-minded children choosing to take up drugs. At the same time we ignore the strong profit motive that brings the unscrupulous to solicit weak-minded children to sample drugs illegally (the hope being that this will lead to a life-long client for their product). Both sides protest moral reasoning, but the latter guarantees that <u>more</u> children will become addicted; i.e. the bottom line is more immorality as a result our "moral" posture (more misery as well). Then there is the universally-acknowledged fact that this addiction leads to more crime as addicts seek to support their habit, and more policemen to control this crime. We are destroying lives, endangering the wealth and welfare of our citizens and wasting huge amounts of America's taxes in ways that only make the situation worse. Insane!

Everyone has a bias whether confessed or not confessed, and there is likely evidence of mine within these pages. Yet there is nothing I wish to sell, no personal benefit that might come my way through guiding a reader toward sharing these expressed fears. My motive is simply to present for your consideration what I feel should disturb you as much as it does me, reasons why our country is losing ground. We are a society in denial. We are apathetic, arrogant, and uncompromising, and as the history we conveniently ignore will prove, there will be a price to pay that we might not be able to meet.

STATUS OF THE AMERICAN EXPERIMENT

The aim throughout these pages has been to reveal the corrosion eating away at a nation that for so many years has been the envy of the world, a nation composed of individuals who, while intensely possessive of the freedom they have come to enjoy, are mistakenly of the impression that God and/or inertia is on their side, that their nation will go on forever regardless of how little effort they give to maintaining it. When approached by suggestions of sacrifice, Americans react in two detrimental ways: The first is that they rebel in a combination of indignation and anger. The second is that they create a cocoon of denial that eases their conscience regarding their first reaction.

If it were simply one bit of corrosion eating away at the pillars of our nation, we might otherwise survive, but when it is not one but many, and when they show signs of uniting to underpin the entire structure, then denial devolves to suicidal.

The really bad part about this is that we appear to have developed a tolerance for corrosion. As alluded to above, there is little recognition of the cards stacked against us, and virtually no acceptance that collectively they present a mortal danger to our nation's future. The evidence is there, but it is hidden in history that entertains but fails to teach.

We lose when we turn our heads from obvious error in the name of a preferred belief. We lose when we answer decay with denial, as if by doing so we keep it from spreading. And we lose when we respond to a decline in life style by bemoaning the terrible luck that providence has thrust upon us. In response to Ben Franklin's comment, "If you can keep it," it would seem that the jury is on its way in with a negative verdict.

Yet there are things we can do. For example, making the decision that a crash campaign to define and establish a suitable alternative to fossil fuel is at least as important as another $100 billion to continue a senseless war. The question is will we. Perhaps a review of our "monsters" will help you make up your mind.

RELIGION ENCROACHING ON GOVERNMENT

Extreme, by definition, is carrying one's beliefs further than is considered reasonable to one's neighbors. Extreme rarely benefits even those who espouse it, whereas it can cause great harm to those who are exposed to it.

In medicine, research, family planning and evolution important decisions affecting our national health and welfare are being made to conform to the spiritual belief of our national leaders. As this continues, we slip ever closer to a theocracy, where reason comes second to ideology and where the young are trained, not to survive and compete in a increasingly threatening world, but to conform to narrow and unsupportable thinking.

This world is a dangerous place, and history tells us much of the danger revolves around religious disagreement. Our founding fathers gave us a way to escape the ravages of this, and we are foolish indeed if we do not seize on their wisdom and keep separate our governing from our spiritual functions. To the extent we do not, we will no longer be free, having surrendered a bit of our freedom to one group's spiritual urge.

Unfortunately, there is evidence that this is already happening. There is a "salting" taking place in the many fingers of government from local to national, not with the most competent, but with those loyal to the spiritual views of the Bush administration—government services controlled by political automatons, their devotion not to the people they serve, but to the 'right thinkers' who hired them. Left in place, we will, among other things, soon find ourselves saddled with judges and justices more influenced by ideology in their administering and interpreting of laws than by scholarly analyses of the lawmaker's intent.

Evidence that it is happening may be found in the decisions passed down from the Bush administration, decisions that place ideology above reason. For example:

> Withholding the so called 'morning after' contraceptive pill because it disturbed the religious right's sense of morality.

> Withholding condoms to HIV-infested countries until they accept a conservative view of its use, <u>even as this results in more people contracting AIDS.</u>

> Restricting family planning and stem cell research for the same reason, and pushing abortion legislation without providing a <u>realistic</u> means of avoiding pregnancies.

History teaches that a diverse society is inherently neither peaceful nor stable. Overcoming this human weakness is an uphill battle, but encouraging a greater diversity (minority resentment) shows a lack of understanding of both history and human nature. What logic suggests a government such as ours benefits its people by doing so? We do not enrich ourselves or our country by waving flags or holy books. We do it by showing character, by behaving better than the next guy, by being moral because it is right not because one fears punishment. Too often we hide behind icons and slogans, as if they excuse otherwise bad behavior. In the fifty years since we placed "under God" in the Pledge of Allegiance, we have had more wars than any of the more secular countries of Western Europe.[107] In addition, we murder and rape our neighbors at rates that shock Europeans. Since these words obviously have not benefited us, it might be that God is not impressed with window dressing, that he prefers substance to slogans. As it is said that there is only a fine line between genius and insanity, there is also only a slight difference between argument and mayhem. Aware of this, as we certainly should be, it makes sense to construct barriers to keep this particular "argument" out of government policy.

Religion mixed with government will not help our country to survive. The question is will we learn this in time.

ENERGY CRISIS

We give only lip service to preserving one the most important engines driving our economy, energy. At the moment, we as a nation cannot survive without oil, yet there is nothing in the wings ready to leap to our aid should the supply of oil become unstable or exhaust itself. And in continuing to rely on energy derived from the burning of oil, we ignore the damage it brings to our environment.

"Unstable" easily defines what we suffered in 1973. And what we are suffering to an even greater extent today, with large nations such as India and China demanding a larger share of a dwindling supply of oil and with our oil dollars feeding Middle Eastern extremism. Government has become more of a

---

[107] When the European Union produced its draft constitution the text made no mention of Christianity or God, the members arguing that Europe's constitution should deal with government, not faith.

hindrance than a help, this because they are stuck on more oil as the solution. If we succumb to what is sure to be increasingly regarded as short-sighted reasoning and refuse to stretch our intellect far enough to examine the long-range consequences of such a restrictive policy, we will see economic turmoil and human suffering that will exceed in its impact anything our country has ever faced before.

We <u>must</u> begin a crash program to develop a sensible alternative to oil, whatever initial price tag it fosters upon the energy-consuming public, and even if this results in a subsequent rise in energy costs for Americans. With a stable energy supply will come, not only less risk of an unstable economy, but a less well-financed enemy. Middle Eastern extremists will not be able to purchase the means of attacking us.

Global warming closely relates to the energy crisis. While one exacerbates the other, so can both be solved when one (energy) is solved. Until then a rising of carbon dioxide level in our atmosphere will cause storms to increase in both frequency and ferocity, land to disappear as polar ice caps melt, dislocations and failure of crops as the average temperature is no longer able to sustain them. History might yet prove that we are not the main cause of this global warming, but there is so much evidence currently available that suggests we are, that we ignore it at our (and our grandchildren's) peril.

Denial is permitting us to go on with our lives as if there will be no day of reckoning. Fearful of disruptions in profits and the economy, we argue that it is not necessary to overburden ourselves with concern now, that the problems of waning energy and global warming have not been proven "to our satisfaction." If either of these two "monsters" reaches the level of global catastrophe, the question of who was right will be less relevant than how our country can survive.

ECONOMICS, EDUCATION AND SOCIAL CONSCIOUSNESS

The structure that supports the greatest economy in the world is souring. Our **balance of payments**, both domestic and international, is going through the roof. We are the incongruity of young adults experiencing the joy of a new credit card and counting on our parents to save us from the worst of our excesses. In the process, we are selling our country to foreigners, not because we want to, but because we have no choice—they are holding too much of our money and want something in return.

In this we receive encouragement but little guidance from government. And the encouragement is that which you might expect of an irresponsible (or ignorant) parent: they tell us it is okay to spend more than we earn, that others in the world, aware of the honor we bestow upon them by permitting them to hold our IOUs (dollars), will never cease to shower us with the goods we Americans feel we deserve.

Closer to the truth is that nations have a habit of penalizing a country that suffers from excessive debt. Increasingly, we see evidence of this happening, a switching of allegiance from the dollar to the Euro. And it feeds on itself—the more talk there is about the Euro being a safer currency, the more confidence is lost in the dollar. Some good comes to our economy as a result of this, but much bad as well. The bad is worse if the switch comes to quickly.

Our cornucopia of "free" goods from abroad is running dry. The uniting of European countries into one economic powerhouse[108], coupled with the rapid

---

[108] The European Union, an organization of democratic European countries committed to working together. Their economic power grows daily.

growth of China and India, is making world investors think hard about the value of the American IOUs they hold. Already the Euro, the currency of the European Union, is being taunted as a "safer" currency. If we do not reduce our international deficit (buy less from abroad, make the products we offer more attractive to foreigners and increase our savings rate to provide sources of investment here at home), the shifting from dollars to Euros will speed up and we will suffer enormous disruptions in our economy.

One way to slow down this deficit, however unpopular and selectively unfair it might be, is to place a large tax on gasoline purchases (purchases of oil from abroad represents a very large part of our deficit). This will force energy conservation while at the same time ensure that this portion of our fuel budget remains in the United States rather than flying to an unfriendly Middle Eastern country. For sure this "tax" will occur in any event, with world competition for fuel increasing so rapidly that the forces of supply and demand will "enact it" whether we approve or not. Had we taken such action in 1973, the time when we were rudely awakened to a serious national vulnerability, conservation and energy alternatives might have already solved the problem. And at a lower cost than we are likely to face in the future.

Such a tax will bring out disingenuous arguments from those whose interests lie in encouraging rather than discouraging consumption, and history has shown that their arguments often land on sympathetic ears (e.g. an image of an old couple unable to get to a pharmacy for badly needed medicine because they cannot afford the gas). For this reason, it is unlikely to happen.

We are falling behind on **educating our young** and fail to see how this contributes to the reduction of our middle class, so important to America's economy.

Job competition from abroad is daily becoming more intense, yet we pull back on the educational achievements expected of our young and simultaneously make it more difficult to attract foreign students. And even as America's middle class continues to lose ground to foreign competition, we show little appreciation of what is within our control.

The case of automobile manufacturing in the United States is a good example of how not to treat a good thing. We were on top, with the "Big Three" composed of American companies. Sales were reliable and wages and benefits could be raised or not depending on management and union's interpretation of how much the market would accept. At the time the head of General Motors made the statement, "Americans are not going to buy Japanese cars," unions were insisting on more and more for themselves and management was routinely giving in, both parties laboring under the arrogant assumption that they could pass costs on to the public with an impunity that would last as long as they wished it to last. We were American manufacturing and the fire in the belly of American labor. We led the world in just about any area we chose to enter.

Not surprising, it did not last.

This demonstrates the kind of penalty abuse and neglect can impose. Today there is less arrogance, with unions having shrunk to a fraction of what they once were and one of the "Big Three" now being a Japanese car maker[109].

The economics of our country are changing, and the speed at which this is happening allows us little time to adjust. However much management and labor battled in the past, each needs the other. With the

---

[109] Toyota

middle class shrinking at an alarming rate, it is inevitable that business will shrink as well.

Management and government, which one assumes are composed of people who know better, are slow to recognize the damage they do when they fail to properly address the shrinkage of the middle class. And the middle class fails to realize how much they contribute to their own decline by pointing fingers rather than looking to self-improvement, complaining rather than rising to the occasion by striving to make themselves more valuable to a changing marketplace. The latter is not easy, but there is no choice. The United States government cannot reverse what is essentially a global trend.

That is not to say, however, that government cannot do something. Or that they should not be held responsible when they take actions that serve only to exacerbate the problem (e.g. a tax cut to the <u>least</u> stimulating segment of our society during an economic slowdown). As was proven during the Great Depression, placing too much faith in "market forces" can produce pain and suffering on a grand scale. As we do with the Federal Reserve's control of the money supply, we must apply human logic and reasoning (and compassion) to avoiding the human suffering the extremes of market fluctuation can bring.

In our current **welfare** policy, with our fear of inviting accusations of political incorrectness by criticizing a system heavily skewed toward a single minority, we have created a situation whereby a large group of Americans are condemned to perpetual second-class status—wards of the state held at a poverty level, even as we spend more and more of the fruits of other American's productive energy to support them. Without more backing from black leaders, only a naïve (or exceptional brave) politician will be foolish enough to wade into the problem with an eye toward bringing real improvement to the system. Thus this monster will continue on, and we will continue to have a resentful underclass demanding more and more while contributing nothing but another generation of bitter, poorly-controlled and hopeless prodigy. Rather than join our society they will be forever earmarked as a separate and unequal part of it.

There is little logic to encouraging illegal immigrants to "crash" our country to do "the jobs Americans do not want to do" while at the same time paying people to do nothing. We need to apply more of a "tough love" approach to welfare, provide negative stimulus to on-going participation in the program, in effect saying nothing is free. Without such a negative stimulus, there is no incentive for a welfare recipient to take that extra step to improve himself to the point where he becomes self sufficient (and self respecting).

Social Consciousness, however sound the thinking when the concept was introduced, too often diverts us from what needs to be done—the civilized lose ground to the uncivilized in the name of civility. How much closer could we get to establishing a more perfect society if we worked through each problem with less fear and more honesty? Fear of brands such as "racist" or "xenophobe" only halt discussion and debate. It permits insults to common sense and decisions that cancel out the good social consciousness was intended to bring about. We accomplish "feel good" at the expense of "real good."

Affirmative action, welfare and political correctness were intended to be good things but we fail to treat them with the respect they deserve, including offering criticism where such criticism is warranted. We take them too much for granted, believing that they will always be what we intended them to be at their start, that we have no need to modify them in accordance with new thinking. Like everything discussed here, it adds up to a growing pattern of corrosion attacking our future. Step by tiny step, the good we seek to do is turning bad through neglect and arrogant assumption.

BROKEN BORDERS

As with America's deteriorating energy situation where sacrifice now to avoid disaster later is rarely taken seriously, we delude ourselves into believing our undocumented immigration situation does us no serious harm. In this we ignore evidence to the contrary. The problem with immigration not only exists but has become huge, with the politics of it so inflamed that it is difficult to discuss it in a reasonable manner.

After World War II, some European countries enacted "guest worker" programs, arrangements whereby aliens received employment in the host country on a mutually-agreed-to <u>temporary</u> basis. Such programs were tightly controlled and came to an end when it was no longer advantageous for the host country to continue to have unassimilated aliens in their midst. Not an easy thing to do to tell "guests" to go home, but both parties knew in advance that this was a likely outcome. Such "trimming" occurs in businesses all over the world, and however unfortunate for the dislocated, the alternative to retaining workers a business can no longer afford is the loss of even more jobs as an economically distressed company no longer has the means of keeping itself afloat.

In the United States we do this a different way. Our "guest worker" program is controlled, not by our government, but by chance. Millions upon millions of undocumented aliens are permitted to decide for themselves whether to enter our country and, if so, how long to remain here. Recent history has shown that our attempts to accommodate this illegal behavior (through partial or full amnesty) have encouraged more such invasions and a greater problem.

There is a naïve assumption among Americans that we can have for ourselves a cheap labor pool that will forever agree to do our most menial bidding. As justification for maintaining this quasi-slavery, we point to jobs that we find distasteful and would rather not do—this "rather not do" is shared by those being paid by the American taxpayer to do nothing (welfare). We view this do-it-yourself immigration policy as a win-win situation, where one side gets workers at a price that conveniently skirts American labor laws, and the other now has a way of avoiding the poverty he left behind in Mexico.

More and more we believe we are so entrenched in whatever this undocumented worker situation has become, that there is no choice but to continue it, that economic hardship will befall us if we force this subclass of labor to return to their own country. While it is true that some such hardship will be unavoidable, the alternative (allowing it to continue) is even worse—sociological, economical and political disaster. **Sociological** because at such numbers we are slowly converting our country into a diverse society that historically has never worked to that society's advantage. **Economical** because our hopes of a permanent, low-paid underclass is not only naïve and immoral but doomed to eventually fall of its own weight as resentment of one's "slave" status begins to fester. **Political** because we are slowly surrendering the right to chose our government (i.e. vote) to those who began their association with America with an illegal act and in whose interest it is to keep such "lawlessness" going.

Reality is millions of *poorly*-educated, *low*-skilled workers competing for jobs that are increasingly demanding *higher*-educated and *higher* skilled workers, the incongruity of this sure to lead to millions more being added to the public dole. Since politicians go with the votes, it remains to be seen whether this will boil down to, not the right or the wrong of it, but which block of voters will be seen to offer the most assurance to a politician of remaining in (or securing) office.

Our quasi policy of undocumented immigration is destined to deliver a serious wound to America. But like with many of our other "monsters," this wound is self inflicted.

A LITIGIOUS SOCIETY

We have a dysfunctional tort system in the United States, one that creates inequity almost as frequently as it dispenses justice. A substantial amount of the public's money goes to support frivolous or overblown lawsuits, and this is having a negative impact on the American dream. Support for this notion that we are an overly-litigious society may be found in the ratio of attorneys to population in the United States, from twice that of England to <u>twenty-five times that of Japan</u>.

The American people, both rich and poor, live in fear that a lawsuit is on their horizon, that a moment of carelessness will result in a lifetime of savings gone. We fear each other—a neighbor's child come to play with our child on our property; what legal disaster will befall us if that child is injured? We fear stopping to help an accident victim—if we so much as touch him will this come back to haunt us in a courtroom? We fear justice will play only a small part in any of this, aware as the system has made us that civil justice has devolved to emotion coupled with ability of a defendant to pay.

We carry our fear to extreme, depriving children of the most mundane recreational activities. "Tag," a game played by all of us when we were young, has been banned by many elementary schools around the nation—too risky from a liability standpoint. It is even affecting our ability to secure for ourselves good health care. Physicians in high-risk specialties are abandoning all or part of their practice or leaving a heavily litigious state for one less legally-tumultuous. Vaccines are receiving the worst of both worlds, less available and more costly. Hospitals, nursing homes, and clinics are closing their doors because they can no longer protect themselves against lawsuits.

While it is true that some benefit has come out of all this litigation (safer practices and products), the extent to which the suits are carried can be considered nothing less than abusive. And some of these "safer practices and products" are counter-productive, such as doctors forced to practice defensive medicine by ordering unnecessary tests or procedures (thus depleting healthcare dollars that could be used elsewhere), or the attaching of product labels that border on the absurd.

This canon of endless and costly lawsuits is supported by the illogical notion that those suffering from someone else's misstep have the right to the wealth of that person (or business) well beyond the damages they suffered. We (and twelve of our "peers") regard it as just and fair to make us (and our attorney) rich as a result of such real or imagined outrage. In this, we (and the jury) conveniently ignore our own contributory negligence, in effect suggesting personal responsibility has no relevance.

The tort system as it is currently exercised in this country is terribly broken. It takes wealth from all of us, such as when product and healthcare costs increase, or when class action suits strip equity from even the smallest and most innocent investor, in effect saying such people also deserve to be "punished." Yet one political party continues to prop up the system, which party by no small coincidence receives financial support from trial lawyers associations. In "defending the little guy," Democrats cause him (and the rest of us) more harm than if they were a bit less solicitous.

A bill in congress attempting to reform the system, introduced each year since 2005, has gone nowhere, primarily because of opposition from Democrats. Thus this outrage to society will continue for the foreseeable future.

SELECTION OF POLITICAL LEADERS.

The key to the slaying of our nation's "monsters" is the selection of competent leaders. It is we who chose the politicians we have learned to distrust, and it is we who stand in the way of what they (and we) must do to save ourselves. The selection of President of the United States (or any American leader) should not be a beauty contest, a reward given to someone we like. The best person for the job might be someone we admire less but who can stand up to the many problems facing our nation. The current candidates for office (2008) offer only more of the same. They tell us what we want to hear, not what we need to know. There appears to be no JFK willing to suggest sacrifice for a greater goal. And no significant public willing to reward such honesty with their vote.

The times we live in are perilous and cry out for leadership, yet we search, not for substance, but for symbols, an attractive personality rather than competency. The Iraq war has the potential to seriously damage our country and possibly for decades, yet the person who brought us to this point has the "moral values" we thought important at the time. That he was not up to the task may be argued, but that we had our eye on the wrong ball cannot be.

We delude ourselves into thinking we have more of a say than we really do, ignoring in our delusion the power of special interests and the media to twist our thoughts away from the meaningful and toward the emotional. A proposed fix for Social Security is presented as an attack upon the system, a strategy whose disingenuous nature should be obvious to us all but that seldom fails to have its desired effect.

"The media bias I detected most often in the White House was neither liberal nor conservative but a tendency to play up conflict and controversy."
George Stephanopoulos, Press Secretary for President Clinton

Once in office, our elected choices quickly begin work to convince us that they should stay there, tossing federal projects our way whether or not those projects have merit. This we also fail to see through, showing our pleasure by re-electing the politician responsible for our "windfall" without chastising him for approving wasteful spending he helped toss to his colleagues. There is little chance of defeating this "pork" monster, few of us willing to put the greater need of the country above our desire to profit locally, and few congressmen willing to risk defeat at the polls merely to save the public's money. If the law were changed to require a vote on each pork item, perhaps the resulting exposure would bring down wrath on those (e.g.) voting on a "Bridge to Nowhere" regardless of where in the country it was to be built. But the way this system works today, it is unlikely that enough of a grass-roots effort will be gathered to bring about such change. Thus our country will continue to suffer overt and nation-damaging pilfering of the public dole. And the financial burden we are forcing upon our children and grandchildren will continue to grow.

We love democracy even as we dislike participating in it. It is difficult to imagine a formula that would encourage more involvement in the election process, but it is sorely needed. When more voices have to be accommodated, we stand a better chance of seeing laws, et. al. passed that more reflect necessity than political viewpoint. And more voices have a tendency to encourage compromise, which tends to temper extremism.

IRAQ

Iraq is arguably the most ferocious "monster" currently eating away at our nation. We have permitted pride to suck us into a war that is not only highly self-destructive but which diverts us from the real threat against America: Islamic extremism. Through misguided ideology, bad intelligence, poor planning and even worse execution we have become embroiled in a diplomatic and military disaster that will live in infamy in our nation's history. Lives, treasure and national reputation, all of it lost to a military adventure that is going nowhere and never should have happened.

That the war is "legal" is probable but irrelevant. Past presidents have made much the same commitment to force, and each time Congress refrained from exercising their constitutional power to counter or even temper it, in effect giving quasi approval to a presidential edict.

That the war was contrived outside the spirit of constitutional checks and balances is relevant, however. Also relevant is that we were guided by ideologues who saw only what they wanted to see, including declaring "the end of hostilities" only weeks into a campaign that has yet to end.

Vietnam is not something that happened so long ago as to be difficult to remember. It is recent American history, a poor chapter at that, and that we forgot (or conveniently glossed over) this history does not speak well for our collective intelligence or for the future of our country.

Even worse for the country is the attitude of our elected officials, both proponents of the war and those in opposition. The American people voted in 2006 to end the conflict in Iraq, yet those they put in office placed image above the people's mandate. Not willing to offer an unflattering image to an electorate they must count upon to maintain themselves in office, they surrendered principles to their opponents' rhetoric—they more feared being seen as "failing to support the troops" than removing those troops from harm's way. As the war droned on with no end in sight, both sides of the isle retreated to sound bites, pejorative slogans and public displays of outrage at their opponents, none of which changed even slightly what was happening in Iraq.

But can we really blame them for their inaction? It is an unfortunate fact of political life that politicians will do nothing if they believe the public will react negatively to whatever action they might otherwise take. Of political necessity, they will shy away from encounters that, as with suggesting Social Security reforms, lends ammunition to their opponents, ammunition that the public is likely to buy into, hook, line and sinker. Restated, the fault for the 2006 mandate failing to produce what the voters had intended lies not in the politicians but in citizens who prove the politicians' fears valid, who fall for the sound bites, pejorative slogans and public display of outrage. "We have met the enemy, and them is us[110]."

"The people can always be brought to the bidding of the leaders. All you have to do is tell them they are being attacked, and denounce the pacifists for lack of patriotism, and exposing the country to greater danger."
— Herman Goering at the Nuremberg trials

---

[110] "Pogo," ibid

What formula might we yet impose upon ourselves that will give us the wisdom and courage to resist such transparent arguments as "support the troops," aware as we should be that such slogans import no logic to a discussion on the merits of the war but are voiced solely to embarrass opponents into submission?

Iraq and world-wide terrorism may almost be considered one issue, the latter being encouraged by our attempts to defeat the former. Our soldiers are where they do not belong, where they are not doing any good and where they are being severely weakened. Unfortunately, it is likely that we will not accept the necessity to leave Iraq (short of the American definition of victory) until it becomes a disaster that all recognize and few can any longer deny. America does not have such resources that she can continue to indulge her pride at such high cost. She does not have such a reputation that she can survive the errors made in Iraq. Her allies are dwindling even as her enemies are being emboldened. Syria, Iran and perhaps others are as much relieved at our failure as they are alarmed by our presence.

The Iraq war will end some day, but its legacy will live on if we ignore what brought it about, principal of which is out of control ideology. Iraq proves we did not learn from Vietnam, but what we need worry about now is whether we will learn from Iraq. If we fail to reflect upon the ease in which we slip into deadly conflicts, then history not remembered will once again come back to visit us.

We need laws that will get us back to the kind of reasoning put forth by our founding fathers, leaders who strongly believed that no Executive should be given the power to commit the country to war by edict, who were wise enough to recognize that it is dangerous (and naïve) to trust so much power to one man. In the modern world, there are rapidly-moving events that require prompt action, but there must be better controls on the extent to which that action will be permitted. And considering our weakness—the ease at which we can be wooed by self-serving politicians—such controls need to be more "automatic." There should be prescribed actions to be taken (or avoided) and prescribed formulas for disengagement. We cannot permit a future president to commit us (or keep us committed) to armed conflict solely on his interpretation of a "clear and present danger." Congress must become a full partner, both in what leads up to the decision and in when the effort is to be discontinued.

As long as *We The People* fail to insist on a return to shared responsibility between the Executive and Legislative branches of our government, we will continue to suffer brave new strategies that are equally as incompetent as the ones that preceded them.

Politically-savvy politicians get their courage from the electorate. This translates into a greater burden upon us to become active in the political selection process. Or if not "active" then at least better informed, enough so that we will not become fodder to a politician's (or his opponent's) well-aimed but disingenuous rhetoric.

Most of all, we must guard against electing a candidate with a Messianic complex, someone who believes God is guiding his hand. There have been many such claims in recorded history, and never has even one of them proved to be correct. Indeed, considering all the things that go wrong during a leader's time in office, God might well take umbrage at attempting to place the blame on him.

FANATICAL ISLAM

The danger inherent in Islamic fundamentalism is very real and not likely to go away. We have only to examine the history of the Islamic movement to understand this, two massive and very brutal invasions to impose their religion upon Western countries. They have proven that when they have the power they also have the will, and thanks to our purchases of their oil, they are again feeling that power. To prevent a third such invasion by people less interested in governing than in enforcing conformity to their rigid religious practices, we must reexamine our attitudes our policies and our defenses.

As with other of America's "monsters," it does not look promising. We are unlikely to come to grips with religious extremism (terrorism) until a major disaster produces a willingness to awaken the sleeping giant within us, whatever nastiness that entails. At present we are gentlemen fighting street-hardened bullies and thinking in doing so that our devotion to civility will see us through to victory. A country with as modest a population as ours and with a delicate attitude toward casualties, cannot compete against suicide bombers. Nor will the WWII tactics of hand-to-hand and house-to-house combat produce any more than temporary success at a high cost. Matters are turning increasingly against our country and our civilization, and the longer we treat this threat with the dignity of the naïve, the more perilous will be our plight.

Another 9/11 might not be enough to provoke serious action on our part. It could take two, maybe more before finally we come to accept whatever sacrifice (in conscience as well as in wealth and lives) is necessary to rid ourselves of this terrible danger. One such sacrifice will be finally coming to realize that we cannot continue an energy policy that has as its centerpiece the purchase of Middle Eastern oil.

The sacrifice to conscience will begin as we come to accept that we must unleash the demon within us, that with our very survival at stake, we must throw everything within reach at the evil so threatening to us all. We may well spend the next 50 years regretting the barbarity of it, but few will suggest restraint at our moment of greatest fear. It does not help, however, that we are at present seen to be arrogant rather than righteous and of stretched patience.

However we might be viewed by the world (or ourselves,) we will not, simply to be seen playing "nice" with fanatics, surrender our hold on civilization.

CLOSING THOUGHTS

As hopefully is apparent from the above, the structure that is the United States of America is truly being eroded and from many sides. These are serious problems, some of them capable of taking us down a notch or two but others exhibiting a potential for harming us in such a way that we will be hard pressed to recover. The monster, Islamic extremism, for example, suffers one of the most serious prognoses.

Yet we argue, some honestly, but many with a bias that does not escape even their own notice. At the upper echelons of our government, the arguments are more transparently disingenuous, yet they find ears willing to believe. And in believing such people feel comfortable in brushing aside, or at least putting off, what more honest voices insist is increasingly urgent. We have at least partial traps for each of the Hydra monsters, but they are unlikely to be employed because they bring with them pain and sacrifice, factors that are deal-killers to a public in denial. Thus the prognosis is not that the jury is still out but that it is so deadlocked that the evil and injustice it attempts to address will go on. Paraphrasing a line in the Declaration of Independence, mankind has been endowed by its creator with inalienable faults, and there is little evidence that He intends to ratchet up the awareness of this in His creations.

What I have tried to present here is not a précis on the misery we import upon ourselves but an outline for some student of the distant future regarding what led up to the fall of the American "Empire." I have, however, no illusions regarding the use to which it will be put. Whoever writes this history, and however they choose to present it, it is unlikely that readers of the future will feel the lessons apply to them; i.e. they will, as we did, learn nothing from it. They will protest that they are not Romans, they are not Ottomans, they are not Americans. They are invincible and unending.

What are the chances of any of the monsters revealed in these pages being tamed? Not all of them or even most of them, but even one of them? And in not being tamed, what might we imagine will be the result? Will they fade away as we continue to deny their presence? Or as we continue to seize on assurances from political prostitutes that we need not be as concerned as the facts suggest we should be?

If it walks and quacks like a duck, no amount of personal or national pride will excuse our refusal to see it as a duck. Hiding our heads in the sand and seeing the world as we would like it to be serves no useful purpose and certainly does us as Americans no credit. (It could well lead to yet another disastrous military adventure.) The unfortunate truth is, without a monumental awakening of our people to the dangers we are so reluctant to see, and without universal acceptance of the importance of sacrifice now for survival later, these monsters will live on, some of them growing to frightening size. We need to believe less and think more. If the fire in the hearts of those who brought the United States into being is not replicated in their posterity, the monsters will gain the upper ground.

"You may never know what results come from your action. But if you do nothing, there will be no result."
Mahatma Gandhi

The proof of the pudding in any of these prognostications may be found in the reader. How many of you will be inclined to emphasize competence during the next election rather than someone of (e.g.) good "family values?" How many are likely to look with doubt on the political prostitutes who tell you the Hydra monsters are no serious threat to America, certainly not enough to require inconvenience on your part? Finally, how many truly believe that you will be passing on to your children and grandchildren a country that is in at least as good a condition as that which was passed on to you?

We have a window but it is closing. How long before it shuts completely depends entirely on us. If we fail to reverse our self-made road to destruction, we will be but one more footnote in the long history of rising and falling empires. Will we prevent this from happening? The odds are against it, not because we do not have the means, but because we do not have the will.

There is reckoning to all this, and the possible magnitude of it should disturb us all.

"A republic, <u>if</u> you can keep it."
Benjamin Franklin